Strategic Political
Communication

Communication, Media, and Politics

Series Editor
Robert E. Denton Jr., Virginia Tech

This series features a broad range of work dealing with the role and function of communication in the realm of politics, broadly defined. Including general academic books, monographs, and texts for use in graduate and advanced undergraduate courses, the series will encompass humanistic, critical, historical, and empirical studies in political communication in the United States. Primary subject areas include campaigns and elections, media, and political institutions. *Communication, Media, and Politics* books will be of interest to students, teachers, and scholars of political communication from the disciplines of communication, rhetorical studies, political science, journalism, and political sociology.

Titles in the Series

The Millennium Election: Communication in the 2000 Campaign
Edited by Lynda Lee Kaid, John C. Tedesco, Dianne G. Bystrom, and Mitchell McKinney

Strategic Political Communication: Rethinking Social Influence, Persuasion, and Propaganda
By Karen S. Johnson-Cartee and Gary A. Copeland

Campaign 2000: A Functional Analysis of Presidential Campaign Discourse
By William L. Benoit, John P. McHale, Glenn J. Hansen, P. M. Pier, and John P. McGuire

Forthcoming

Inventing a Voice: The Rhetoric of First Ladies of the Twentieth Century
Edited by Molly Meijer Wertheimer

Activist Communication
By John P. McHale

Political Campaign Communication: Principles and Practices, Fifth Edition
By Judith S. Trent and Robert V. Friedenburg

Reelpolitik II: Political Ideologies in '50s and '60s Films
By Beverly Merrill Kelley

Strategic Political Communication

Rethinking Social Influence, Persuasion, and Propaganda

Karen S. Johnson-Cartee
and
Gary A. Copeland

ROWMAN & LITTLEFIELD PUBLISHERS, INC.
Lanham • Boulder • New York • Toronto • Oxford

ROWMAN & LITTLEFIELD PUBLISHERS, INC.

Published in the United States of America
by Rowman & Littlefield Publishers, Inc.
A wholly owned subsidary of The Rowman & Littlefield Publishing Group
4501 Forbes Boulevard, Suite 200, Lanham, Maryland 20706
www.rowmanlittlefield.com

P.O. Box 317, Oxford OX2 9RU, United Kingdom

British Library Cataloguing in Publication Information Available

Library of Congress Cataloging-in-Publication Data

Johnson-Cartee, Karen S.
    Strategic political communication : rethinking social influence,
persuasion, and propaganda / Karen S. Johnson-Cartee and Gary A.
Copeland.
        p.   cm. — (Communication, media, and politics)
    Includes bibliographical references and index.
    ISBN 0-7425-2881-2 (cloth : alk. paper — ISBN 0-7425-2882-0 (pbk. :
alk. paper)
    1. Social influence.   I. Copeland, Gary.   II. Title.   III. Series.
HM1176 . J65   2004
302'.13—dc22   2003017722

Printed in the United States of America

♾ ™ The paper used in this publication meets the minimum requirements of American
National Standard for Information Sciences—Permanence of Paper for Printed Library
Materials, ANSI/NISO Z39.48-1992.

To my late grandparents, Robert Maddox and Grace Mills Maddox and Early Blair Johnson Sr. and Mazie Trent Johnson, who inspired in their children and grandchildren the will to succeed.

—Karen S. Johnson-Cartee

To Karen and Michael Cartee, Beth Bennett, and Jeremy Butler. Colleagues and friends who have always been supportive in the good times and caring in the bad. Without their support and household goods, I would be a poorer person.

—Gary A. Copeland

Contents

List of Illustrations   ix

1   In Defense of Social Influence and Social Marketers   1

2   Social Psychology: Understanding Human Behavior and Social Influence   9

3   Social Influence Models   51

4   Identifying and Targeting Those You Want to Influence   75

5   The Individual in a Mass-Mediated World   109

6   Propaganda Strategies   137

7   Propaganda Tactics and Principles   163

Appendix A   The Personality Strength (PS) Scale and Weighting   193

Appendix B   Goebbels's Propaganda Machine   195

References   203

Index   227

About the Authors   231

Illustrations

FIGURES

2.1 Sociological Terminology and Accompanying U.S. Cultural
and Subcultural Examples   11

2.2 Observed Sorority Norms, Mores, Folkways, and Rituals   34

3.1 Newcomb's Schematic Illustration of the Minimal
A-B-X System   57

3.2 Overlapping Meanings   65

3.3 Communication Networks   71

4.1 VALS   97

4.2 Gutman's Conceptual Model of Means–End Chain   105

5.1 An Explicated Version of the Ball-Rokeach and DeFleur (1976)
Dependency Model of Mass Media Effects   131

7.1 Jowett and O'Donnell's (1992) Model of the Process
of Propaganda   178

TABLE

6.1 Typing Propaganda by Desired Outcomes   145

Chapter One

In Defense of Social Influence and Social Marketers

Today, social influence per se is often distrusted in America. Often portrayed as being sinister, manipulative, and undemocratic, social influence and the professions that engage in the practice of social influence are often viewed as less than respectable. Yet those who engage in social influence, whom we identify as social marketers, are both prevalent and pervasive in American society. Advertising executives, public relations practitioners, and direct mail experts are readily recognized as engaging in social influence or social marketing. Others such as lobbyists, trial attorneys, diplomats, religious leaders, charity directors, political candidates, corporate executives, and a host of others may not be as obvious to the layperson. Nevertheless, they all have one thing in common: these professionals desire to reach designated audiences with carefully crafted images that the audience will ultimately accept as their own. As a result, we are literally bombarded with competing images of people, products, corporations, nations, religions, and so on (Combs and Nimmo 1993; Edelstein 1997; Jowett and O'Donnell 1999; Pratkanis and Aronson 1991).

Ironically, though social marketers are so pervasive within our society, they collectively share a bad reputation, even within their own professions. Attorneys are suspicious of other attorneys. And they are even more distrustful of professions outside of their own that engage in social influence, such as lobbyists, for example. Indeed such distrust often leads to public ridicule. One has only to consider the widespread telling of trial attorney or preacher jokes in our society.

Social marketers have a bad reputation in part because the idea of influencing people and society through a process of social influence is often perceived as evil in a democracy. Social influence is often confused with social control or at the very least social power. Indeed, the synonyms most often associated with "influence" are control, power, authority, sway, or rule.

Yet social influence and the marketers who practice it may be good or evil, ethical or unethical. Such judgments should be reached only after considering both the means used to attain the goal or objective and the end product brought about by the practice of social influence. Social marketers often experience the same prejudice as that which was prevalent in Victorian England. In that day, a young, wealthy woman whose father was "in trade" (a proprietor of business or industry) would never have been considered for marriage by men of the aristocracy; it just wasn't done. But not so in the United States; money more than class was the great leveler: if you had money, it propelled you into the social circles you desired. Pedigrees, while nice, were not a requirement. Today, persuasive communicators are often presented as if they are "in trade" even though other commercially based occupations such as chief executive officers, divisional managers, fiscal officers, and transportation managers are not viewed negatively. Indeed, marketing, advertising, and public relations are presented as the poor stepchildren of business, undesirable but necessary in the modern marketplace. Such nonsensical biases obscure the frequently constructive role of social influence in contemporary life. Consider for example, the public information and charitable donation campaigns associated with the International Red Cross, the Names Project AIDS Memorial Quilt, Reading Is Fundamental, Inc. (RIF), Project Literacy United States (PLUS), or the United Negro College Fund. Surely no one would suggest that these worthy causes should go unpromoted within our society. Often, prejudice against the concept of social influence or those who practice it regrettably discredits or ignores the many wonderful programs that depend on social marketing to maintain their viability. This prejudice may be in part related to the false dichotomy of argumentation techniques.

A FALSE DICHOTOMY OF ARGUMENTATION

Today, researchers continue to disagree as to the relative merits of social influence, particularly persuasion and propaganda. This is in large part because of misconceptions and faulty reasoning. For a number of years, researchers accepted a scientifically influenced false dichotomy in evaluating argumentation (see Kecskemeti 1973). Facts (or that which could be proven and verified by science) were deemed rational and therefore superior, both argumentatively and morally. And emotional appeals used in argumentation were considered to be manipulative and therefore immoral, ultimately creating what researchers considered to be irrationally based responses.

This false dichotomy ignores the realities of persuasion and propaganda. As Dodge ironically observed, an unemotional argument may be used to propagate opinion, but such "argument is so notoriously ineffective that it would seldom deserve the name" (1920, 242–43). Facts (information bits) are not sufficient in and of themselves to influence. Rather, facts accompanied with an identifiable attitude valence (positive or negative) toward the object (or fact) are a necessary precondition for influence. Anyone interested in bringing about social or political change does well to remember this dictum: *facts inform; emotions inspire*. "In other words, persuasion [and propaganda] requires, ideally speaking, complete emotional and affective resonance between the persuader and the audience" (Kecskemeti 1973, 86). Emotion is a highly persuasive device in that it, in effect, eliminates any "distance between the source and the audience" (Kecskemeti 1973, 86).

TWO MEANS OF SOCIAL INFLUENCE: PERSUASION AND PROPAGANDA

Jowett and O'Donnell have noted that "the terms *propaganda* and *persuasion* have been used interchangeably in the literature on propaganda, as well as in everyday speech. Propaganda employs persuasive strategies, but it differs from persuasion in purpose" (1999, 2; emphasis in original). And that purpose may be best understood in terms of the means of the message structure. Persuasion utilizes messages that tell individuals to adopt a new belief or attitude, or to engage in a new behavior for their own personal benefit. For example, "you should brush your teeth everyday, because if you don't your teeth will get infected and ultimately fall out." Propaganda, on the other hand, utilizes messages that tell individuals the attitudes, beliefs, and behaviors found desirable by their social groups. For example, "you should brush your teeth everyday, because people within your group find people with halitosis to be disgusting."

As Miller (1987) noted, persuasion as a communication process, issue, or problem is one of the most often studied areas in human communication research. Yet, it has been defined in myriad ways (Miller 1987; Nimmo 1978). Miller offered a working definition of persuasion in 1980, one that we choose to adopt here. He wrote, "the term 'persuasion' refers to situations where attempts are made to modify behavior by symbolic transactions (messages) that are sometimes, but not always, linked with coercive force (indirectly coercive) and that appeal to the reason and emotions of the intended persuadee(s)" (Miller 1980, 15). For the most part, then, persuasion may be viewed as seeking to modify behavior "by changing existing responses, by reinforcing existing responses, or by shaping new responses" (Miller 1987, 451; Miller 1980).

Sproule (1991) contends that while employing persuasive communication strategies, the majority of advertising, marketing, public relations, and political campaigns are propagandistic in nature in that messages are targeted at groups within society who may share characteristics important to the source of the message. For the purposes of this work, we will primarily focus on propaganda, for propaganda is marketing directed toward individuals in social groups. The French sociologist Jacques Ellul has defined *propaganda* as communication "*employed by an organized group that wants to bring about the active or passive participation in its actions of a mass of individuals, psychologically unified through psychological manipulation and incorporated in an organization*" (1968, 61, emphasis in original). In other words, groups use propaganda to manipulate their own group members or those belonging to another group. Thus, propaganda may be used internally (within a group) or externally (directed at another group whom the propagandist desires to influence). In short, propaganda works to influence people as members of a group.

However, Ellul's definition ignores a very important component of the propaganda equation, the predispositions of the intended audience. Kecskemeti provides us with a more complete understanding of the process, for he views propaganda as "streams of instrumentally manipulated communications from a remote source that seek to establish resonance with an audience's predispositions for the purpose of persuading it to a new view that the propagandist prefers" (1973, 844). In short, propaganda is not **brainwashing**—or the introduction of new ideas, attitudes, and beliefs—contrary to the individuals' cognitive structure. Rather, propaganda is a **resonance strategy,** the discovery of culturally shared beliefs and the deliberate reinforcement and ultimately aggrandizement of those beliefs (T. Schwartz 1972, 1976). A resonance strategy takes advantage of cultural or group beliefs, values, and so on, in order to "evoke" meaning within people. Thus, the resonance strategy utilizes messages "harmonious with the experience of the audience" (Patti and Frazer 1988, 301).

Lasswell's (1927) rather businesslike definition of propaganda emphasized the *management* of a group's attitudes and behaviors through a careful *orchestration* and *dissemination* of the group's *significant symbols.* Or more simply, "the deliberate attempt by the few to influence the attitudes and behavior of the many by the manipulation of symbolic communication" (Qualter 1985, 124). And the propagandist does this by manipulating the group's "common beliefs, shared values, and overlapping expectations. The aim is to enhance members' identification with the group (nation, state, corporation, university, special interest association, etc.)" (Nimmo 1978, 110). Kecskemeti explains:

> To be persuasive, the propaganda theme has to be perceived as coming from within [the group]. The propagandist's ideal role in relation to the propagandee is that of alter ego, someone giving expression of the recipient's own concerns, tensions, aspirations, and hopes. (1973: 864)

In order to achieve the position of an alter ego, the propagandist must first analyze the predispositions of significant groups deemed crucial to the successful fruition of the organizational leaders' objectives, and then and only then does the propagandist craft messages intended to resonate with the groups' preexisting belief structures. After the production of these messages, the propagandist selects a group-perceived, credible source/channel to deliver the message. Such efforts ultimately maintain or exert social control. And as such, some researchers characterize propaganda as a purveyor of ideology (Burnett 1989).

Clearly, this should be a research-driven process, in that the propagandist must first discover what are the commonly shared beliefs, values, and expectations, before crafting persuasive messages consistent with the group's shared worldview and ultimately disseminating them. Bogart writes:

> Propaganda is an art requiring special talent. It is not mechanical, scientific work [alone]. Influencing attitudes requires experience, area knowledge, and instinctive "judgement of what is the best argument for the audience." No manual can guide the propagandist. He must have "a good mind, genius, sensitivity, and knowledge of how that audience thinks and reacts." (1976, 195–96)

And just as importantly, the propagandist's job is ongoing, revising and adapting communicated messages to the audience based on a monitoring and an analysis of the audience's responses to earlier propagandistic messages (Jowett and O'Donnell 1992; Qualter 1962).

Our review of the persuasion and propaganda literature indicates that not only are there discrepancies among researchers as to the merits and distinctiveness of various social influence processes, but there also exist internal inconsistencies within the arguments of individual researchers Choukas 1965; Dodge 1920; Doob 1948, 1966; Jowett and O'Donnell 1992; Lasswell 1927, 1938, 1972; Lee and Lee 1939; Pratkanis and Aronson 1991; Qualter 1985). Below we provide what we consider to be an internally consistent outline of the persuasion and propaganda processes.

Shared Characteristics

Persuasion and propaganda sources are both *motivated* through their own projections of desired outcomes. Both persuasion and propaganda sources seek to influence their audiences through **reasoned acts,** which have been strategically crafted to sway audiences. Which suggests that both persuasion and propaganda are deliberate (intentional and premeditated) and systematic (organized and methodical). In addition, both persuasion and propaganda may be either one-to-one or one-to-many, that is, personal or mass communication. Both propaganda and persuasion sources carefully select language, music, and images appropriate to the personal and cultural values of the intended receiver or audience (Jowett and O'Donnell 1992; Perris 1985; Short 1983; Ward 1985). And, both persuasion and propaganda are end-oriented in that appeals are used to shape perceptions, which will then be used by individuals in evaluating and/or responding to environmental stimuli in a desired manner. External evaluators may judge such persuasion/propaganda strategies and their induced outcomes as either undesirable and evil or desirable and good. Again such judgments are made relative to the external evaluator's own psychological and/or sociological frames of reference.

PERSUASION ALONE

Persuasion sources craft messages designed *to exert influence on individuals (shape perceptions or impressions)* through the tapping of **psychological mechanisms,** that is, affect, personality, cognitive schema, and so on. While persuasion may occur through interpersonal or mass communication channels, persuasion is far more effective on the interpersonal level, because the opportunity for true interaction allows the source to adjust the message in response to the perceived needs and reactions of "the receiver." Such simultaneous situational analysis and adjustment, which some call **feedback,** increases the potential power of persuasive messages. Persuasion as primarily executed through mass communication is best characterized by interaction, which suggests turn-taking or exchanges. The nature of mass communication inhibits continuity and dynamism, because temporal delays in responses and the monitoring of those responses, and the resulting adaptations based on those monitorings, take time—time that breaks up continuity and segments exchanges. Persuasion is most often depicted as benefiting both the persuader and the recipient in that in some small measure the perceived needs of the recipient are satisfied (see O'Donnell and Kable 1982). Such an observation rests on the assumption that the recipient must perceive the adoption of the persuader's message or idea as being in their own best interest before committing to adoption. Researchers describe persuasion as being more accurately characterized as transactive in that interpersonal communication (which most often typifies persuasion situations) involves "a more continuous and dynamic process of co-creating meaning" (Jowett and O'Donnell 1992, 21).

PROPAGANDA ALONE

Propaganda sources craft messages designed *to exert influence on group members (shape perceptions or impressions)* through the tapping of **sociological mechanisms,** that is, group-shared normative configurations. Propagandistic appeals may be used both interpersonally and through mass communication. However, propaganda, as the term is currently used, normally refers to appeals made through mass communication channels. Propaganda is influential to the extent that its messages are crafted consistently with an accurate, intensive, and exhaustive analysis of a group's normative configurations. Ultimately, the successful propagandist utilizes the group's own norms in a process called resonance to influence group members. The propagandist also makes adjustments as necessary; however such adjustments are not immediate but made over time as the environmental monitoring warrants. Furthermore, propaganda's influence rests not on the recipient's perceived satisfaction of individual wants but on the recipient's perceived satisfaction in participating and bringing about the ultimate satisfaction of group or societal goals. While it is the propagandist who chooses the desired outcome and works to channel the recipients' collective actions toward the achievement of that objective, the involved recipients and the propagandist find satisfaction in the process (although this is disputed by Doob 1948; Pratkanis and Aronson 1991).

When George W. Bush asked America's children to send one dollar to the White House in order that Afghan children might be fed, he used a psychological appeal, tapping the children's need to feel empowered in America's struggle against terrorism. This is far different from ad campaigns arguing, for example, that "as Americans we enjoy the highest standard of living in the world; but, because we have so much, we can't imagine the millions of diseased children who live in the streets, who have no decent food or place to sleep in the world's cities." Such an ad uses collective guilt or a sociological mechanism to induce contributions. Ads may transpose scenes of well-dressed, well-nourished, healthy children playing in an idyllic American park or school playground with scenes of the squalor typical of Calcutta, Mexico

City, or Ocho Rios—here again a powerful sociological mechanism is being used.

CONCLUSION

Persuasion and propaganda as means of social influence have many similarities, but they also have important differences. Primarily, persuasion targets the individual through reason and emotion to encourage the recipient to consider the benefits or the costs of accepting or rejecting the message. Propaganda, on the other hand, evokes preexisting shared meanings among audience members to gain social acceptance of the message.

For any individual to become a successful social marketer, he must be well grounded in not only communication theory, but in social psychology as well. It is essential for those engaged in social influence to understand what works and why. This is particularly true for those engaged in political communication, where in the realm of politics, the stakes are often quite high—for the individual communicator as well as for society. While we will touch on other social marketers besides the political communicologist, we will primarily focus on those working within the body politic, for here rests our primary interest.

This book will introduce the reader to the fundamentals of social influence, social psychology, and social influence models. Second, the book will review social influence as a strategic process, examining the means used to identify and target those the social marketer wishes to influence; reevaluating the importance of individuals as social creatures in a mass-mediated world; and, finally, analyzing and framing propaganda strategies, tactics, and principles.

Chapter Two

Social Psychology: Understanding Human Behavior and Social Influence

From the outset, we, the actors on the social scene, experience the world we live in as a world both of nature and of culture, not as a private but as an intersubjective one, that is, as a world common to all of us, either actually given or potentially accessible to everyone; and this involves intercommunication and language.

—A. Schutz (1962)

INTRODUCTION

Those engaged in social marketing must be cognizant not only of the psychological influences on individuals, but also the social influences on individuals as they go about their daily lives as members of groups and of a society. An anonymous British statesman once remarked, "The great mystery of all conduct is social conduct. I have had to study it all my life, but I cannot pretend to understand it. I may seem to know a man through and through, and still I would not want to say the first thing about what he will do in a group." Such recognition of the significant influences of social roles on individuals requires that a competent social marketer be thoroughly versed in the field of sociology. We turn now to an examination of the sociological contributions to the understanding of human behavior for social marketers.

CULTURE

The study of social psychology has its roots in the basic human concern with the ramifications of mass society. Early psychologists observed:

9

Taken singly, all individuals are rational in their behavior, but taken collectively, they cease to be rational—as witnessed by the outbursts of violence, panic, enthusiasm, and cruelty in which crowds indulge. A sharp difference must therefore exist between individual and collective psychology, which accounts for the radical transformation of the individual's psychic state and disposition when in a social setting. (Moscovici 1985, 347)

And for the last one hundred years or so, psychologists and sociologists have explored the role of social relationships whether "actual, imagined, or implied" in influencing the individual's behavior (see Allport 1985, 1). Sociologist Émile Durkheim's work *The Division of Labor in Society* (1893; 1947) established the basic tenets of social influence. Turner and Beeghley have noted that Durkheim's choice of a book title may well be misleading, for while he discussed the division of labor, his emphasis was on the creation, maintenance, and adaptation of social organizations and/or society (1981, 334).

Durkheim emphasizes the significance of the social frame or an individual's frame of reference in understanding the processes of social organizations (cf., Mortensen 1972, 3–27). Goffman (1974) has described the **social frame** as the basic organizational pattern that people use to organize what they perceive and which ultimately defines and gives character to that perception. More colloquially, the social frame has also been called a frame of reference, because individuals refer to their stored social frames to make sense of their environment. According to Durkheim, when humans meet with no social frame of reference, they have no readily available means to define the situation; therefore, they experience uncertainty and ultimately anxiety. To combat this uncomfortable state, people engage in interactions intended to create a "commonness" among participants by which all subsequent future social interactions will be judged. Durkheim called this negotiated "commonness" the "morality" or "moral facts" of the society and the totality of that morality, "collective conscience." While at first we might not understand Durkheim's terminology (especially given today's sociological terminology), *The Division of Labor* provides us with a clear definition of this collectivity. Durkheim asserted that "[T]he totality of beliefs and sentiments common to average citizens of the same society forms a determinate system which has its own life; one may call it the collective or common conscience" (1893, 32). This concept embodies what modern day sociologists and social psychologists call **culture** or "the system of ideas, such as values, beliefs, and norms [thus mores, folkways, and rituals which] constrain the thoughts and actions of individuals" (Turner and Beeghley 1981, 336; see figure 2.1). Figure 2.1 reviews these sociological constructs' definitions.

Figure 2.1   Sociological Terminology and Accompanying U. S. Cultural and Subcultural Examples

Norms: "Shared convictions about the patterns of behavior that are appropriate or inappropriate for the members of a group; what group members agree they can, should, might, must, cannot, should not, ought not, or must not do in any given situation. As used here, *norm* refers to expected rather than actual behavior" (DeFleur, D'Antonio, and DeFleur 1973, 618; emphasis in original).

Examples:

- Do unto others as you would have them do unto you.
- Absolute personal honesty is the distinguishing characteristic of University of Virginia college students. Immediate expulsion for dishonesty, which not only includes academic dishonesty, but also such acts as using a fake identification to obtain alcoholic beverages or for writing a bad check.

At the Societal or Cultural Level, Norms are Called Universal Norms, Which Are Often Classified as: Mores, Folkways, or Rituals

Mores: "Intense feelings of right and wrong which come down to us from the past. The mores define basic rules of conduct, and an individual who violates them is severely sanctioned by society" (DeFleur, D'Antonio, and DeFleur 1973, 618).

Examples:

- Monogamy in marriage is ideal; nonmonogamous relationships receive society's disapproval.
- People should bathe regularly in order to avoid becoming an olfactory problem, which receives society's scorn.

Folkways: "Norms that do not specifically apply to any particular group within a society but are simply established as common practices. They specify modes of dress, etiquette, language usage, and other routine matters not regarded as having much moral significance" (DeFleur, D'Antonio and DeFleur 1973, 615). And as such, violations of folkways rarely provoke strong negative reactions.

Examples:

- Females other than the bride should not wear white to a wedding.
- White shoes should not be worn after Labor Day.

Rituals: Practices performed for the purpose of symbolizing, honoring, and reinforcing significant aspects of group-condoned behaviors.

Examples:

- Initiation ceremonies performed for pledges of college fraternities and sororities.
- The performance of wedding ceremonies.

Cultural Traits

When studying culture, researchers attempt to "identify, describe, and classify individual culture *traits*—the smallest meaningful units of cultural content" (DeFleur, D'Antonio, and DeFleur 1973, 113; emphasis in original). Sociologists have identified four categories of cultural traits:

Material Traits. All the material and technological products that a culture produces as well as the skill patterns and past experiences required to effectively use the products are considered to be material traits.

Normative Traits. The institutionalized expectations (of individuals within the culture) of individual and group behavior, including specialized role-patterns within the culture are considered normative traits. Therefore, cultural norms, folkways, mores, laws, regulations, and rituals are considered normative traits.

Cognitive Traits. The various belief components within a culture's shared version of reality are categorized as cognitive traits. Heavily influenced by language, scientific, religious, and political beliefs are considered to be cognitive traits as well as the myths, songs, or legends handed down through generations.

Value Traits. All the emotionally held orientations of a culture, which assign value or lack thereof to environmental objects or human behavior. Value traits "are the basic sentiments by which men orient themselves toward the higher goals and ideals by which they interpret what is worthwhile, what is sordid, what is humorous, what is sacred" (DeFleur, D'Antonio, and DeFleur 1973, 114).

For example, refrigerators or freezers in the United States could be considered to be a small meaningful unit of cultural content. You're asking yourself, "How in the world could a refrigerator be considered a 'meaningful unit of cultural content—a cultural trait?'" Well, Karen thought the same thing when she read that in 1974; the text she was reading offered no explanation for that assertion. And as Karen frequently does when she is faced with something she doesn't understand, she simply stored it away with all the rest of those seemingly irrelevant bits of information that she doesn't quite know why she wants or needs to recall. However, more than twenty-six years later, Karen now understands why refrigerators and freezers may be considered cultural traits of American society. Indeed, the widespread use of refrigerators and freezers in the United States explains a great deal about the way Americans live. Karen gained insight into the significance of refrigerators after having visited numerous European nations where the typical refrigerator is little more than an American dorm-room size refrigerator (about 2 ft. by 2 ft. by 2 ft., or in the more privileged homes, 2 ft. by 4 ft. by 2 ft.). Freezers are not widely owned, and if the tiny refrigerator has a freezer compartment, it is not larger than about four inches tall. The result: everything in Europe is sold in much smaller sizes. People rarely use ice, and if they do, it is one cube. And most go to the grocery everyday. And, for the most part, shoppers only purchase what they predict will be used by the household that day and the following morning. While milk, butter, eggs, yogurt, jams, and cheeses are found as staples in European refrigerators, little else is. Europeans buy only what they truly need. And this behavior is continued with nonrefrigerated foodstuffs as well. What Europeans call a larder or pantry is often little more than a shelf or two in a cabinet.

All this is possible because Europeans, whether living in large cities or small villages, have grocery stores, butchers, bakers, confectioners, vintners, and produce markets within easy walking distance. Grocery store parking lots, if they even have a parking lot, are very small. Indeed, the very pattern of the food-supply industry is on a much smaller scale than in the United States. While Europe has chain grocery stores, these chains are a system of small stores. Shopping for food is a neighborhood exercise. There is no need to get into the car and drive. Here in America everything is very spread out. Most Americans would not think of walking to the grocery store or budgeting the time to go once a day. For instance, Karen drives 15 miles each way to go to a grocery store; therefore, she goes to the store once a week, loading up both the trunk and the back seat of her car with groceries. Her pantry looks like a small 7-Eleven, and if there were an unexpected flood, tornado, or multitude of guests, Karen wouldn't have to go to the store.

Cultural traits do not, however, occur in isolation. Rather they form **cultural configurations,** which are the "patterns of interrelated traits that together account for some broad pattern of behavior" (DeFleur, D'Antonio, and DeFleur 1973, 114). And such cultural configurations provide important clues as to how society operates. Indeed, **ideology** or the "complex of beliefs and values providing an overall rationale for a society in being or for one that is envisaged" (DeFleur, D'Antonio, and DeFleur 1973, 616) is an example of such a cultural configuration.

The Caribbean islands provide us with a readily available environment in which to observe conflicting cultural configurations in operation. Many Caribbean governments believe that they are now facing what they term "a cultural crisis." Specifically, we will consider the experience of the island of Aruba, where the native islanders' cultural configuration of the work ethic is now faced with a competing work ethic that recent immigrants brought to the island.

On Aruba, the weather is ideal, a uniform sunny 86 degrees Fahrenheit with strong tropical winds cooling the islanders. Because the island is outside of the hurricane belt, Aruba is an ideal year-round vacation destination. As a former Dutch colony, Aruba has a strong educational system; it is not unusual to find high school graduates who read and speak at least three foreign languages. Such a prowess in languages makes Aruba an ideal vacation spot for international travelers.

The islanders are a charming people, noticeably happy with each other. Arubans are easygoing, unworried, and have an ingrained ability to enjoy life. While Americans are often accused of living to work, the Arubans only work to live. And live well they do. Islanders enjoy one of the highest standards of living in the Caribbean; seafood is plentiful, and, with Venezuela less than twenty miles off its coast, vegetables, meats, and fruits are also easily obtained. Heavily influenced by the Latino culture, islanders like to sleep late in the mornings and enjoy their afternoon siestas.

Aruba as an outstanding vacation spot is a secret that couldn't be kept. And within the last twenty years, it has become a tourist mecca with a wide variety of new resorts, hotels, restaurants, and casinos. Such rapid growth put a strain on the limited pool of potential service industry employees on the island. And for this reason, the new businesses began hiring not only native islanders but also began recruiting people from as far away as the Philippines to come to live and work on the island. Because these immigrants came from rather poor economies, they were often willing to work longer hours for less money than the native islanders. For this reason, the hotels and resorts began hiring more and more immigrants as employees. And as a result, the majority of employees in the tourist industry are now non-natives who are poorly educated by Aruban standards and who do not speak English, Dutch, or German, the three languages most needed for the tourism industry.

In addition, Aruban officials worry that the immigrants do not share the warm, open, hospitable, and easy, relaxed nature of the native islanders. They fear the tourist experience on the island is no longer representative of the real character of the island and its people. Some worry this will eventually hurt the tourism industry. The government clearly faces a dilemma. (This discussion has been based on a personal conversation that the authors had with the Aruban prime minister in December 1993.) Aruba's fate is yet to be decided.

Cultural Configurations as Political Mythologies. Unfortunately communicologists have not been as vigilant in examining cultural traits and cultural configurations as they have those beliefs that deviate from the majority; it has been the variation in human behavior that has most intrigued researchers. However, communication researchers will often turn to both sociologists and political scientists when faced with social behavior that cannot be explained through either psychological means or through contemporary observed behavior. For example, communicologists will turn to political scientists when needing to explain the paradox of small-town pastoralism.

Despite the fact that the majority of Americans live in urban areas, small-town pastoralism or the rural ethic is venerated by Americans. "Americans have high esteem for small towns, farmlands, and the values found there" (Johnson-Cartee and Copeland 1997b, 77). The interdisciplinary research group known formally as the Oxford Analytica (three hundred interdisciplinary researchers from Oxford University) defined this rural ethic as "the Jeffersonian ideal of independence, thrift and hard work symbolized by the traditional American family farm" (1986, 100). This ethic is abundantly apparent in both news reports (Gans 1979), product advertising (Combs and Nimmo 1993), and political advertising (Johnson-Cartee and Copeland 1997b). Johnson-Cartee and Copeland describe the use of small-town pastoralism in political advertising:

> Political candidates are often shown walking through towns and villages, talking and listening to the voters there. Candidates often say that they are going to the people to hear their concerns, but "the people" are the icons of rural America—farmers, general store owners, or a local postmaster. (1997b, 77)

Subculture

In many societies, categories of individuals may exist who share their own internal culture, and this shared internal culture may be clearly differentiated from that held by the entire society. Such an internal culture shared by a category of individuals is called a subculture. A **subculture** is the "pattern of norms, beliefs, attitudes, values, and other cultural elements that are shared within particular groups or segments of a society but that do not normally characterize the society as a whole" (DeFleur, D'Antonio, and DeFleur 1973, 117). In a diverse population, one would expect to see a rather large number of subcultures. Occupational groups such as medical doctors or trial attorneys form subcultures in American life. Religious groups like the Amish or the Branch Davidians or American youth gangs such as the Crips and the Bloods are all subcultures.

For a time, many lay persons believed that the waves of immigrants, which at first produced distinctive cultural neighborhoods within major American cities, had gradually dispersed throughout America; consequently, this belief produced the political myth of the great American melting pot. However, in 1963, Glazer and Moynihan found that identifiable ethnic and religious subcultures continued to exist as identifiable neighborhoods in urban centers. A visit to Los Angeles or New York City in the twenty-first century will provide evidence to suggest that this is still true more than thirty-seven years later. And to the extent that various economic classes share cultural patterns of norms, beliefs, attitudes, values, they too form subcultures. One international economic class deserves special attention, because the world's peasants form the largest subculture on earth (Guthrie 1972).

Peasantry. Despite the size of their economic class, few social scientists have studied the social psychology of peasantry (Guthrie 1972). Peasants are the rural poor; they work small patches of land, or they work as day laborers on larger farms. They are uneducated, living in villages where the necessary conditions for development and the emergence of a merchant class are non-existent (Guthrie 1972). They exist primarily in Europe, Asia, Central and South America, and Africa, but heavy concentrations are also found in the United States. Peasants do not constitute an ethnic, religious, or racial minority; rather, in most instances, they represent the majority of the population. And what is most interesting about the world's peasants is that despite living on different continents, having different language systems and cultural, religious, ethnic, and racial identities, the peasants of the world share certain cultural traits:

1. Mutual distrust in interpersonal relations with those outside of the extended family and circle of close friends.
2. Perceived limited good—there is only so much to go around and the total supply cannot be increased.
3. Dependence on and hostility toward government authority.
4. Strong extended family structures.
5. Lack of innovative spirit.
6. Fatalism.
7. Limited aspiration.
8. Lack of deferred gratification (or the refusal to delay rewards in order to receive greater rewards in the future).
9. Limited view of the world—little knowledge of the world beyond the confines of their village or neighborhood.
10. Low empathy—inability to imagine themselves in some other role or in another's shoes (adapted from Guthrie 1972, which was condensed from Rogers 1969, 19–41).

It is obvious that someone from outside the peasant class made these assessments about peasantry. Such assessments, if accurate, make it highly unlikely that such a people will be able to improve their lot in life, for such subcultural traits are, in effect, self-destructive. These traits prohibit modernization and advancement. And indeed, the perpetuation of peasantry has been a concern of those nations wishing to improve their people's economic position, in order to more successfully compete in the international marketplace. Initially, Western social scientists asked to develop means by which the peasant classes could advance within the economic structures believed that improved educational opportunities would wipe out such self-destructive behaviors within the subculture. However, in some cultures, social scientists discovered that education did not change this cultural configuration of peasant attitudes and behavior (Foster 1965). Foster suggested that peasants share an image of the world that is one of "limited good" in that peasants can't visualize having more or achieving more, for they view everything in terms of shortages and finite supplies.

> Broad areas of peasant behavior are patterned in such fashion as to suggest that peasants view their social, economic, and natural universes—their total environment—as one in which all of the desired things in life such as land, wealth, health, friendship and love, manliness and honor, respect and status, power and influence, security and safety, *exist in finite quantity* and *are always in short supply*, as far as the peasant is concerned. Not only do these and all other "good things" exist in finite and limited quantities, but in addition *there is no way directly within peasant power to increase the available quantities.* (Foster 1965, 296; emphasis in original)

Clearly governmental leaders or outside agencies such as UNESCO, UNICEF, or the Peace Corps who try to improve the quality of life for a peasant village by reducing infant mortality or by eliminating infectious diseases would confront substantial barriers to change. Highly innovative approaches are called for in dealing with the peasantry.

Rogers and Kincaid (1981) tell the story of the Korean peasant village Oryu Li, a miraculous tale of modernization. The 103 thatched huts in the village were "cramped between the tracks of a railroad and the steep foothills of a mountain range along the edge of a narrow valley" (Rogers and Kincaid 1981, 2). More than five hundred people lived on this tiny span of land. The village was so poor that it had no school, no running water, no public bath house, and no market. The lone business was a bar serving the native rice wine to male patrons. Tiny plots of land, barely an acre in size, grew rice that was the only source of income for Oryu Li families. According to Rogers and Kincaid, Oryu Li is a prototype of the Korean village: poor, overpopulated, underdeveloped, and lacking in cooperative trust and social structures (1981, 2). Although Koreans often make what we would view as personal decisions within the confines of their family or close circle of friends, they still have not developed the necessary cooperative trust and the attending social structures necessary to facilitate collective decision making within a village to achieve village-defined goals (Rogers and Kincaid 1981, 16).

In 1968, the Planned Parenthood Federation of Korea (PPFK) had established a program meant to encourage the adoption of birth control usage.

This was no easy task in the Korea of the late 1960s. Women were subordinate in all respects to the men in their family, and they had no status with their husband, his family, or the community until they produced sons. Clearly birth control would be difficult to sell to women whose only source of status and security was through the ability to produce male children.

A regional PPFK change-agent established a mothers' club, a village-level organization whose female members were of child-bearing age. Mothers' clubs were to encourage family planning in Korean villages and to serve as the channel for the diffusion of birth control information and also the physical diffusion of birth control devices. The PPFK modeled the mothers' clubs after the traditional rotating credit clubs called *kaes.* Such clubs are used in a variety of Asian, African, and Caribbean cultures. Women pay a small fee to the *kae* each month, and at the monthly meeting, one woman is awarded the sum collected. The person receiving the money is rotated through all members of the *kae;* and then the process begins again. In this way, the poor are able to make a major purchase once a year or once every two years; the *kaes* are typically twelve or twenty-four members in size.

At first the Oryu Li mothers' club met in secret with only nine women participating. Because the village had once adopted communism during the North Korean occupation, the South Korean government was now highly suspicious of public meetings in the village, and for this reason, family members discouraged such activities. In addition to this politically based fear, the men of the village openly disapproved of birth control, and the women feared angering their husbands. Eventually, they did begin to meet publicly, and when they did, the group leader urged the women to placate their husbands and families by showing them additional respect and by preparing extra-delicious meals twice during each month, coinciding with the mothers' club meeting days. These newly found wells of respect and culinary expertise were attributed to the influence of the club's meetings and activities (see Rogers and Kincaid 1981, 11).

In 1971, the Oryu Li mothers' club won a piglet for showing promise in family planning. Not used to cooperative trust or cooperative efforts, the women held several meetings deciding how to care for the pig and ultimately what they should do with it. After much deliberation, they devised a solid strategy, ultimately breeding the pig to produce additional piglets to serve as a source of income for the group and the village.

A new family moved to the village after experiencing financial reverses in another area of Korea. The mother of the family, a Mrs. Chung, had graduated high school, because she was from a far more prosperous area in Korea. The original mothers' club leader turned the reins of power over to the better-educated woman, promising to help the new leader as much as she could.

Mrs. Chung also received additional training from the PPFK, which made her, in effect, a paraprofessional aide to the regional change-agent.

Under the new leadership of Mrs. Chung, the mothers' club grew in numbers, and the members adopted a series of goals unrelated to the original birth control agenda. The club would now work to improve cooperative relationships within the village and to improve the village itself. The members formed a mothers' club bank where money made by the women on profit-making projects would be saved until sufficiently sizable to start and complete an agreed-upon village improvement. As a group, they bought cloth and produced school uniforms for neighboring villages with more prosperous economies; the profits from this enterprise went into the club's bank.

Mrs. Chung quickly recognized that the local bar was a source of problems for many of the women in the village. Village men would drink and gamble away money needed for their families. Mrs. Chung helped coordinate a negative information campaign against the wine shop, and group members participated in a number of money-making projects until the club saved enough money to buy out the bar's owner. And in its place, they founded a cooperative store selling staples and making additional profits for the club's bank.

The group planted two thousand government-donated chestnut trees on the slopes nearby, hoping one day to reap the profits from selling the chestnuts. The women by themselves built concrete storage facilities to house *kim chee*, the native dish of pickled vegetables. And Mrs. Chung convinced each woman to pawn her gold wedding ring to finance the rebuilding of the brick-kitchen cooking stands in each member's home. Nearby Korean soldiers whom the women had befriended by sharing their *kim chee* agreed to haul sand for the construction project, and the women recruited those of their husbands who were experienced in brick laying. The wedding rings were retrieved from the pawn shop only after the women had earned additional money from other collective projects (see Rogers and Kincaid 1981). During the next two years, a new bridge, a road, and a sewing factory were built using proceeds from the mothers' club money-making projects and from the monetary prizes given by the PPFK to the club for being the most outstanding mothers' club in Korea.

By 1973, fifty-three women were members of the club, and all fifty-three were practicing birth control. Almost all fertile women in the village were now members. The national rate of birth control adoption was only about 36 percent among women of child-bearing age in 1973 (Rogers and Kincaid 1981, 5). The Oryu Li women had accomplished what once had seemed impossible—the village women had 100 percent birth control adoption; not one new birth was recorded in the village in 1973. And most importantly, the village women had learned "the three basic means of village improvement: cooperation, self-reliance, and diligence" (Rogers and Kincaid 1981, 17).

Social Organizations

This interest in culture and the resulting norms, mores, folkways, and rituals led to other research into social organizations of all sizes and descriptions. Sociologists distinguish between **social categories** and organized groups; a social category is an unstructured number of individuals who share common characteristic(s) but who do not share common norms, roles, or goals (DeFleur, D'Antonio, and DeFleur 1973). All college graduates in the United States may be said to be a social category, but they do not participate within an organizational structure of college graduates nor do they necessarily share any norms, roles, or goals. Although social categories "lack a pattern of social organization, [their] collective behavior [as individuals] is seldom if ever completely unstructured" (DeFleur, D'Antonio, and DeFleur 1973, 347). Such a statement may seem contradictory, but in practice it is not. For example, an audience at a rock concert is certainly an unstructured number of people who do not hold the same norms, roles, or goals. However, audience members may have observed audience behaviors at previous concerts, thus engaging in social learning and ultimately acquiring what could be termed as collective behavior. For example at such concerts, lit matches or cigarette lighters held high by audience members indicate their high level of satisfaction with the band's performance and this serves as a symbolic request for additional musical numbers. It also communicates a show of respect and thanks.

Recent research has documented the potential significance of social categories in influencing an individual's unconscious behavior. Tajfel's work (1969, 1972, 1982) explains the process of **social categorization** by which individuals first classify themselves and their own normative behaviors into a labeled social category (e.g., "Chinese"), then classify others like themselves who share the same normative behaviors into the now-shared social category ("Chinese"), and finally classifying others who are unlike themselves and who do not share the same normative behaviors into a separate and distinct social category from their own (e.g., "'Korean"). This simple act of social categorization, in effect, establishes **in-groups** (those the individual identifies with and approves of) and **out-groups** (those the individual rejects and disapproves of) with all the resulting discriminatory activities and hostilities between groups that one might expect (Brewer 1979; J. C. Turner 1975, 1982, 1983; Whillock 1995). Such predicted discriminatory behavior may indeed be real in the case of the Chinese and Koreans. On a recent trip to Los

Angeles' China Town, Karen and her husband were enjoying a delightful dinner at an authentic Chinese restaurant. Karen's husband, Michael, studied and lived in Korea during his college years and has retained a love for the country's cuisine; thus, he inquired as to the location of an equally good Korean restaurant. The waiter quickly informed Michael in quite a huff that "this is not possible" (because there were no good Korean restaurants in Los Angeles), because "Koreans do not know how to cook." Such social categorization leads to the following reasoning by those in the in-group: *"We are superior as a people. Therefore, the way we view the world is superior. Our version of reality is The Truth, spelled with the capitalized 'Ts,' because it is the belief of the in-group that their Truth is the final universal authority. Thus, it is the in-group's strongly held belief that their religion, their politics, their governmental system, their artists, their intellectuals, their musicians, their cultural artifacts, and their social behaviors are all superior to any others in the world. Therefore those in the out-group who do not share this 'universal authority' of Truth are judged by the in-group to be ignorant, irrational, immoral, unethical, evil, and inferior. And all things associated with the out-group such as their religious, cultural, social, or political views are also judged as being inferior by the in-group."*

Clearly such social categorization produces sharp divisions within a society. And social categorization encourages two perceptual tendencies: (1) perceived homogenization within each group (high degree of similarity within each group); and (2) perceived polarization of the groups' affects (the groups' positions or character profiles depicted as being antithetical or in opposition) (Allen and Wilder 1978; R. Brown 1986; Mackie 1986; Tajfel 1969, 1982; Wilder 1981, 1984). The process of social categorization produces:

- **Ethnocentrism:** the practice of viewing one's social category as being superior in terms of ideas, values, codes, and achievements and of viewing those outside one's social category as being inferior; such practices lead inevitably to one approving of those like one's self and disapproving of those unlike one's self (Peffley and Hurwitz 1993). Which leads to:
- **Ultimate Attribution Error** (Pettigrew 1979, 1981): "the tendency to attribute negative acts by members of out-groups to innate characteristics while discounting positive traits as exceptional" (Sigelman and Tuch 1997, 87). Which leads to the production of ideologies justifying the second-class citizenship of members of the out-group (Bar-Tal, Graumann, Kruglanski, and Stroebe 1989; Jackman and Senter 1983; Stroebe and Insko 1989). Which produces the:
- **Initial Discriminatory In-Group Behavior Directed at the Out-**

Group: Such actions deny members of the out-group equal access to the relatively scarce valued goods and services within society, and often on arbitrary grounds created by the in-group theout-group are treated unfairly in all manner of situations (see DeFleur, D'Antonio, and DeFleur 1973, 614). Which encourages:

- **Intragroup Cohesion** (solidarity or unity within each group): Members of a social category have shared the experiences of being labeled and ultimately the consequences of that labeling within social interactions, and through these shared experiences they perceive themselves to be so "intermeshed and interdependent as to form a more-or-less unified whole" (see DeFleur, D'Antonio, and DeFleur 1973, 614; Ehrlich 1973). Which leads to both the:

- **Exacerbation and Magnification of Perceived Differences, Discriminatory Behaviors, Intragroup Cohesiveness, and Intergroup Hostilities:** Peoples' perceptions of social category differences are intensified; in-group discriminatory practices increase as a result, ultimately producing an increased intragroup cohesion and the creation of out-group negative **metastereotypes** (out-group stereotypes of in-group–held stereotypes about the out-group) (Sigelman and Tuch 1997, 99), which eventually produce out-group distrust and hostility directed at the in-group, resulting in increased ethnocentrism (Sigelman and Tuch 1997). Which inevitably creates "self-fulfilling prophecies when mutually stereotyping groups interact" (Hamilton 1981; Sigelman and Tuch 1997, 87).

And the cycle feeds upon itself, producing an unhealthy social environment (Brewer 1979; J. C. Turner 1975, 1982, 1983) characterized by its **distortions,** the shared conceptual biases developed as the result of social categorization, from which individuals view the world. Such distortions as viewing mechanisms have all the resulting acuity of one who is looking through the bottom of a coke bottle to see the moon (see Anderson 1988).

J. C. Turner (1985) modified Tajfel's social categorization theory (1982) by adding the concept of social identity to the equation; the result was Turner's **self-categorization theory** (see also J. C. Turner 1987; Turner and Oakes 1989). Turner maintains that self-categorization is responsible for the observed conformity or cohesiveness (solidarity) within social categories (cf., Lewin 1948). **Conformity** should be viewed as the possible outcome of an individual's interaction within a group at a particular occasion; the relational nature of conformity suggests that the individual evaluates the opinions of others as well as his or her relationships with others and ultimately decides to accept or give the appearance of accepting the observed group norm (Hollander 1975, 1976). **Cohesiveness** or **solidarity** may be viewed as the extent of mutual interest and identification among group members that fosters an impression among the members that membership in the group increases the likelihood of achieving their goals (Lewin 1948; Littlejohn 1992). **Mutual identification** "is a function of the degree to which members are mutually attracted to certain goals or repulsed by certain negative forces" (Littlejohn 1992, 297; Lewin 1948). However, it must be remembered that individual members do not have to have identical or even similar attitudes, but rather, the members perform their group tasks interdependently yet effectively to achieve mutually desired goals (Newcomb 1953; Littlejohn 1992). In such situations, members may be said to perform complementary roles.

Rather than the group exerting normative influences on the individual, for J. C. Turner, it is the individual who cognitively assesses his world through social categorization—the identification of a social category whose members are similar to the individual. Once this assessment has been made, the individual engages in **self-identification** that mentally associates one with the identified social category. When this is done, the individual evaluates not only his or her own behavior, but also the identified social category's behavior as well; a comparison is made between the two, and the perceived similarities become normative behaviors associated with identified social category and the individual. And the individual begins to adopt other behaviors of the identified social category, because the adoption serves to validate the individual's own view of the external world (J. C. Turner 1987).

A Case Study of the Effect of Social Categorization in the Business World. Such social categorization may have a dramatic impact in the business world. Often an individual's identification with a social category may well subconsciously influence that individual's behavior within an organization such as a corporation. For example, corporate managers have been found to (1) have the tendency when interviewing potential employees to judge the candidates on how well they "fit" the company mold and (2) have the tendency when evaluating an employee's performance to judge not the employee's work quality but the employee's "fit" within the organization (Loden 1985; Loden and Rosener 1991; Morrison 1992; Thomas 1991). But these evaluative decisions have been found to be based on the managers' assessments of how much the potential employee and employee are like the managers; in other words, the manager evaluates others as to whether they share the same social category with the manager (Loden 1985; Loden and Rosener 1991; Morrison 1992; Thomas 1991). This is not surprising, in that in general people naturally like those they can identify with, and thus, they seek out those who are similar to themselves. And in business, this may mean giving those like themselves a job or a promotion. However, such social category-driven judgments may well hurt both the people they affect and the organization.

The "comfortable fit" or "is this person like me?" criteria have resulted in years of discrimination against women and minorities in the workplace (Loden 1985; Loden and Rosener 1991; Morrison 1992; Thomas 1991). At diversity workshops, facilitators often allude to the very real power of WGITS (pronounced widgets)—"the white guys in ties" who assist those like themselves and who discount those unlike themselves to avoid potential conflict that they perceive as being negative in the workplace. Researchers and news reporters have identified such discriminatory practices as structural barriers within an organization and allude to the proverbial "glass ceiling" for women (Loden 1985) or "brick wall" for minorities (Sigelman and Tuch 1997). As hypothetical as it sounds, the concept of a glass ceiling or brick wall within organizations preventing women and minorities from advancing has been documented over and over again. In 1990 *Fortune* magazine surveyed 799 of the major corporations in the United States. The magazine found that only nineteen women were among the nation's top executives. Less than 1 percent of chief executives in the United States are women, African Americans, or Hispanics (Morrison 1992). Yet, 30 percent of middle management are members of these same groups. Few minorities and women have broken through that glass ceiling/brick wall barrier. Frequently these barriers breed employee dissatisfaction, which leads to high employee turnover, forcing significant company expenditures to pay for the necessary advertising, recruiting, and training for new employees. This turnover ultimately hurts the bottom line of the company's profitability (Loden and Rosener 1991). And such perceived injustices create tensions among employees, leading to the escalation of unexplored and unresolved negative conflicts among employees and between management and their employees. This leads to potential Equal Employment Opportunities Commission complaints. These complaints result in the company's loss of man-hours during the discovery and court appearance phases of the complaint; a large cash outlay in attorney and court fees; and, if found to be in violation of the EEOC regulations, punishing court fines and hefty economic compensation packages for the complainants (Loden and Rosener 1991).

Although not as obvious but equally as chilling as those negative effects on individuals and the organization, structural barriers are also indirectly harmful to the culture and productivity of the organization. By avoiding differences and perceived potential sources of conflict, the company, in effect, strangles creativity and innovative problem solving. Thus both the employees and the organizational structure itself remain unchallenged, often resulting in underproductivity and inefficiency. And as the organizational culture stagnates, it loses its vitality and ultimately loses the employee's personal loyalty to and identification with the company, which further weakens the employee's performance and the company's overall health (Tjosvold 1991). Conflict, then, when managed effectively, is a positive source of organizational creativity, problem solving, and vitality.

Conceptually similar to social categories, the **mass** is a great body of people, who "in theory at least, exemplif[y] the *complete lack of social organization*" (DeFleur, D'Antonio, and DeFleur 1973, 430; emphasis in original). Blumer has provided us with what some view as the classic definition of mass:

> Mass is devoid of the features of a society or community. It has no social organization, no body of custom or tradition, no established set of rules or rituals, no organized group of sentiments, no structure of status roles, and no established leadership. It merely consists of an aggregation of individuals who are separate, detached, anonymous, and thus, homogeneous as far as mass behavior is concerned. It can be seen, further, that the behavior of the mass, just because it is not made by preestablished rule or expectation, is spontaneous, indigenous, and elementary. (1951, 185–89)

For this reason, social philosophers such as John Stuart Mill (1806–1873) feared "the mass." Mill's renowned *Liberty* was first published in 1859; in this treatise, Mill describes the mass as a "collective mediocrity" whose "thinking is done for them by men much like themselves, addressing them or speaking in their name, on the spur of the moment, through the newspapers" (Mill 1956, 80). Mill urges lone individuals to stand against this collective mediocrity for the good of the world (1956, 81–86). For Mill, just because behavior was customary among the masses did not make it right or moral. He wrote that "the despotism of custom is everywhere the standing hindrance to human advancement" (1956, 85).

Even more damning than Mill's assessment of the mass is Aldous Leonard Huxley's (1894–1963) depiction of the mass, which he calls a crowd.

> A crowd is chaotic, has no purpose of its own, and is capable of anything except intelligent action and realistic thinking. Assembled in a crowd, people lose their powers of reasoning and their capacity for moral choice. Their suggestibility is increased to the point where they cease to have any judgment or will of their own. . . . In a word, a man in a crowd behaves as though he had swallowed a large dose of some powerful intoxicant. He is a victim of what I have called "herd-poisoning." Like alcohol, herd-poison is an active, extraverted [sic] drug. The crowd-intoxicated individual escapes from responsibility, intelligence and morality into a kind of frantic, animal mindlessness. (1971, 60)

During the Michigan State University's March 27–28, 1999, riot, after losing to Duke University in the NCAA basketball tournament, MSU students demonstrated **mob anarchy**—the state of complete lawlessness and the resulting disorder characterized by emotional contagion. **Social-emotional contagion** is the process by which violent emotions such as hate, anger, or fear infect members of a mass, overcoming the normal thought processes and inhibitions experienced by individuals (as a result of psychological or sociologically imposed constraints within their own experiences) and creating a mass psychology of dramatic efforts (see DeFleur, D'Antonio, and DeFleur 1973, 356). Reacting to their team's defeat, the MSU rioters, though an unstructured and diverse mass, engaged in collective behavior produced by the emotional contagion of drunken disappointment. Such an emotional contagion gives birth to a mass hysteria, short circuiting normal individual thought processes and ultimately producing the most elemental forms of *homo sapiens*'s conduct: anger, violence, greed, hatred, and cruelty. Deprived of such constraints while operating on pure emotion-driven, drunken impulses, the rioters became more like the fiercest of animal competitors than civilized man.

Very different from social categories or masses, human **groups** may be viewed *"as a number of individuals who interact recurrently according to some pattern of social interaction"* (DeFleur, D'Antonio, and DeFleur 1973, 31; emphasis in original). Groups are formed when three necessary conditions coexist: (1) potential members are available (2) who share certain goals (material, emotional, physical, etc.) and (3) who engage in coordinated interaction to achieve these shared goals (see DeFleur, D'Antonio, and DeFleur 1973, 31). Groups may be either formal or informal. **Formal groups** are heavily routinized with written rules and regulations governing the groups' interaction patterns. Examples of formal groups would be the Kiwanis Club, the U. S. Air Force, or the college volleyball team. On the other hand, **informal groups** are loosely organized, highly flexible, with no written regulations. Examples of informal groups would be social cliques at school or at work.

Researchers use the same cultural or societal constructs to describe group behavior. While universal norms operate on the societal level (e.g., murder is wrong), other norms are the product not of the society but of a particular group. Urban gangs may require new members to murder someone as part of their initiation; while deplorable, such acts may be viewed as representative of a group norm. Researchers characterize groups in terms of four observable social interaction patterns:

> Sociologists identify these as a system of *norms*, or rules for governing the behavior of group members; a system of *roles* for coordinating their activities; a system of *sanctions* for maintaining social control; and a *ranking system* for assigning different

degrees of importance to particular roles. (DeFleur, D'Antonio, and DeFleur 1973, 31, emphasis in original)

These four social interaction patterns will now be examined in some detail.

Characteristics of Group Norms. It has been said that norms are the "social glue" that hold groups together. Deutsch and Gerard suggest that norms exert two types of influence within groups: **normative influence,** which is the "influence to conform to the positive expectations of another," and **informational influence,** which is the "influence to accept information obtained from another as evidence about reality" (1955, 629). Further research suggests that norms may be characterized by the function they perform for an individual. **Descriptive norms** indicate what is commonly done within a group or culture, and **injunctive norms** are those that have a sanctioning force in that they detail what is approved or disapproved within the group or culture (Cialdini, Reno, and Kallgren 1990). Injunctive norms have the component of "social desirability." In other words, injunctive norms establish what is socially correct in polite society.

The operation of a rotating gourmet supper club provides a ready example of such normative group influences. Such clubs rotate the hosting of dinner parties among its members. Membership in the group exerts normative influences on individual behaviors. For example, a member of a rotating supper club will want to prepare a meal for other members at the same level or above that of the culinary expertise exhibited by other members at previous club functions. Such efforts would be said to represent the normative influence within the group. In discussing the merits of a new gourmet restaurant, members who have not personally been to the restaurant will likely accept the judgment of other members concerning the quality and presentation of the food. This acceptance of other members' versions of reality rather than waiting to experience the restaurant for oneself is a demonstration of the informational influence of the group. In addition, when preparing a meal for club members, a member will take into account how the group members in the past have presented the meal. The decision to have a sit-down dinner or a cocktail buffet, the decision to seat spouses together or separately, or the decision to serve wine according to each course rather than serving one wine throughout the meal are all examples of individual decisions influenced by descriptive norms. A member who chooses to cater the meal when it becomes his or her turn to prepare dinner may well receive the group's scorn or rejection, because individual effort and creativity in food preparation is what is valued within the group. This is an example of violating an injunctive norm.

Although group membership does exert normative influences on individual behaviors, that influence may be most powerful in the presence of other group members. In other words, individual members may choose to deviate from group norms when separate from the group. Aquilino (1993) found that married couples when interviewed together responded very differently on questions concerning the benefits of marriage, spousal contributions to housework, and likelihood of divorce than when they were interviewed separately.

This brings us to an important distinction when analyzing human conduct—*public compliance* with group norms versus private acceptance or *internalization* of group norms. They are not always one and the same. For example, members of the Baptist faith may well observe public compliance of church norms by not drinking alcoholic beverages; they may well drink privately within the confines of their own home. Thus, the norm of consuming no alcoholic beverages was not internalized.

In a ground-breaking experimental study, Asch (1951) documented the power of social desirability and the resulting public compliance. Asch placed a subject in a setting where a majority of participants were actually Asch-trained confederates who expressed passionately their opinion as to the length of various drawn lines. This expressed opinion was observably incorrect in that the confederates identified the shorter lines as those being the longest and the longest lines as those being the shortest. Roughly one-third of the subjects rejected their own estimation as to the various lengths of the lines and ultimately accepted the majority opinion, which was incorrect. The subjects reported feeling considerable anxiety when confronted by the impassioned majority. Asch concluded that one-third of the subjects who disregarded what their own eyes told them were trying to avoid social isolation by agreeing with the majority. Thus, they were seeking social acceptance through publicly complying or agreeing with the majority's version of reality despite the fact they knew it to be incorrect.

However, in discussions about Asch's experiment, it is often overlooked that two-thirds of Asch's subjects resisted the influence of the confederates. When Asch placed two subjects rather than a lone subject with the confederates, the subjects were far more likely to express their disagreement with the majority opinion. In this situation, only 5 percent went along with the majority. Indeed, individuals may resist normative demands made by the majority, if competing normative choices are present because of multiple group memberships. In addition, people who value public individuation are likely to offer resistance to overt influences directed to change opinions.

When an individual's social judgments will likely become public knowledge, the power of normative influence is increased; and, when individuals are faced with normative pressure when interacting with multiple group members, the influence to conform is intensified (Deutsch and Gerard 1955).

When norms within a group represent extreme social judgments or when group pressure is highly intensified, the conformity to group norms is greater (Campbell, Tesser, and Fairey 1986). When an individual anticipates interaction with group members in the very near future, the individual is more likely to conform to group norms (Lewis, Langan, and Hollander 1972). And the more difficult the decision-making process and the more uncertain the appropriate outcome, the more likely for group members to conform (Luchins and Luchins 1955). However, the more information an individual has about a topic and the more self-confident the person is of his or her own judgment, the less influence the group may exert (Snyder, Mischel, and Lott 1960).

J. M. Jackson (1965) has summarized some observable patterns of the functioning of group norms, and he calls these identified patterns the structural characteristics of norms. The structural characteristics of norms are observable when:

1. an individual observes both what is appropriate behavior within the group and how the group rewards appropriate behavior;
2. an individual considers a potential act but evaluates that anticipated behavior by comparing it to behaviors that are deemed appropriate or inappropriate by the group;
3. an individual evaluates the intensity of feelings or the strength of approval or disapproval of specific behaviors exhibited by the group and considers the potential sanctions or rewards (or reinforcements) an individual would likely receive after the performance of such behaviors;
4. an individual plots the group's distribution of feelings about such behaviors on an approval–disapproval continuum (with approval positioned on the far left of a line and disapproval positioned on the far right of the line), which ultimately establishes the individual's perceived range of tolerable behavior for the group that the individual recognizes as a negotiated group norm;
5. an individual assesses a point on the approval–disapproval continuum where the majority of group members approve of the conduct, representing for the individual the group's ideal behavior; and
6. the high crystallization of norms (universal agreement within the group concerning the norm) yields more effective organizational behavior, and the low crystallization of norms yields dysfunctional organizational behavior (when members' viewpoints do not coincide on what is appropriate or inappropriate behavior).

Thus, the functioning of social norms within groups is the complex integration of six social judgments.

A historical example of the extreme power of some groups' normative influence on their members is the documented solidarity of Nazi Germany's Wehrmacht. In a groundbreaking study in 1948, Shils and Janowitz determined that during World War II, the Allies' propaganda war, which dropped millions of propaganda leaflets over German troops and continuously broadcast radio propaganda directed at German soldiers, was totally ineffective in bringing about desertion or a collapse in morale. Rather, the Wehrmacht (German soldiers) continued to display "extraordinary tenacity" throughout the course of the war (556). Shils and Janowitz concluded that the soldiers' reference group—the combat unit—provided continuous motivation and support even when faced with overwhelming odds. The "spatial proximity, intimate association, and the military organization itself" left the German soldier well protected against Allied propaganda (1948, 557). The German army worked to build group solidarity (cohesiveness) among its combat units. For example, military policy dictated that men who had shared victories on the battlefield were to remain together as fighting units. Thus, such conscious reinforcement of group norms built a powerful mutual identification.

At times, norms may be in transition. This is particularly true today in the Southern United States. Thousands of people and businesses have exchanged the cold winters of the North for the sunny delights of the Sunbelt. This has introduced individuals into the South who were raised in a culture very different from the one they now call home. This has caused a strange blending of the old and the new. And it has highlighted the distinction between those whom society columnists call "Old Money" and those they call "New Money." Marilyn Schwartz (1993) provides a humorous commentary on social categorization based on the observation of normative behaviors of women with "new money" in the Old South. She writes,

No matter how much money you have, how much coaching you have and how many sponsors you have, there are ten ways you can always tell that you're new money in the Old South.

1. Your plastic surgeon buys an entire table at the charity ball you're chairing.
2. Your bathroom is bigger than the town you were born in.
3. Your silver pattern wasn't inherited from your grandmother, it was recommended by your hairdresser.
4. The newer your money, the smaller the vegetables you serve at your dinner parties.
5. Your paintings match the sofa.
6. When people talk about you they know how much money your house cost rather than who your grandfather was.

7. No little pearl earrings from Grandmother; your earrings are big enough to double as barbells in your aerobics class.
8. You've never heard of homemade cheese straws; your specialty is the miniature frozen quiches from Sam's.
9. You don't have a file of family recipes, you have a file of caterers.
10. Your pearls are fake. But your money is real. (1993, 96)

Roles. A social role "defines the rights, duties, and obligations of any group member who performs a specialized function with the group" (DeFleur, D'Antonio, and DeFleur 1973, 40). In corporate America, roles are defined by written job descriptions and company manuals. But in a social clique, one might find the person who always decides where to eat, or the person who always convenes the group to go to the movies, or the person who is the recognized clique clown. Members of groups come to expect certain behaviors from various group members. "Roles are configurations of norms" (DeFleur, D'Antonio, and DeFleur 1973, 40) in that such specialized activities form an "organized system of mutual expectation" (41). And for this reason, role expectations and role behavior are both critical to the study of groups. For when an individual's actual role behavior deviates from the group's role expectations, then disharmony occurs, threatening the very existence of the group. And for this reason, groups exercise social control or sanctions.

Social Control or Sanctions. Social control is the group's application of sanctions to ensure that members will: "(1) abide by the group's norms, (2) perform required roles in a prescribed manner, and (3) coordinate their activities in such a way that group goals can be achieved" (DeFleur, D'Antonio, and DeFleur 1973, 42). Such sanctions may either be positive or negative. **Positive sanctions** serve as rewards for performing above and beyond the group's expectations in some area of desired behavior. This serves as a powerful reinforcement to continue to adhere to group goals. **Negative sanctions** are used to rebuke or punish someone for failing to follow group norms or for failing to sufficiently perform their assigned group roles and duties. This works to discourage deviation. Equally important to the understanding of group behaviors is a recognition of the group's social ranking system.

Social Ranking System. Different roles within the group have different degrees of significance to the group. Group roles may be viewed as existing on a hierarchical structure with more significant roles located at the top and less significant roles near the bottom. The president of a citizen's group like the League of Women Voters would be at the top of the league's social ranking system in that the president's performance is critical to the success of the organization. A telephone receptionist, on the other hand, might be positioned near the bottom. However, this does not mean that the telephone receptionist is not valued as an employee. Rather, such roles because of little power, few responsibilities, or little visibility are judged by the group members as falling low in the group hierarchy. In formal situations such as governmental or corporate organizations, roles are usually assigned to individuals by virtue of their education, professional experience, and perceived abilities. In informal situations, the individual who organizes group activities among a circle of friends may well be considered the group's leader and therefore would be positioned at the top of the social ranking hierarchy. As a result of social ranking, individuals will receive status or prestige by virtue of performing the identified role at that particular level in the system. For example, a senior partnership in a law firm is viewed as a very prestigious position within the law firm, because the role indicates a high level of power within the firm. But if you take the individual who is a senior partner in the law firm and move that person into another group, say, a racquetball club, then the prestige will be related only to his or her ranking within the racquetball set.

A Case Study in Social Interactions: The American College Sorority. Contemporary social sororities on college campuses provide us with a ready example for examining patterned social interactions in a microcosm. Many sociologists view college sororities as "mating" and "hostess" training schools for America's economically privileged, college-age women, for the social skills learned in college help secure their future life in desired social circles, ultimately culminating in the selection and acquisition of a socially desirable marital mate. In sorority life, young women learn confidence and poise in a variety of social situations. These social situations involve the discovery, learning, and mastering of social etiquette, which involves norms (as well as folkways, mores, and rituals). In addition, the sorority reinforces lifelong commitments to healthy lifestyles, scholarship, achievement (personal best), and service. Although few female college students see their social sororities in this manner, a close examination of such groups reveals a number of shared characteristics and/or behavior patterns that promote the achievement of a social prowess deemed appropriate for the young woman's desired social status in life and future mate (see figure 2.2).

Perhaps one way to identify a given sorority's normative patterns is simply to ask a variety of students on campus what the "rap" is on a given sorority. You will quickly find that students share a common stereotype about the nature of the young women who belong to each sorority. And frequently, those women within the sorority actually agree with the stereotype. In Karen's late 1970s experience at the College of William and Mary, the stereotypical characterizations made about sororities on campus involved physical descriptions of the women with accompanying personality traits (as tasteless as they may be): the large and unattractive, and/or athletes; the beautiful but very easy; the beautiful with trust funds; and, the beautiful but campus leaders; or the above average looking but goody two-shoed. Clearly such stereotypes (as cruel as they may be) give a clue as to: (1) the society's evaluation of the group and (2) why the women themselves joined the group. On another campus, sororities may be classified as to what area of the state they call home, their religious affiliation, their parents' wealth, or their major in college. Whatever the classification system, it does provide us clues as to what behaviors are likely to form normative patterns within the group (see figure 2.2).

To maintain stability and solidarity, college sororities exercise techniques of social control both through positive sanctions establishing a rewards system to reinforce approved social behaviors and through negative sanctions establishing a punishment system to discourage deviance. In Karen's, positive sanctions included being selected to receive an historical bejeweled sorority pin for significant contributions to the sorority during the previous month. Positive sanctions might be as simple as the chapter president recognizing the member's accomplishment during a chapter meeting. Negative sanctions were used to punish those who deviated from accepted roles, such as those who failed to attend chapter meetings, failed to attend sorority/fraternity swaps or parties, failed to meet other significant behavioral expectations, or failed to perform required formal roles within the sorority. In such cases, negative sanctions ranged from the assessing of fines to expulsion from the sorority. Such sanctions characterize group behavior when confronted with individual deviancy, the lack of personal compliance. The campus social sorority provides us with a ready example of the normative social interactions performed by members; however, the social sorority may also be viewed as being influential in the campus society outside of their membership. We now turn to a theoretical area that will address such potential external influence.

Reference Group Theory. During the twentieth century, researchers expanded their interest in social organizations and the various manifestations of their social influence. Specifically, early research emphasized the recurrent interactions among members of a formal group, also known as a membership group. As the researchers observed social behavior and as they inquired as to what motivated such behaviors, they often found that normative patterns of social interaction within a group might well influence the behavior of others outside the group. This occurs when individuals outside the group desire to join the group, and in aspiring to the group, these individuals observe the group's normative patterns and adopt them as their own, seeking

Figure 2.2   Observed Sorority Norms, Mores, Folkways, and Rituals

- Fine china and silver at sorority functions
- Full-course meals served
- Meals are served to the young women by people external to the sorority (servants)
- Required appropriate table etiquette
  a. appropriate attire
  b. appropriate thank-yous said to the servers
  c. appropriate dinner conversations observing the proprieties
- Well-decorated and often refurbished surroundings within sorority houses
- Family-like subunits within sororities providing appropriate socialization to new pledges who are known as "little sisters" (those recruited and who have agreed to join)
- Pledge training classes on desirable conduct within the sorority
- Rules and regulations concerning pledge and ultimately initiate's behavior
  a. required attendance at dances, balls, initiation ceremonies, or swaps (fraternity/sorority parties)
  b. expectation of following formal etiquette: formal invitations, stationery, thank-you notes
  c. requirements to wear sorority colors on chapter meeting days; requirement to wear pledge or initiation pins on days of observed sorority milestones
  d. required minimum GPA
- Sanctions established for violating the rules and regulations of the sorority
  a. verbal or written rebuke
  b. social ostracism
  c. demerit system
     —fines
     —assignment of undesirable duties, e.g., cleaning kitchen, washing windows
     —expulsion from the sorority
- Systems established for rewarding adherence to or the exceeding of expectations of desired behavior
  a. scholarship banquets or ceremonies for highest GPA, most improved GPA, for A-B members
  b. awards for achievements in sports
  c. awards for being selected cheerleader, majorette, mascot
  d. awards for achievements in community service
  e. awards for induction into academic honoraries
  f. awards for superior assistance in achieving group goals
  g. awards for being elected to college political office
  h. awards for holding prestigious offices in other groups
  i. special recognition and ceremonies for women who receive fraternity lavalieres, pins, or who get engaged
  j. awards for members who receive recognition from national headquarters
- Presentation of new little sisters at a formal pledge dance, introducing them to the campus community as part of the sorority family
- Initiation ceremonies combining a series of elements:
  a. the demonstration of the continuity of life by representing life's stages
  b. presentation of secret-mystical, shared bonds (handshakes, motto, oaths, signs)
  c. the presentation of religious and/or spiritual undertones designed to promote the approved "spiritual" system of the sorority
  d. an emphasis on the mind, the body (beauty), and the soul (spirit)
  e. the promotion of service as a life-long goal
  f. the promotion of sisterhood or life-long loyalty to your sorority sisters

the approval and perhaps eventual validation (formal support) by the group's acceptance of them as members. Thus, the role of groups in exerting social influence once perceived as being limited to the group's influence on its own members was expanded to include the potential group influence on individuals outside the group who wish to join. For example, a young woman going through the experience of sorority rush (the formal process by which sororities and a pool of eligible members mutually evaluate one another, seeking social similarities or compatibility) may well adopt the normative fashion style associated with the particular sorority she wishes to join. Her observation and adherence to the sorority's norms is an impression management strategy designed to achieve group recognition, approval, and ultimately acceptance. For this young woman, the sorority to which she aspires serves as a reference group.

Indeed group membership may be viewed as "varying along an ingroup-outgroup dimension" (Levine, Bogart, and Zdaniuk 1996, 533); such a depiction recognizes that "the relationship between a group and its members changes over time, and members occupy different roles in the group, depending on the length and quality of their relationship with it" (Levine, Bogart, and Zdaniuk, 1996, 533). According to Levine, Bogart, and Zdaniuk, five categories of group-membership may be described:

> "Prospective members" have not yet joined the group, but may do so in the future. "New members" have recently joined the group and are undergoing socialization in order to acquire the knowledge and skills needed for full membership. "Full members" have successfully completed socialization and thereby earned all the privileges and responsibilities of membership. "Marginal members" once had full member status, have lost this status because they violated group norms, and are undergoing resocialization. Finally "ex-members" once belonged to the group, have left it, but may still be influenced by their group experiences. (1996, 533–34)

Reference groups, then, are those groups to which an individual belongs or aspires (Riley and Riley 1959, 548). And as such, reference groups were said to exert influence on an individual's self-evaluation by providing a point of comparison and exerting influence on an individual's adoption of values, beliefs, and attitudes (Kelley 1952; Merton 1957). College students who want to be accepted by a law school often do away with their jeans, T-shirts, and baseball caps during their senior year in college. Both men and women leave behind the unkempt look so favored by most college students and instead adopt "law student attire," the socially prescribed traditional modes of dress considered appropriate for the respective genders and for attorneys in informal social situations. For most, this means an adoption of what stereotypically constitutes the "preppy look," loafers, khaki pants, skirts, button-down shirts and blouses, and pullovers. By changing their clothing behaviors, these students are anticipating their joining of the law student body and are adopting the normative dress code of their future reference group.

Reference Group Functions. Kelley (1952) distinguished between the **normative** and **comparative** functions of reference groups. To the extent that individuals turn to groups for guidance in adopting attitudes and/or behaviors, these groups exert a normative influence. And to the extent that reference groups serve as standards of comparison for self-evaluation and the evaluation of others, the groups serve a comparative function. Newcomb (1950) distinguished between **positive reference groups**—or those groups valued by an individual and who serve as a positive source for normative guidance such as a successful graduate student association and those groups that function as **negative reference groups**—who are rejected by an individual and serve as a negative source for normative guidance such as those students who were arrested in the MSU riots.

Sometimes reference groups function as **primary groups,** because as the term suggests, such groups play a key role in crafting an individual's attitudes and values. Noted sociologist Charles Horton Cooley, the first to identify and define primary groups, wrote:

> By primary groups I mean those characterized by intimate face-to-face association and cooperation. They are primary in several senses, but chiefly in that they are fundamental in forming the social nature and ideals of the individual. The result of intimate association, psychologically, is a certain fusion of individualities in a common whole, so that one's very self, for many purposes at least, is the common life and purpose of the group. Perhaps the simplest way of describing this wholeness is by saying that it is a "we"; it involves the sort of sympathy and mutual identification for which "we" is the natural expression. (1929, 23–24)

The most common primary group is the family unit—parents, siblings, and the extended family. Primary groups do not have a formal structure, but they are important nevertheless. Peer groups whose members share similar interests are also important primary groups for the individual. It should be noted that research indicates that primary groups and membership groups exert the greatest normative influence on members as compared to other types of reference groups such as those that individuals do not belong to but aspire to join (Kaplan 1968; Siegel and Siegel 1957; Walsh, Ferrell, and Tolone 1976).

A Further Clarification. Because researchers came to recognize the influence on an individual's behavior of reference groups to which people aspire, they came to view such nonmembership groups in a different light. Researchers eventually acknowledged the potential influence of a nonmembership group that serves as a reference point for an individual. Nonmembership groups may never serve as a means for direct social comparison or social interaction. Such groups either do not function as a group within the "real world," or they do exist, but are only known through an individual's "imagining" of group characteristics. Often people never intend to join, thus avoiding the expenditure of time, money, and effort often required for organizational membership (Shibutani 1955; Stern and Keller 1953; R. H. Turner 1956). These "imagined groups" are based on the individual's personal demographic and psychological assessment and resulting values, belief structures, and assumption of other people out there who share these same belief structures and values. Thus, such "imagined" groups exert influence only on those who have created them. Riley and Riley (1959) provide an example of an "imagined" group. They write that for most Americans, the national political parties are only "imagined" in that the parties are the creations of an individual's mind, for they have no direct experience with them. Yet people will behave toward such imagined groups as if they were real.

> The fact that people vote as members of groups, and that groups themselves tend to remain stable, ensures a fairly stable division of the electorate into two major parties—thus maintaining the system and thereby providing a balance between the conservatism of the right and the demand of the left for change. (Riley and Riley 1959, 559)

Although such imagined groups do not produce the level of normative influence usually exerted by membership groups, these "imagined" groups may have significant consequences, nevertheless. When public issues that the individual has no readily available reference group to turn to for guidance arise, the individual's perception of the social majority's viewpoint (as often presented through the mass media) may prove influential on their own opinion (Charters and Newcomb 1958). Thus the *perceived social majority* may exert influence on the individual who is temporarily without a reference group.

Researchers came to develop a theoretical conceptualization that explained how the process of social influence works within groups and within societies. Researchers knew that once an individual had selected a group as a reference point for his or her own behavior in guidance-seeking or in self-comparisons, the individual tended to conform to group expectations of behavior. For this reason, researchers hypothesized that group members usually share homogeneity (similarity) in attitudes and values. And researchers suggested that groups develop group sanctions, which reward compliance and punish deviancy. Researchers discovered that groups that were successful in their exertion of normative influences were those groups who (1) held and propagated unambiguous norms (Hyman, Wright, and Hopkins 1962) and who (2) directed messages at group members who attached a greater degree of personal salience (importance) to membership than the average member (Braungart and Braungart 1979; Suchman and Menzel 1955). Such observations and conclusions assisted researchers in their development of greater explanatory processual models of social behavior and ultimately the development of social-influence processual models.

To Summarize. In our review of the sociological contributions to the understanding of human behavior, it has become obvious that the majority of the research emphasizes the desirability of social control (through internal and external group behaviors) and the preferred maintenance of the social-structural stability of systems (whether they are groups or cultures).

DANGERS OF CONFORMITY: AN ALTERNATIVE PERSPECTIVE

While the majority of research has emphasized the desirability of conformity, liberal social philosophers and some social science scholars have taken an opposite perspective. The writings of British social philosophers John Stuart Mill and Aldous Leonard Huxley as well as the writings of American social critics such as Fromm (1941); Gardner (1961); Janis (1972); Riesman, Glazer, and Denney (1950); and Whyte (1956) represent the vibrant tradition of the glorification of independence and individualism. For these writers, conformity is not necessarily a prized commodity. They emphasize that "a society built on rigidly structured patterns of behavior wastes individual talent and loses the capacity to act in novel ways" (Hollander 1976, 412; Gardner 1961). And some organizational scholars suggest that strict insistence to conformity will eventually lead to severe limits on organizational effectiveness in that the organization will not be able to adapt to the ever-changing environment in which it exists (cf., D. Katz 1964). The dangers of conformity are perhaps best typified by the writings of Janis (1972, 1973).

Indeed, John Stuart Mill has written eloquently on the desirability of eccentricity:

> It does seem, however, that when the opinions of masses of merely average men are everywhere become or becoming the dominant power, the counterpoise and corrective to that tendency would be the more and more pronounced individuality of those who stand on the higher eminences of thought. It is in these circumstances most especially that exceptional individuals, instead of being deterred, should be encouraged in acting differently from the mass. . . . Precisely because the tyranny of opinion is such as to make eccentricity a reproach, it is desirable, in order to break through that tyranny, that people should be eccentric. Eccentricity has always

abounded when and where strength of character has abounded; and the amount of eccentricity in a society has generally been proportional to the amount of genius, mental vigor, and moral courage it contained. That so few now dare to be eccentric marks the chief danger of the time. . . . There is one characteristic of the present direction of public opinion peculiarly calculated to make it intolerant of any marked demonstrations of individuality. The general average of mankind are not only moderate in intellect, but also moderate in inclinations; they have no tastes or wishes strong enough to incline them to do anything unusual, and they consequently do not understand those who have, and class all such with the wild and intemperate whom they are accustomed to look down upon. (1956, 81–85)

Groupthink

Janis suggested the groupthink hypothesis after reading and contemplating Arthur Schlesinger's *A Thousand Days* (1965), an account of decisions made during President John F. Kennedy's short-lived administration. In particular, Janis was fascinated by Schlesinger's description of the decision-making apparatus that approved the Bay of Pigs scenario (Janis 1976, 406). Janis was dumbfounded in that he could not imagine how such a group comprised of such uniformly noteworthy individuals could have been "taken in by such a stupid, patchwork plan as the one presented to them by the C. I. A. representatives" (406). For Janis, the Bay of Pigs fiasco could only be explained as the product of group solidarity that had gone awry. In other words, the members of Kennedy's inner circle cared more about maintaining each others' approval, that is, the maintenance of the "we," than crafting a solid strategic and tactical foreign policy initiative (Janis 1972, 1973, 1976). Janis desired that "groupthink" take on an invidious connotation, because for Janis, the concept "groupthink refers to a deterioration of mental efficiency, reality testing and moral judgment that results from ingroup pressures" (1976, 407) seeking concurrence or agreement. After reviewing several other "historic fiascoes," Janis's normative analysis arrived at what he considered to be the "major defects in decision-making which contributed to failures to solve problems adequately" (1976, 407). These defects are summarized below:

1. The group fails to survey the universe of alternatives available to them, with the resulting group discussion focusing on only a few alternatives.
2. The group fails to reconsider their decision after resting and reflecting on their decision. They fail to examine the potential negative consequences of their decisions, including the potential pitfalls involved in implementation.
3. Early decisions to reject possible solutions are never revisited. Thus, the group does not have the advantage of comparing potential gains and

losses from previously rejected alternatives with those of the accepted decision. As such, the group ignores any knowledge gain generated through group discussion, which might affect the assessment of previously rejected alternatives.

4. The group fails to obtain multiple, independent experts who are capable of analyzing the various alternatives from a variety of perspectives and ultimately supplying sound projections of potential positives and negatives associated with each. The use of information from multiple expert sources is desirable as it exposes decision-makers to various expert presentations, providing them with the opportunity to judge the veracity or acuity of each presented alternative.

5. Members selectively attend to information provided by media accounts and available expert sources that supports preconceived policy notions.

6. The group fails to craft contingency plans in the event of a policy decision failure. Group members continue to support the original decision, even when opportunities arise to abort or change course. (See Janis 1976, 407–8.)

Littlejohn has commented that Janis's observed defects are "merely the manifestation of a lack of critical thinking and overconfidence in the judgment of the group" (1992, 298). Clearly, those groups that are ongoing and whose members anticipate future interactions with each other are more likely to produce behavior symptomatic of groupthink (Hollander 1976, 415). Janis suggested that a number of shared symptoms of groups exercising groupthink become readily apparent upon comparative analysis; these include:

- An *illusion of invulnerability* creates unfounded optimism.
- A group-constructed narrative produced by the group's history *rationalizes* the decision.
- A self-judged *inherent morality* in what the group wishes to accomplish protects members from soul-searching or self-criticism.
- *Stereotyped* or demonized out-group leaders provide reinforcement for both the in-group's inherent morality and its narrative rationalization of the decision.
- Forces applying *direct pressure* within the group strain toward symmetry by discouraging dissent among group members.
- Individual members may demonstrate outward compliance but maintain internal dissension, because discouraging group forces invoke *self-censorship*. This self-censorship ruins any possibility for alternative ideas to be voiced.
- Specific group members work to protect the leader and the other group

members from contrary information or dissension once a decision has been made. These *mind guards* also call for group solidarity to maintain optimum performance. (The emphasized words reflect Janis's own terminology; see Janis 1972, 1973, 1976.)

Janis has suggested a number of means to avoid the potential of groupthink. His suggestions (1972, 262–71) are condensed in the following discussion.

The decision maker/leader should empower all members by encouraging them to critically evaluate all information and opinions presented. The leader should avoid prejudicing the discussion by deliberately refraining from voicing an opinion or inclination. The organization itself should rely on multiple, independent decision-making clusters with designated leaders to arrive at independent recommendations rather than on one decision-making group and leader.

Internally a decision-making group should work in independent subunits when considering proposed alternatives. Upon subunit consensus, the various subunits should present and defend their recommendations to the entire group. A genuine debate of recommendations should occur.

In addition, group members who represent different areas or departments should obtain information and guidance from their home areas or departments at the end of each deliberation session. Ultimately, their comments should be brought back to the decision-making group for consideration and review.

Independent experts not part of the initial decision-making group should observe and critically evaluate policy discussions. In addition to these outside challenges by independent experts, the leader should appoint a "devil's advocate" from within the group for each day of deliberation to critically evaluate and expand group discussion.

The group should constantly monitor forces within the environment, particularly those identified as "a problem out-group" or "enemy" to assess any changes in the behavior or rhetoric of the out-group. This monitoring should be done with the assistance of experts who understand the out-group's cultural environment. At all times, multiple scenarios of likely out-group behavior should be constructed and reassessed upon any out-group action.

And ultimately, after reaching a preliminary consensual decision, group members should have the opportunity to reflect on the wisdom of such a decision and to reevaluate the pros and cons associated with this choice. After that time, the group should reconvene, and the group leader should encourage free and open discussion for members' assessments and about the proposed policy itself (see Janis 1972, 262–71; Littlejohn 1992, 298–99).

A host of researchers in the ensuing years have tried to test and refine Janis's concept of groupthink (see Mansfield's review of the literature, 1990, 257). By Mansfield's count, nineteen academic articles were generated on the subject by 1990, and groupthink was widely included in many communication theory texts such as Littlejohn (1992). Groupthink remains, at least for these authors, a highly contrived, rather naive depiction of group dynamics within high-level decision-making circles in the United States. For a far more theoretically based account of faulty group decision making, please review Graham Allison's classic *Essence of Decision: Explaining the Cuban Missile Crisis* (1971). However, Janis's work remains a useful guideline in the creation of mechanisms to introduce dynamism to discussions, provide significant challenges to traditional thinking, and invigorate group processes through outside influences.

Other Potentially Dysfunctional Group Influences

Latané and Darley (1969) first identified the tendency of individuals to develop a sense of **personal detachment** within organizations or groups where they have highly specialized roles. In such situations, the individual will not volunteer to solve problems or to contribute to problem-solving, because "the problem" is someone else's, and because of structural barriers, which promote alienation, the individual feels detached or unconnected with and unaffected by the problem. Such **diffusion of responsibility,** while maintaining clear chains of command and responsibility, often hinders creative problem solving.

In addition, researchers have identified the **risky-shift phenomenon** or **choice shift phenomenon** (Clark 1971; Dion, Baron, and Miller 1970; Kogan and Wallach 1964; Pruitt 1971; Vinokur 1971). Individuals participating in a group are far more likely to engage in risky behaviors or extreme behaviors than if they are acting alone. Moscovici and Zavollini (1969) suggested that this observed phenomenon is created by group polarization in that "the opinion of a group involved in a decision process will tend to be more extreme in the direction of the norm than the initial opinions of its members" (Moscovici 1985, 397). Other researchers (Fraser 1971; Fraser and Billing 1971; Gouge and Fraser 1972; McCauley 1972) have validated the group polarization effect; McCauley has made it clear that observed group opinion polarization does not imply a corresponding individual members' attitude polarization (1972). Indeed, it may be safely said that "groups are more extreme and more strongly for or against than individuals" (Moscovici 1985, 398). A telling example comes to mind: Karen has seen grown men and women (presumably alumni), as well as enthusiastic college students, at an Auburn University vs. University of Tennessee football game (held in Auburn at the Jordan Hare Stadium) pelt Tennessee fans and players with rotten oranges. For the life of us, we cannot visualize these same Auburn orange-pelters walking down a street in either Auburn or Knoxville, pelting with rotten oranges individuals who are wearing Big Orange T-Shirts or displaying the Big Orange color.

NONCONFORMITY AND POTENTIAL MINORITY INFLUENCES AND INNOVATION

Nonconformity Characteristics

Independence. Just as conformity has been viewed as a relational concept that describes the outcome of an individual's participation in social interaction, independence should also be viewed as a relational concept characterizing the outcome of an individual's interaction in a social situation (cf., Hollander 1976). Individuals who deviate from the group's norms are said to exhibit independence in their relations with the group and other group members. Group pressures, as we have previously discussed, work against deviant expressions of opinions. For this reason, group processes present a number of impediments to independence. Hollander has identified these impediments: (a) risks of disapproval, (b) lack of perceived alternatives, (c) fear of disrupting the proceeding, (d) absence of shared communication, (e) inability to feel responsibility, and (f) sense of impotence (1976, 416).

Clearly deviant behavior within an organization or group will often meet with disapproval, ostracism, or even ejection from the group. Yet, it is sometimes through deviancy that significant and positive social change ultimately occurs. For example, prior to the 1960s, newly elected members of the United States Senate were told by senior members that they must serve a lengthy apprenticeship before fully participating in Senate business, and as part of that apprenticeship, they were explicitly told "don't rock the boat," "to get along, go along," and "go with the crowd." Clearly such advice discouraged new members from developing independence within the group (see J. F. Kennedy 1956; Matthews 1960). Those who did exercise independence were nicknamed "mavericks" and as such, these "wild horses" often found themselves in losing corrals, frequently relegated to serving on overlooked and often rather insignificant Senate committees—an undesirable prospect for someone seeking national attention for future electoral plans. And in some instances, mavericks were placed on Senate committees that actually hurt their chances of reelection in their home state, because the purview of the committee didn't have anything to do with their home state. In other words, their Senate committee assignments precluded the maverick senators from bringing home the bacon to their constituents (cf., Matthews 1960). However, by the early 1960s, a new breed of senator was finally emerging as senior members of the body, and they opened up the opportunities for significant contributions from all members during Senate deliberations (cf., Ornstein, Peabody, and Rohde 1985; Ornstein 1983).

Often offering a wide variety of alternatives in a decision-making situation is resisted by members who dislike brainstorming and prefer more channeled and thus constricted discussions. In addition, in trying to interject alternatives into the discussion, individuals may face the displeasure of group leaders who are often oriented to arrive at the easiest and quickest consensus, and for this reason, those who voice alternatives may be viewed as engaging in unnecessary and disruptive behavior (Maier and Hoffman 1965). In some circumstances, group members may disagree with the group leader's assumptions about group goals or group decision-making processes; yet, those in disagreement risk being viewed as impolite or obnoxious if they do voice their opinions. Thus, their differences in opinions remain unvoiced and therefore unshared and unknown. Fundamentally, the common denominator of Hollander's (1976) first four impediments is a reluctance to speak because of the fear of retribution.

Hollander's last two impediments to group influence emerge as the by-product of group processes that foster alienation. Individuals fail to identify with the relative successes and failures of the group, and, instead, focus only on the single microcosm of behavior that is in their own responsibility domain with the resulting attitude of "it's not my problem." If the individual's alienation from the group becomes too severe, then a feeling of impotence inhibits independent action, for the individual contribution will simply be ignored or ridiculed and as such is not worth the expenditure of energy.

Independence and Innovation. Much is unknown about independence, because the predominant strain of social science research has focused on conformity and ignored the concept of relational independence (Hollander 1976; Moscovici 1985). Moscovici (1976) found the various functional models of society biased in their emphasis on conformity or the desirability of the social-structural stability of systems, the resulting norm-enforcement mechanisms, and ultimately the significance of social control. "The advocates of this approach [functionalism] essentially look at the adaptation processes through which social systems become long lasting and protect themselves against change, regarded as a social evil" (Mugny and Pérez 1991, 1). Such a perspective is biased toward the status quo and biased against social change or innovation.

Moscovici (1976) rejected this functionalist notion of social-system immobility (see Balandier 1985), and instead posited that social systems are dynamic entities responding to internal and external changes in their environments with the resulting evolution of the social systems' normative patterns. With this perspective, a social system either maintains the status quo or evolves, depending on the outcomes of the system's interactions with internal and external factors. Moscovici was particularly interested in the role of the minority in bringing about social change within the social system; this social change he called an **innovation** (a change in an idea, a custom, a judgment, an action, or a device) (e.g., Moscovici and Faucheux 1972; Moscovici and Lage 1976; Moscovici, Lage, and Naffrechoux 1969; Moscovici and Neve 1972).

We now highlight Moscovici's conception of the stages in an innovation process (as exemplified in the previous citations of his works), coupled with some clarifications made by others (as indicated by citations). First, a minority voices an alternative opinion to the majority's opinion. Then the majority immediately tries to restore consensus through various social influence strategies (which we have discussed elsewhere in this chapter) (cf., Mugny and Papastamou 1980). However, the minority refuses to yield to the majority's efforts. Consequently, the majority continues to engage in attempts to restore consensus. And, if the minority continues to have a united front, voicing a distinctive and consistent opinion through a wide variety of situations, it will likely force the majority to question the validity of their own opinion (Moscovici and Nemeth 1974). Yet, the minority has no power to force their opinions on the majority, because obviously they are not great in number. And there will be no social pressure on the majority to change their position, because those in the minority are usually not liked, considered by the majority to be troublemakers or deviants. Rather the minority's influence rests in its presentation of information and/or evidence that undermines the majority's confidence in its own position (Price and Oshagan 1995). One example of this is in a tribal village, where a few innovative individuals have accepted the practice of boiling water (as practiced by Peace Corps members) before drinking, cooking, bathing, or washing with it. After a time, they are likely to report to the majority that their families are healthier than in previous years. And the majority's independent confirmation of this may encourage their questioning of their own beliefs. Under some circumstances, such minority influence may result in: (1) overt acceptance by the majority of the minority position; (2) both public acceptance and private internalization or acceptance (conversions) (Kimball and Hollander 1974); or (3) a reexamination of the question, producing lively discussions and thought-provoking ideas that ultimately lead to change (Mugny and Pérez 1991; Nemeth and Staw 1989).

Mugny and Pérez have built on the work of Moscovici and others, becoming much more specific about the mechanisms of innovation and the process that brings it about. They write:

> The mechanisms of innovation are rooted in the *conflict* that minorities are capable of creating in others and introducing into the social system. Here, it is no longer a form of dependence that underlies influence, but rather the minority's style of behaviour [sic], which is instrumental to the instigation and management of conflict. Through their consistent, coherent, and committed action along an ever-so-long journey, minorities manage in the end to make "something" change, in individuals and in society. (1991, 3; emphasis in original)

Mugny and Pérez distinguish between the compliance-seeking majority influence, which is direct in that people tend to accept the majority opinion when "the majority is present and psychologically salient," and that of the conversion-seeking, minority influence, which is "indirect, latent, or delayed" (1991, 4). Previously, we have discussed how the majority opinion within social systems exerts pressures on members to conform. At this point, we will focus on the potential minority influence within a social system. For example, the Greek system (sororities and fraternities) at a university in the Deep South has historically been segregated by race and by religion. A minority of Greek leaders represented on the Greek ruling council want to end segregation, offering a plan to integrate the Greek chapters. The majority immediately responded by defending the tradition and exhibiting hostile communication behaviors. However, after a number of opportunities to formally discuss the issue, some chapter representatives, although publicly denouncing the minority's position, will privately agree. And over time, the size of that group exhibiting private acceptance will become larger, ultimately emboldening them to join those in the minority. And over a long period of time, the council's policy may well change from segregation to integration.

Mugny (1982) and Mugny and Pérez (1991, 12) have argued that the relationship between the majority (that exercises power) and the minority (that rejects the power) is one of antagonism; thus, through the minority's consistent behavioral style, social conflict is repeatedly injected into the social system. "Indeed, in order to present itself as an innovative alternative in the face of a dominant normative system, the first thing the minority must do is to explicitly break away from that norm, thus preventing negotiation with the power structure by avoiding compromise" (Mugny and Pérez 1991, 12).

Communication Styles. Mugny and Pérez (1991) distinguish between the minority's **behavior style** and its **negotiation style**. "Behavior style refers to the strategies used to express antagonism with respect to a dominant norm, whereas negotiation style refers to the strategies adopted by minorities" to bargain with the majority (Mugny and Pérez 1991, 13). By the minority's expression of disparate beliefs and the inevitable introduction of social conflict, the majority perceives the minority as an out-group, defined in pejorative terms and ultimately discriminated against (Mugny and Pérez 1991, 14). For example, a country club in the New South experienced a tremendous influx of new members (who aren't native Southerners) who do not necessarily share the original members' definitions of genteel past times. Indeed, a sizeable minority of new female members proposed the country club sponsor bowling teams to compete with other area bowling teams. The "Old Guard" of the club were absolutely horrified at the prospects of having the club's name associated with a bowling team, which they consider to be the height of déclassé activities. One grand dame of the club who sat on the board of directors warned the convened group "that first it would be sponsoring a bowling team, and next, mark-my-words, they will be chewing tobacco in the women's locker rooms." A ranked tennis player responded, "Oh, Dear G——, I knew we shouldn't have let that riff-raff join." And in this way, the majority stigmatized the minority, defining it in pejorative terms, and ultimately discriminated against it by refusing to sponsor the teams. However, the minority got even by funding their own teams, using the logo "Just some more Riff-Raff from ——— Country Club."

Psychosocial Identification. Mugny, Kaiser, and Papastamou (1983) and Mugny and Pérez (1991, 12–16) (and a host of others, as indicated by additional citations within the text) determined that **psychosocial identification** (the psychological processes of social comparison and social identification) (see previous discussion) yields the following generalizations and examples:

1. An in-group favoritism exists intragroup; for example, the majority opinion (in-group) exercises more authority and control intragroup.
2. In-group communication within intragroup is more effective when expressing extremist positions, ultimately increasing the conflict's significance (e.g., adoption required for membership, self-identification by acceptance of the extreme opinion) (Mugny and Pérez 1985, 60); for example, Right to Life leaders use intragroup the strategies of exaggerated claims, extremist rhetoric, and the intensification of perceived conflict with both the more moderate internal/out-group as well as external/out-groups. Such practices help produce and maintain intragroup solidarity.
3. The in-group negates an anti-norm, in-group minority by categoriz-

ing them as a stigmatized out-group. For example, the in-group community of Jews may disapprove of the minority Hasidic population,
often ridiculing or discriminating against them.

4. However, in-group members favor members of the intragroup over
members of an external group, categorized as an out-group (Martin
1987); for example, in-group Jews would favor Hasidic Jews (an internal out-group) more than Muslims, an external group identified as an
out-group.

5. And correspondingly, "An anti-norm, ingroup source [internal out-
group] exerts more direct influence than an out-group [external]
source, especially when the context brings out the intergroup nature
of the influence relationship; an out-group [external] source can nevertheless induce more latent influence" (Mugny and Pérez 1991, 63;
cf., Doise, Gachoud, Mugny 1986). For example, during the course of
a war, an internal out-group (minority) who proposes the destruction
of all military and civilian enemy targets will exert more direct influence on the in-group (majority) who supports the destruction of only
strategic military targets than the enemy, external/out-group, which is
currently waging war against the group. However, the external/out-
group may exert more indirect influence on the in-group than the
internal out-group by consistently behaving in a humane manner. For
example, the humane treatment of prisoners, the swapping of prisoners of war, the immediate investigation and subsequent punishment
of soldiers violating the Geneva Conventions, and the providing of
protection for civilian populations by the enemy is more likely to exert
indirect influence on the in-group to continue their military targets-
only policy than the internal/out-group cries for annihilating strategies.

6. Out-group communication to in-group members is more effective
when adopting a more compromising style that argues out-group positions as being "desirable" rather than as being "essential" (Mugny and
Pérez 1985). For example, the out-group (minority) within modern-
day Protestantism, the Religious Right would be more effective in
influencing the in-group (majority of Protestants) if their communication style were more compromising, arguing, for example, that
abstinence before marriage is "desirable" or "preferred" rather than
their current argument that abstinence before marriage is obligatory
or required to be a Christian.

7. Even when the minority is categorized as an out-group and consequently discriminated against, the minority may still bring about
change, "although of an indirect, private, or delayed nature" (Mugny

and Pérez 1991, 15). For example, in the introduction of minority employees to a corporate sales force, the in-group initially stigmatized the minority employees as an out-group and often discriminated against them. But as the minority employees proved to be both competent and efficient, and increased sales to minorities, and demonstrated through example the profitability of culture-sensitive sales techniques, the in-group came to accept and utilize the techniques exhibited by the out-group.

8. The more members of the majority perceive themselves to be similar to the minority, the more likely they will be to accept the minority's alternative viewpoint, and the greater the degree of conflict the minority may safely introduce (Mugny and Pérez 1985). However, when members of the majority perceive themselves to be psychologically distant from the minority, the more the minority should attenuate the conflict (extend the time rather than heighten the intensity) (Mugny and Pérez 1985). Within the minority (intragroup), the members are dogmatic and rigid in their communication styles, for it is more effective in the reinforcement of their normative patterns. However, when the minority communicates with the majority, a more equitable communication style is appropriate (Mugny and Pérez 1991, 69; cf., Pérez, Mugny, and Roux 1989).

9. When members of the majority are seeking a positive social identification for themselves, the potential minority influence increases when the psychosocial identification made by the majority member about the minority is positive and is compatible with the majority member's own desired positive social identity, but—

10. In order for this to happen, the member of the majority must be able to cognitively separate the social comparison activity from the validation activity that deduces (or inferentially determines) the minority's basis (or organizing principle) for its claims, then applying such principles to a variety of social situations, real and imagined. This "trying on" of the minority's organizing principle may gradually create acceptance of the minority position. For example, within a given social system, the majority is racially prejudiced, and the minority is vocally opposed to racial prejudice. And if the majority in the course of their daily lives have the opportunity to "try on" the appropriateness of the minority belief (as in coming into contact with minorities), the majority may well change their behavior toward people of different races over time.

11. However, the application of the minority's organizing principle to various social situations does not always yield positive influence or accep-

tance; rather, it often increases the majority member's disapproval of the minority, thus offering a stiffened resistance to minority influence (Mugny and Pérez 1991, 112–16). For example, within a Kansas school board, the majority of members disapprove of the teaching of evolution, and a vocal minority support the teaching of evolution. The more the majority has the opportunity to hear the minority's discordant views and the more the majority "tries on" the minority's organizing principle to their own social construction of reality, the more righteous they will view their own beliefs, producing an increase in resolve to defeat the minority viewpoint.

Mugny and Pérez conclude *The Social Psychology of Minority Influence* with this observation:

> Minority influence follows more winding paths than majority persuasion. The factors that ruin its credibility and make it conflictual do not, paradoxically, destroy the influence. They only defer it, making it all the more imperceptible and underground by transferring its effects from the specific positions defended by the minority to the principles that underlie those positions. Since they are principles, they are of a more generalized order, acting as new norms, and hence in the long run, are likely to be activated and affect other attitudes and other behaviors. It is indeed a kind of constructivism, in all of its aspects, that is at the heart of a minority influence and accounts for the fact that in spite of the many manifestations of resistance to the change advocated by minorities, it nevertheless ends up taking effect sooner or later, and in the eyes of each of us, appears to occur "just naturally." (1991, 162–63)

In Conclusion. Social structures contribute greatly to an individual's behavior. Anyone wishing to engage in social marketing must have a thorough grounding in social psychology and the resulting ramifications on social influence.

Chapter Three

Social Influence Models

The early models of communication were linear models also sometimes known as "transportation" models. These linear models viewed communication as a process that started at the sender and shipped or transported the message to the destination receiver. The classic Shannon and Weaver (1949) model is such a transportation model. Source, transmitter, channel, noise, receiver, destination were the six parts identified as a communication system. Information would be transported from the source to the destination.

However, it was quickly noted (e.g., Berlo 1960) that human communication didn't function in such a linear fashion. One of the obvious deficiencies of Shannon and Weaver's model was that it did not include feedback. When people communicate they become involved in a process that is mutually engaged. People respond continuously to the communication process in multiple channels—communicating and providing feedback constantly. While one person may be speaking the other person is sending verbal and nonverbal feedback, helping the speaker to be better understood by the other.

As such, it was said that people interact with one another or that communication was an interaction. Meaning is a result of not just the actions of the person speaking but of the interaction of all involved. "Interaction establishes, maintains, and changes certain conventions—roles, norms, rules, and meanings—within a social group or culture. Those conventions literally define the reality of the culture" (Littlejohn 1992, 169). Others would believe that the process of communication went beyond interaction into a process they call transaction.

TRANSACTIONAL COMMUNICATION MODELS

"Transaction" is defined as "two people engaged in mutual and simultaneous interaction" (Smith and Williamson 1977, 46). A transaction, then, is a negotiation attempting to create meaning. Stewart wrote that "from a trans-actional perspective, human communication is a process of meaning-creating rather than idea- or message-sending. When you're communicating, you're not transmitting ideas to others but 'evoking' [through symbols] their own ideas or meanings" (1973, 16).

Consider the diagram of the communication process below.

Person A <⇒ Person B

"The arrows indicate that both persons in the communication situation are participating simultaneously. They are mutually perceiving each other, and both persons (not just the sender [the speaker]) are making adjustments to messages exchanged within the transaction" (Smith and Williamson 1977, 31). And as Nimmo (1978) and Garceau (1951) have suggested, communication is characterized as dynamic, continuous, circular, unrepeatable, irreversible, and complex. For each communicative interaction is highly dynamic and complex, and the bi/multidirectional nature of the interaction is indicative of its continuous and circular aspects. And with each interaction, we are forever changed, for our subjective knowledge—our image of the world—has been altered; and once the change in the image has been created, we cannot recreate the initial communication experience nor can we reverse the process.

The transactional model corresponds with the idea that "one cannot not communicate" (Watzlawick, Beavin, and Jackson 1967, 49). Watzlawick and his coauthors came to this conclusion by reasoning that

> Behavior has no opposite. In other words, there is no such thing as nonbehaving or, to put it more simply: one cannot not behave. Now if it is accepted that all behavior in an interactional situation has message value, i.e., is communication, it follows that no matter how one may try one cannot not communicate. (1967, 48–49)

Therefore, the interactions depicted in the model are not just verbal messages. Messages are defined as "selectively perceived behaviors to which each person in an interpersonal transaction adapts his or his own behavior" (Smith and Williamson 1977, 79). Knapp has argued that "the verbal components carry less than 35 per cent of the social meaning of the situation; more than 65 per cent is carried on the nonverbal band" (1972, 12).

There have been a number of systems proposed as a means to group these message systems. One such system was suggested by Smith and Williamson: message cues may be codified into four message systems: language (linguistic and paralingusitic), gesture (kinesics), space (proxemics), and sexuality (1977, 80). The language message system consists of linguistic and paralinguistic grammars. The linguistic grammar deals with words, sentence structures, the rules for logical presentation. The paralinguistic grammar provides rules for verbalization as well as the verbalization itself: for example, vocal loudness, inflection, and tone.

The gesture message system consists of bodily movements that people use to regulate or supplement the linguistic communication. This gesture system is traditionally called kinesics by those who study nonverbal communication (e.g., Birdwhistle 1952, 1970). Gesticulating hands on the part of the speaker adds emphasis to the linguistic message. A listener who begins shifting nervously from foot to foot may be indicating an eagerness for the current speaker to end so that the listener may begin to speak. These movements are themselves communication messages.

The space message system is traditionally called proxemics. It is "the study of how man unconsciously structures microspace—the distance between man in conduct of daily transactions, the organization of space in his house and buildings, and ultimately the layout of his towns" (E. Hall 1963, 1003). The nearness of which one stands next to another person or how the communicators' shoulders are aligned in relation to one another are examples of how we use space to create meaning (E. Hall 1966).

The sexuality message system consists of the "use of the body to integrate interpersonal transactions [body rhythms, touching, body image]" (Smith and Williamson 1977, 81).

Each message system may be viewed as operating on three levels of meaning: denotative, interpretive, and relational (Smith and Williamson 1977, 85–91). "The denotative level of meaning is that to which the message literally refers" (Smith and Williamson 1977, 85). The interpretive level of meaning operates when "cues tell the other person in the transaction . . . how the message is to be interpreted" (Smith and Williamson 1977, 86). For example, John strikes out for the sixth time in one baseball game. His friend Alfred says, "You're a real pro." By perceiving the intonation of Alfred's voice, John will create an interpretative level of meaning from this message cue. John will realize that sarcasm was intended and will ignore the denotative meaning. The relational level of meaning is created upon the perception of the relationship between the individual and the other communicator (Burgoon and Hale, 1984). For example, Mary tells Susan, "You wear too many cosmetics; it looks like you have two inches of paint on your face." The relational level of meaning that Susan generates from perceiving the message cues is that Mary thinks herself superior to Susan. It is significant that the same message cues between the same two people may generate different levels of meaning in different contexts.

Years ago, on the *Johnny Carson Show,* the comedian and his guests were discussing animal shows, and one of the guests used the word *bitch,* the proper term for a female dog. However, the same word used colloquially is a derogatory term for argumentative or nagging females, and the network censors at that time considered it to be profane, and as a consequence, would routinely censor or "blip" the term. Because the censors had let the term *bitch* through this particular broadcast, Carson and his guests repeated the word over and over again, thinking they were "getting around" or "pulling the wool over the eyes" of the censors. However, Carson and his guests were not really slipping by, for "the meaning of the message depends on the context" (Smith and Williamson 1977, 81).

Other Social Influence Models

Leon Festinger's **social comparison theory** (1950; 1954) suggests that people evaluate their own beliefs and opinions by comparing them to the beliefs and opinions of others. According to Hardin and Higgins:

> Social comparison theory rests on the assumptions that (1) social comparison processes are initiated when external reality is ambiguous and difficult to grasp; (2) a dualism between physical and social realities exists; and (3) physical reality takes precedence over social reality. (1996, 29)

Generally people select "others" based on their perceived similarity. For this reason, people turn to a reference group and its members for comparison points. Particularly, when people hold beliefs that are not supported by a physical reality, they will turn to the social reality of a reference group to validate their own beliefs and attitudes (Festinger 1950; 1954). For example, individuals who insist on blaming their own economic problems on identifiable minorities within the American population will frequently join hate groups who either covertly or overtly seek the destruction and elimination of the identified "out-group." Such hate groups provide the needed validation of a distorted personal reality.

Chris Rock, whom *Time* magazine in 1999 crowned as the "best comic in America" (Farley 1999, 66), is not just a comic; he is the straight-shooting, hard-hitting social critic of the new millennium. Rock recently made these insightful observations about contemporary social behavior in America:

> "There's nothing scarier than a broke white man. The broker they are, the madder they are. That's why white people start forming groups and blowing up s—. Freeman. Aryan Nation. Klan. Poor, pissed-off white people are the biggest threat to the security of this country." (as quoted in Farley 1999, 66)

Individuals engage in social comparison for various motives: "avoiding invalid opinions . . . maintaining a cognitive structure (a need for cognitive clarity), and maintaining certain conclusions that are pleasing, even if not entirely accurate (which is essentially, a drive for self-validation and esteem enhancement)" (Price and Oshagan 1995, 188; Kruglanski and Mayseless 1987). The social comparison theory posits that "an opinion, a belief, an attitude is 'correct,' 'valid,' and 'proper' to the extent that it is anchored in a group of people with similar beliefs, opinions, and attitudes" (Festinger 1954, 272).

Pressures for conformity exist within the group to achieve group goals and for individuals to validate their attitudes and values by comparing them with other group members (Festinger 1950). If group members disagree on matters considered salient to the group, then one of two things will likely occur: (1) members will change their views in order to achieve group conformity or (2) the group structure will change by either adding new members or expelling discordant members (Festinger 1950; 1954). When group members are faced with uncertainty within the group, they will increase the rate of interaction in order to resolve the uncertainty (Festinger 1950).

For example, one regional hospital had recently announced that they had bought their competitor. The social marketers involved had warned the hospital's board of directors about the likely negative fallout from the proposed takeover, but the board had decided to go ahead with the planned acquisition. And as the marketer predicted, a huge public outcry from both the general citizenry and the medical community dominated the news. The board met in an emergency meeting to decide what to do. They could not come to consensus; the members knew they needed to negotiate a strategy, presenting a united front to the community. Thus, ultimately, they agreed to meet again and again until the issue was resolved. The group had made a conscious decision to continue to engage in negotiation in order to increase their mutual agreement with what would at the end become the board's strategy. Consequently, as uncertainty or disagreement increases, most typically, the willingness to continue to engage in interaction increases in order to meet group goals.

The social regulatory functions of conformity produce a shared reality that ultimately "acquires objective reality" (Sherif 1936), for the members act on this constructed reality as if it were real. Hardin and Higgins have summarized the role of shared reality in social judgments:

> (1) experience of reality or meaning is created and maintained for the individual when it is mutually shared with others; (2) social interaction is predicated upon and regulated by the establishment of shared reality; and (3) the shared reality that is

achieved in social interaction in turn functions to regulate the self, closing the self-society circle. (1996, 30)

These functions of shared reality may be expressed in the following statistical metaphor: "When an experience is recognized and shared with others in the process of social interaction, it achieves reliability, validity, generality, and predictability" (Hardin and Higgins 1996, 35–36). In other words, such shared reality plays an important role in social regulation.

One might expect that the group would exert the most social control or social regulatory behavior when new group members are recruited. And indeed, that is the case; efforts to seek compliance with group norms are particularly strong when newcomers enter the group (Levine and Moreland 1991). Groups indoctrinate newcomers with the necessary knowledge and skills to fulfill the role of a group member; as part of this indoctrination, the group motivates and encourages the mastery of group lore, its shared mythologies (Van Maanen and Schein 1979). Recruits wishing to belong eagerly receive group messages and are openly receptive to influence (Van Maanen 1977). However, if there are a few recalcitrant newcomers, group members markedly demonstrate increased effort to bring them into the fold through repeated contacts (Levine 1989); such accelerated attention is particularly true for those newcomers who aren't sure they belong in the group (Levine and Ranelli 1978). For example, sorority pledges who are uncertain whether they made the right decision in pledging a particular sorority will receive far more attention from the sorority sisters than those pledges who do not express any misgivings.

Heavily influenced by Festinger (1950) and Heider (1946), Newcomb (1953) presented his own **theory of co-orientation,** which explains the processes pressuring for conformity in social interaction. A communicator feels rewarded when his or her attitudes are reinforced by another participant in the interaction who shares the same attitudes. If there are differences in attitudes, then communication participants work to build consensus. In Newcomb's terminology, this process is a "strain toward symmetry" (1953, 345). He meant that participants work toward a unanimity on the given issue.

Newcomb (1953) presented a model of co-orientation that he called the A-B-X System (figure 3.1). The A-B-X System is used to describe two individuals who may be characterized by their frequent interaction (engaging in conversation). This simple communication act may be represented as: "(A) transmits information to another person (B) about something (X). Such an act is symbolized here as AtoBreX" (Newcomb 1953, 393). According to Newcomb, "the minimal components of the A-B-X System . . . are as follows:

1. A's orientation toward X, including both attitude toward X as an object to be approached or avoided (characterized by sign—positive or negative—and intensity) and cognitive attributes (beliefs and cognitive structuring).
2. A's orientations toward B, in exactly the same sense. (For purposes of avoiding confusing terms, we shall speak of positive and negative *attraction* toward A or B as persons, and of favorable and unfavorable *attitudes* toward X.)
3. B's orientation toward X.
4. B's orientation toward A (1953, 393–94).

Newcomb then assigns the description of (+ + or − −) to define A and B holding the same attitudes and attractions for X. This similarity he calls **symmetry.** When A and B hold different attitudes and attractions for X, the description of the situation is (+ − or − +). This dissimilarity he calls **asymmetry.** Note that (+) designates positive or favorable positions while (−) designates negative or unfavorable positions.

For Newcomb (1953), the strain toward symmetry within communicative acts is advantageous in that a participant is able to safely predict the other participant's attitudes and behaviors. And second, communication is made easier in that communicators don't need to explain themselves, for they are already understood. And such symmetry helps reduce errors in communication. And third, individuals feel validated in their assessment of X, because another person like them feels the same way.

Newcomb presents the following postulate:

> The stronger the forces toward A's co-orientation in respect to B and X, (a) the greater A's strain toward symmetry with B in respect to X; and (b) the greater the likelihood of increased symmetry as a consequence of one or more communicative acts. (1953, 395)

And now in plain English: the greater the need for Bob to please Alice, the harder he will work to reach an agreement on how they both feel about going

Figure 3.1   Newcomb's Schematic Illustration of the Minimal A-B-X System

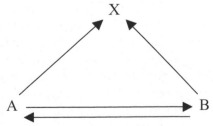

Excerpted from T. Newcomb (1953), An approach to the study of communicative acts, *Psychological Review* 60: 394.

to church every Sunday, and the greater the likelihood that after repeated interactions he will be more and more willing to attend with her each Sunday.

However, symmetry does not always occur even between two people who love each other. The achievement of symmetry varies when a discrepancy occurs between A and B toward X $(+\ -$ or $-\ +)$. The strength of the discrepancy rests on the intensity of attitude toward X and the strength of attraction toward B. When a discrepancy occurs, it usually means that attitudes held toward X are very intense and important for A to continue to hold.

For example, Karen and Mike are married, and they still love each other after more than fifteen years of marriage. Mike loves to duck hunt, killing hundreds of birds each year. Karen finds this repugnant. However, Karen's love for Mike overshadows her disgust at his hobby. And Mike's love for Karen overshadows his knowing her disgust for his hobby. Thus, Mike continues to duck hunt at every opportunity (Canada, Mexico, and Scotland). And Karen tries not to think about it. Such tacit agreements are even used to maintain friendships. Sometimes friends agree to disagree in order to protect their friendship, but they will continue to engage in friendly debate. In other cases, they may avoid speaking about matters of disagreement.

For Newcomb, "symmetry is only a facilitating condition for co-orientation, not a necessary one" (1953, 398). The probability of symmetry varies with why individuals are involved in the group. Newcomb highlights two important distinctions that describe the forces that bring individuals into a conversation: "constrained (enforced) vs. voluntary association, and association based upon broad as contrasted with narrow common interests" (1953, 398). The less two people are attracted to each other, the more likely that their efforts to achieve symmetry will be limited to those critical points of agreement toward X that maintain the existence of the interaction. In other words, the conditions of association determine how hard A and B will try to reach symmetry on attitudes toward X. For example, Sally is involved in a charity organization. She has been made the public relations chair for an upcoming educational event. On the other hand, the director appointed another woman as the advertising chair. Sally knows she must work with the advertising chair to produce an effective, integrated campaign. However, she has had to work with this woman before, and she knows her to be rude, obnoxious, and condescending. This is not going to be a pleasant experience, and she resolves herself not to even attempt to engage in the more relaxed social exchange she normally prefers with colleagues. This said, Sally will limit her co-orientation efforts to those focused on coordinating the public relations and advertising campaigns. And the advertising chair only seeks symmetry with regard to the integrated campaign plan.

In addition, within groups there is a specialization of roles. Rather than coinciding, roles are often complementary. And for this reason, symmetry is replaced with a strain toward **complementarity.** Because A and B have different roles within the group, they may not have the same attraction toward X but rather a complementary one. For example, in a social/charitable organization, the social chair may differ from the eye foundation committee chair as to the amount of money to spend on a social dance function for members. Thus, they have different priorities and different attitudes toward X (the cost of the dance). The two chairpersons subscribe to the same group norms (social collegiality and charitable gift-giving) but prescribe differentiated behavior with respect to their two roles. Thus, Newcomb (1953) writes that the demand for co-orientation will dictate a strain toward symmetry not toward X (the cost of the dance) but toward the role system and the code (the social collegiality and charitable gift-giving), which may be viewed as a strain toward complementarity.

In some situations, symmetry is not desired. This is particularly true when A has committed an act X and does not want B to know of act X. A might feel guilty about having done X, or A may feel threatened if B finds out about the act. For example, Bill bought another hunting rifle, but he doesn't want Susie, his wife, to know about it. Bill knows they really needed a new washing machine more than he needed to buy his sixteenth hunting rifle, and he feels guilty and a little ashamed and doesn't want Susie to know. Or Paula had an affair with Stephen, but she doesn't want her husband Ralph to find out about the affair with Stephen, because he would divorce her if he ever discovered her failure to live up to her marriage vows. She doesn't feel guilty; she enjoyed the affair; she just doesn't want to get caught.

And frequently individuals have multiple group memberships that place conflicting attitudinal demands on them. These conflicting attitudinal demands are called cross-pressures (Sears 1969). A woman may be a Christian, and she chooses to worship at her family's church, which supports creationism and denies and dismisses evolution. Yet, she also holds a Ph.D. in biology and teaches evolutionary theory in her courses. She views the Bible as a series of parables and analogies; she does not observe religious fundamentalism. And therefore, she believes evolution is not inconsistent with Christianity. In this case, her strains toward symmetry with B^1 (church members) in regard to X (evolution) is outweighed by her strains toward symmetry with B^2 (biological sciences), whose orientations toward X are viewed as contradictory with those of B^1.

For some people, holding multiple group memberships with conflicting attitudinal demands is much more stressful than our lady biologist finds. In such conflicted situations, individuals may change their own attitudes about themselves (A), about others (Bs), and/or about the X in question rather than exist in a stressful state. They may try to change a B's orientation toward X, or they may subconsciously cognitively distort one B's orientation toward X. Or they may, after much internal struggle, come to accept the asymmetry as our biologist did. Research indicates that during such cross-pressure contexts, an individual's response to a group's cues (symbols, reminders) will work to motivate conformity to the extent that the individual values group membership (salience), has knowledge of the group's norms, and has sufficient social rank to withstand pressure (Kelley 1955, 287).

Newcomb concludes that for the most part successful groups (long-lived) have certain properties we might expect: (1) "_Homogeneity of orientation toward certain objects_" (group members share attitudes, values, and judgments made about Xs), (2) "_Homogeneity of perceived consensus_" (they believe that they all agree), and (3) "_Attraction among members_" (interpersonal attraction increases with frequency of interaction) (1953, excerpted from 402–3). Grunig (1984) among others has adapted Newcomb's model to the study of publics, message reception, and public relations communication models; and Rogers and Kincaid (1981) have built upon Newcomb's work to construct their own Network Convergence Model. A discussion of Rogers and Kincaid's work follows.

Network Convergence Model. Rogers and Kincaid in _Communication Networks: Toward a New Paradigm of Research_ lament the psychological bias in mass communication research (see also Watzlawick 1967). Clearly oriented to a sociological perspective, the two researchers view the majority of contemporary research as the atomization of human behavior (Rogers and Kincaid 1981, 37–43; see also Lazarsfeld 1970, 40). The majority of mass communication research has focused on micro-effects or the effects on an individual. This orientation has led to a wide variety of approaches such as attitude change, cognitive processing, psycho-physiology, and abnormal psychology. Much of social science research is focused on problem solving in the public or societal domain. For this reason, the micro-effect emphasis in such research has produced a tendency for social scientific research to assert **individual-blame** or **person-blame** for problems manifested in an individual's life rather than examining the society as a whole. Indeed, according to Rogers and Kincaid (1981), such emphasis on person-blame permeates the writing concerning social problems (also see Caplan and Nelson 1973; Fee and Krieger 1993; Waterston 1997). Researchers feel overwhelmed when confronting problems that exist within a given culture or society, and rather than dealing with such complex, multifaceted system problems, the researchers accept the society as it is, warts and all (see Rogers and Kincaid 1981). And instead, the researchers focus on the individual participants within the system whom they believe to be far more open to change than the system as a whole.

Today such sentiments from Rogers and Kincaid may well fall on deaf ears in that American society now considers that the politically correct stance is to champion self-responsibility. Social scientists who urge us to examine the social network of a young anorexic girl, or to look at the family history of a convicted wife-abuser, or to consider the day-to-day physical realities for an unemployed black man in Detroit, are often ridiculed for such sociological suggestions. During the past twenty years, it has become popular to place the blame for societal problems on the individual rather than accepting that something may be wrong with society. And most unfortunately, such individuals often need our help far more than our condemnation.

Caplan and Nelson (1973) tell the story of a Detroit job-training program that helped inner-city blacks learn skills necessary for the auto industry. After being gainfully employed by the industry, many of the trainees ultimately lost their jobs because they had arrived late for their shift work. Such on-line industries where each worker performs one critical task in the construction of a car (or other piece of machinery) as it moves down the assembly line, place a premium on punctuality, for if one person is late or absent, either overtime must be paid to the current workers or the entire line shuts down. The training program supervisors blamed the trainees for the loss of their jobs and labeled them "lazy." The supervisors pointed to the demonstrated lack of work ethic represented by the trainees' tardiness and assigned person-blame.

Rather than settling for the obvious, Caplan and Nelson, as outside evaluators, examined the physical realities of each trainee's life and discovered that the men were so poor that (1) they did not own an alarm clock and (2) they did not own cars. The trainees had to rely on Detroit's rather unreliable mass transportation system. The training supervisors had no experience with what it means to be that poor, and therefore their empathy (Broome 1991) or breadth of perspective (Culbertson 1989) was severely limited. Caplan and Nelson (1973) urged the federally funded training program to buy inexpensive alarm clocks for their trainees. The alarm clocks could have made a difference. By anticipating the inevitable tardiness of the bus, the trainees could set their alarm earlier than normal to put themselves in the position of catching an earlier bus that was far more likely to get them to work on time. But it was not to be; the training program's director ignored the recommendation.

In an effort to avoid such psychological bias in their own research, Rogers and Kincaid (1981) borrowed from the theoretical traditions of symbolic interactionism, general systems theory, and the pragmatists as well as from Newcomb's (1953) co-orientation model to craft their own network convergence model. Georg Simmel (1922) is credited, for instance, with recognizing the uniqueness of each individual's social circles, for no two people have the same group affiliations. Simmel called this pattern of group affiliations and interpersonal interactions, the **web of group affiliations.** Simmel's web corresponds with Rogers and Kincaid's notion of the personal network (1981). Rogers and Kincaid accepted Sapir's (1935) definition of **society** as being a "highly intricate *network*" (emphasis added) characterized by dynamic and relational processes that work to achieve mutual understanding among participants when they engage in social interaction intended to achieve a "commonness" among network members. Therefore, an individual is not influenced simply by a network of interactants but by networks of networks

When individuals meet, as we have said before, they experience the anxiety of facing the unknown; therefore, they engage in conversation, working to establish a commonness or mutually agreed upon situational reality. Individuals then engage in information-processing that "involves perceiving, interpreting, understanding, believing, which creates—potentially at least—new information for further processing" (Rogers and Kincaid 1981, 56). The process is repeated over and over as long as the two individuals continue to interact. When individuals meet in a group setting, the same process occurs, although involving more participants and becoming far more complicated as the behaviors are carried out within the personal networks. Rogers and Kincaid call this process of seeking a commonness among participating individuals within a network **congruence.**

The **congruence model** is represented by "three levels of abstraction: (1) the physical level, (2) the psychological level, and (3) the social level" (Rogers and Kincaid 1981, 56). An explanation for each level follows:

- **Physical Level.** An individual assesses the physical level within the person's visual domain; the individual arrives at an understanding of the physical world as it presents itself; however, the individual's understanding will evolve as the physical world changes, and the person continues to attend to it.
- **Psychological Level.** When this individual talks with another, the same process of perception, interpretation, understanding, believing, and information processing occurs over and over again, as the two individuals seek a commonness. The individual is seeking a commonness—a meeting of the minds—not just on the behavioral physical level but also on the psychological level; and the other individual is engaged in the same set of behaviors as well. If they are successful, it may be said that

they have reached a mutual understanding that then is constantly evolving as the result of continued interaction, producing additional perceptions, interpretations, and information.

- **Social Level.** When two or more individuals agree on a common reality or commonly shared value, the reality or the value itself becomes "true" in that it has been validated by the consensus of the group. The establishment of such truths involves multiple members of the social world, interacting to achieve commonness, ultimately engaging in the same perception, interpretation, and information processes characterized by intrapersonal and interpersonal communication. This communication structure may be characterized as the network's members engaging in congruence-seeking behaviors on the social level.

Thus, on all three levels of abstraction, physical, psychological, and social, it may be said that:

> Convergence is dynamic: it always implies movement and goal orientation or purpose. It requires study of the direction and rate of change, and study of the networks of two or more persons who exchange information. Movement in one direction, toward one point, always implies movement away from other points (divergence). Convergence and divergence are two aspects of the same process. (Rogers and Kincaid 1981, 66)

When network interactions do not yield agreement, four possible variations result: "(1) mutual understanding with agreement, (2) mutual understanding with disagreement, (3) mutual misunderstanding with agreement, and (4) mutual misunderstanding with disagreement" (Rogers and Kincaid 1981, 56). Such a wide range of outcomes for network interactions highlights the uncertainty of individual information processing and the uncertainty of **information circuits**—the patterns of interactions among group members who attempt to share information. It must be recognized that perfect understanding between two people is never possible, for people cannot transmit meaning; they have to socially construct meaning, and the degree of convergence produced by social interaction is dependent on the variances in language symbol systems held by each individual and all of the members' evaluations or perceptions about past interactions, present interactions, and future expectations of interactions. Both the socially constructed meanings or understanding as well as the **divergence** or unshared meanings held by both interacting individuals may be represented by Venn diagrams.

When two people meet from two distinctly different cultures with different language systems, there is literally very little in common. E. T. Hall (1959) has told us that there are few shared universals—the fear of snakes, the fear of fire, and the fear of darkness. Two people meeting in such a situation could be represented by diagram A in figure 3.2.

When two people of the same culture find each other attractive and begin the courtship rituals customary in their society, they will come to know and understand more about each other than when they first met. As they share common experiences and begin to develop commonly negotiated under-standings of those experiences, their relationship will evolve, and their shared meanings or convergence will increase. When they make the decision to marry, the situation could be represented by diagram B.

After years and years of marriage, couples develop a solid history of shared meanings. Often observers remark how they finish each other's sentences, or how they seem to know what the other is thinking without their having said anything. Such closeness in understanding may be represented by diagram C on page 65.

SYSTEMS THEORY

In 1651, Thomas Hobbes in his classic work *Leviathan* first introduced the concept of "a system" to study and analyze political behavior (1909). The system concept is very similar to the biological constructs found in physical sciences that approach various organisms as systems. Systems theory as it is typically discussed in organizational communication today finds its roots a bit more contemporaneously.

The leading exponent and primary promulgator of systems theory is Lud-wig von Bertalanffy (1968), a Canadian biologist, who believed that all sci-ences held concepts and principles in common. He attempted to define these principles and concepts by arguing that they functioned together in the form of a system. These systems applied not just to one specific area of knowledge but to all areas. He first presented his general systems theory in 1937 but would not publish until after the conclusion of World War II. His book *General System Theory* would call many people's attention to his views.

Bertalanffy set out to show how there was commonness among the various bodies of knowledge, particularly the fields of biology, psychology, and soci-ology. Bertalanffy wished to construct a theory that was holistic rather than atomistic. He rejected the common notion of examining smaller and smaller parts and wanted to look at the whole as "he saw the whole to be greater than the sum of its parts. He believed that the complex interaction of parts makes it necessary to study total units as systems" (Ferguson and Ferguson 1988, 38).

Hall and Fagen (1968) have listed four things that are common to every system. Systems consist of objects. Objects may be people, communication

Figure 3.2   Overlapping Meanings

Diagram A

Diagram B

Diagram C

channels, or procedures. Objects need not be some actual physical thing. Systems have attributes. An attribute is some quality that is part of the objects or the system. Those properties that make an object distinctive within the system are the object's attributes.

Objects in systems maintain internal relationships with one another. These internal relationships point to the interactions between the various objects that comprise the system. The relationships actually go beyond interaction to interdependence. The concept of relationships among and between objects is one of the most important concepts within systems theory and frequently is at the heart of most definitions of a system (e.g., Broom, Casey, and Ritchey 2000; Katz and Kahn 1966; J. G. Miller 1978).

Systems, finally, function within an environment. A system may or may not interact with its environment. Whether a system interacts with its environment or not distinguishes two types of systems—closed and open. A closed system is one that is conceived of as having no interaction with its environment. It is cut off from objects and energy. Closed systems are viewed as constantly moving toward chaos, which borrowing from physics is called *entropy*. Closed systems cannot survive over a long period of time. Think of a refrigerator that is unplugged. It is a closed system, and everything left in the refrigerator is heading for chaos.

Systems that interact with their environment are known as open systems. Open systems can draw energy and objects from their environment and can influence the environment. Open systems follow the law of negative entropy as long as they import more energy from the environment than they use (Katz and Kahn 1966). A refrigerator that is plugged into the electrical system is an open system as it is drawing energy from outside the system. Open systems respond to changes in the environment and also affect the environment in which it is situated. The refrigerator will respond to the effects of an increasing room temperature on the interior temperature by starting its compressor to combat the change.

Systems that include human beings are perceived of as being open systems (e.g., Allport 1968). It is with open systems that General Systems systems theory is primarily concerned.

A classic example of a system is the human body. The body is a system that is composed of a number of objects such as organs, tissue, secretions, and the like. These objects each have attributes. The heart is composed of muscle tissue and four chambers. It pulls in blood from one side and pushes it out the other. The attributes of the brain would be different from those for the heart. The objects within the body possess an internal relationship to one another. These subsystems are organized to operate together. What happens to one object of the body affects the other parts of the body. A malfunctioning heart can affect the blood flow to the brain, reducing the oxygen to the brain, consequently decreasing the ability of the brain to function. Finally, the body is an open system that reacts to its environment.

All systems have the attribute of wholeness or synergy. Simply put, the whole system is greater than the sum of the parts. The various objects within the system create a whole that is distinct from the product that the objects might create individually.

John Lennon, Paul McCartney, George Harrison, and Ringo Starr as four solo acts would not have had as much influence on rock and roll as they did as the Beatles. How many Ringo Starr CDs do most people own? Working together created a synergy that transformed music. Together the Beatles viewed as a system was synergistic, or demonstrated the characteristics of wholeness.

One of the difficulties with the systems approach is defining where the boundary of the system exists. The boundary defines what the system is. Those objects within the boundary are part of the system; those objects outside the boundary are part of the environment (Parsons 1969). What designates the beginning of one system and the ending of the other? The answer may be mostly point of view. One could define a university department as a system. The department would respond to the environment of larger units with which it interacts, such as the school or college in which it resides or the university. A department might be viewed as an object within the larger system of schools and colleges (e.g., the School of Communication or the College of Arts and Sciences). From a larger perspective, these schools and colleges might be viewed as objects of the university as a whole, which could be viewed as the system. Accepting an even more macroscopic view might be to see the public university as one object in the state government which could be the system that is studied. The correct view really depends on the perspective of the observer. One attempt at being more specific at setting appropriate boundaries believes that where a system exists with a high concentration of relations, the area where the relations are less concentrated distinguishes the boundary of the environment (Kramer and de Smit 1977).

Continuing with the university example, one could see the departments as objects that comprise the system, or, more appropriately, they might be viewed as subsystems. The departments serve as subsystems of the suprasystem of colleges and schools and the colleges and schools are subsystems of the suprasystem university. So the university might be seen as a system comprised of the subsystems of the colleges and schools, which are themselves comprised of the sub-subsystems of departments. This embedding of systems within systems or subsystems within subsystems implies that there is some type of order. Smaller units subsumed by larger suggests an ordering from less powerful to more powerful. Every complex subsystem (and system) has some subsystem (or system) more powerful—suprasystem—and less powerful—subsystem. In terms of organizations the suprasystems might be seen as "natural, technological, human, political, socioeconomic and market environments" (Creedon 1993, 58), while subsystems are internal (see also Brody and Stone 1989). This ordering is called hierarchy.

Arthur Koestler in *The Ghost in the Machine* (1967) called this phenomenon of always having a superior suprasystem and an inferior subsystem the Janus effect after the mythical two-faced Roman god. He notes that members of a hierarchy perpetually have one face turned toward subordinates and the other toward the superior. The two faces of every system are depicted: "One is the face of the master, the other the face of the servant" (48).

Systems strive to achieve some purpose or obtain a goal state. In other words, they are goal oriented. The system will act to make changes when it feels that its ability to achieve its goal is being impeded. The threat to achieving goal status may come from inside the system or it may come from the environment (external to the system). The system will react differently in attempting to correct the error, depending on where the threat is perceived to originate. Correcting internal errors is often easier than dealing with external threats.

The system's attempts to strive to reach its goal is one example of its attempt to maintain an equilibrium. This balance is usually called homeostasis. Homeostasis includes not only attempting to maintain the ability to achieve goal state; it also deals with any threats (major or minor) to its well-being. This homeostasis may be viewed as the maintenance processes that regulate the system (Daniels and Spiker 1991).

At the same time, a system must adapt to changes from the environment. An inability to adapt will usually lead systems to fail to be able to reach their goal. Adaptability allows the system to cope with changes from the environment while still pursuing the system's goal. The ability to alter how the goals will be achieved is called equifinality. This simply means that there is more than a single way to reach the goal. For example, you could probably think of at least two ways to drive to a nearby grocery store. If getting to the store is the goal, the various streets that you may take to get there represent equifinality, that is, the different methods to obtain the goal of getting to the grocery store.

The ideas originally disseminated by Bertalanffy were quickly picked up by those people who were interested in studying the workings of organizations (e.g., March and Simon 1958; Katz and Kahn 1966). People studying how organizations function found that the concepts of systems theory nicely modeled how organizations function. Organizations have objects, attributes, and interrelationships; demonstrate wholeness; operate within an environment; have a goal; are hierarchical; and attempt to maintain homeostasis while adapting to changes from the environment. Systems theory provided a set of concepts that could be applied and easily understood in regards to the functioning of an organization.

The new systems approach was far superior to the machine model of organizations. The machine model viewed "members of organizations as passive instruments that perform assigned tasks, receiving but not initiating action" (Buck 1966, 105). Observation of organizations quickly indicated that these were not realistic elements of successful organizations.

Systems theory also found its way into the explanations of communication within organizations. For some such as Lee Thayer (1968), it is communication that maintains the system/organization. Communication is how the organizational system interacts with its environment and establishes relationships. The study of this organizational communication has been "predominated" by the use of systems theory (P. R. Monge 1982, 245).

The usefulness to social marketing of the systems theory has been particularly adopted by those social marketers in public relations. For almost two decades, public relations researchers have suggested that systems theory is uniquely suited to analysis of public relations activity in society (Cutlip, Center, and Broom 1985; Grunig 1984; Pavlik 1987). "A system is a set of interacting units which endures through time within an established boundary by responding and adjusting to change pressures from the environment in order to achieve and maintain goal states" (Cutlip, Center, and Broom 1985, 184).

The system theory's concepts of maintenance functions and systemic adaptations are the stuff of public relations, for instance. Pavlik writes:

> Homeostasis, or maintaining balance between an organization and its public, is often one of the primary functions of public relations. Open systems also change and adapt. Because they exist in a changing environment, they must do so to survive. Public relations often plays a key role in the adaptive behavior of an organization. (1987, 127)

While systems theory is one of the explanative theories in public relations, it is not without its critics. Pearson (1990) warned that the use of systems theory to explain public relations "may simply provide the profession with a highly technical, and sometimes obfuscating and mystifying language" (232). It has also been negatively critiqued by feminist scholars (e.g., Creedon 1993; Fine 1993).

NETWORK ANALYSIS

Previously we have discussed that one of the most important aspects of systems theory is that of relationships. These relationships help define the organization. When applying systems theory to organizations the interrelationships usually can be defined as the communication that happens between people.

Researchers have studied the communication between people in organizations. They frequently study who talks to whom and the topics about which people communicate. These studies are usually grouped under the heading of network analysis. Communication networks are "the regular patterns of person-to-person contacts that can be identified as people exchange information in a human social system" (P. Monge 1977, 243). Communication networks are communication relationships. Network analysis "represents a very systematic means of examining the overall configuration of communication relationships, both formal and informal, within an organization" (Johnson 1993, 33).

The human social system of interest currently is the organization. The organization might be a public relations firm, a manufacturing plant, a university, and so on. An organization is viewed as two or more people established as a cooperative system with a goal of producing some outcome. These people are working interdependently with input, throughput (the process that transforms input into output), and output (Rogers and Agarwala-Rogers 1976).

In an organization, the most important resource is information. How that information is dispersed or withheld from individuals can define how an organization functions. Those with information can decide to pass it along to someone else or deny a person the information. This control of information is a powerful influence in how well organizations function.

The information in an organization is often broken into two types—absolute and distributed. Absolute information is conceptually all the knowledge or information that exists within an organization. It may be known only by a single person but it is conceptually part of the absolute information that is within the organization. The second type of information is distributed information. Distributed information is that information that has been shared with others within the organization. One of the issues with distributed information is whether those people who need to know the information have received it. A converse to this issue is whether people who should not have the information have received it.

By measuring who actually talks to whom, one can see the way an organization actually works, how information flows through an organization. The charts of organizational communication are often at variance with the formal organizational chart (organigram as Rogers and Agarwala-Rogers [1976] called the formal organizational chart) which is supposed to describe how information is to flow through an organization. This organizational chart is a formal network. Peter Monge defines a formal network as "those designated by someone with authority to prescribe who should communicate with whom" (1977, 253). The way in which information actually flows in an organization is called the emergent or informal network. These networks "evolve from day-to-day interactions among people, irrespective of whether someone has specified that they communicate" (Monge 1977, 253).

The exchange of communication between people in an organization promotes more than simply imparting information. People in communication with one another usually also deal with other types of social functions such as construction of social reality, the use of power (often the giving or receiving of information), and the development of the corporate culture.

Communication networks are constructed out of a group of people who communicate with one another and the relations among that set of communicators. Communication networks are often graphically portrayed similar to the network in figure 3.3. The circles represent nodes. A **node** may be an individual or it may represent some other social or work unit, such as a

Figure 3.3 Communication Networks

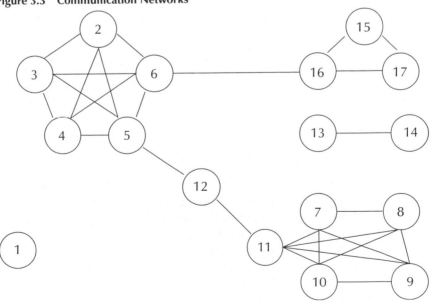

department or a business. The lines between the nodes indicate that the nodes interact with one another. The lines are called **links** (Farace and Mabee 1980).

The fundamental property of the network analysis is the links between nodes. The links reveal the relationships that exist (Rogers and Kincaid 1981). The links have properties beyond simply indicating that two nodes are in communication. There are a number of attributes that may be assigned to a given link (e.g., Johnson 1993). We use the five attributes reviewed by Littlejohn (1992; see also Monge 1987) as they tend to be link attributes commonly found in the research. Littlejohn identifies five attributes—symmetry, strength, reciprocity, content, and mode—of a link.

Symmetry deals with the equality of the flow of information. A symmetrical link is one where the two nodes receive and give information in generally equal quantities. An asymmetrical link indicates that one of the nodes generally gives information and the other node simply receives information.

The frequency with which the nodes communicate is considered the strength of the link: the greater the frequency the stronger the link. Weak links would be those where there are few communications among the two nodes (Richards 1985).

The perception that a node has about another linked node is called **reciprocity**. Specifically, reciprocity measures whether each node is in general agreement with the strength of the communication. If both nodes have similar judgments of the frequency of communication, the link is reciprocated. When one member of the link feels that communication with the other node is less than the other believes, the link is unreciprocated.

Content is another property of the link. There are many classification schemes for the content, for example, Redding's (1979) task, maintenance, and human function. There are even those that suggest that different organizations require the creation of different content classification schemes (Farace, Monge, and Russell 1977). For our discussions here, we'll grossly classify content into two groups—work-related information and social information. Links within a network may represent only work-related interactions where information about social issues are not included, or the link may represent communication about social issues but not contain much information about the tasks within the organization. As with most things about communication, this is much too simple. People tend to not just talk about one topic exclusively. There is an overlap in the types of communication in which people engage (e.g., Farace and Mabee 1980; Johnson 1993). A link that has approximately equal amounts of work-related and social information being shared is known as a **multiplexed link** in that the information carried over it is about both major communication functions.

The question of how the communication is carried out is the issue of mode. The communication might primarily be face-to-face, electronically mediated, or on paper. Understanding the channel through which the nodes communicate is another aspect of the link.

Communication Relationships in Networks. Consider the network represented in figure 3.3. Assume that each node is a person within an organization. The links indicate with whom the person communicates, if anyone. The type of communication represented by the network could be one that deals with work-related information or social information, or it might represent multiplexed communication. For the purposes of this discussion the content is not important. However, for a person concerned about network analysis the type of content represented by the network researcher would be very important.

Groups are people (nodes) who communicate with one another. Actually there are four criteria for a cluster of nodes to be labeled a group. A group must consist of at least three persons; each person must be linked with all others in the group; a minimum of half the communication of members is within the group; the group can be sustained if there is a linkage break or a member departs.

There are three groups in the figure 3.3. One group is comprised of nodes 2, 3, 4, 5, and 6. A second group is comprised of nodes 15, 16, and 17. Nodes 7, 8, 9, 10, and 11 comprise the third group.

The groups are linked together by relationships called bridges and liaisons. Nodes 6 and 16 are bridges. As you can see by the diagram, a **bridge** is a member of one group who has communication links to another group.

Liaisons are nodes that are not members of a group but serve as a link between two groups and perhaps more. Node 12 is an example of a liaison; it is not a member of either group 1 or group 3 but it provides a communication linkage between the two groups. Another name for a liaison is a linking pin (Johnson 1993). They are necessary to hold the organization together by serving as coordinators of communication flow within the organization (Likert 1967). Practically, there are few actual liaisons in organizations. The relative infrequency of actual liaisons is a symptom of what Johnson called "the generally low level of communication between diverse groups in organizations" (1993, 47).

Characteristics of people who come to fulfill the role of liaison within an organization have been studied. People who take on liaison positions usually demonstrate more openness in their communication with people (Reynolds and Johnson 1982). The perception of openness on the part of liaison will help the person establish contacts with different groups.

Liaisons have also been noted for having superior cognitive abilities. People who must serve to connect differing groups with communication that may not be easily interpreted by another group must be able to receive information from one group, interpret it, and pass along the relevant information to the other group (Johnson 1993).

Nodes who are not "jacked-in" to the network are **nonparticipants** or **isolates.** Node 1 is an example of a true isolate. There is no communication between this node and anyone else in the network. Nodes 13 and 14 are isolated from the network but do communicate with each other. These two nodes create an isolated dyad. They share communication with each other but not with the rest of the network.

Differences between those who are participants and those who are isolates have been researched. Not surprisingly, participants are more outgoing and more influential than isolates (Goldhaber, Yates, Porter, and Lesniak 1978). More unsurprising findings are that participants have higher satisfaction with their communication than isolates (Roberts and O'Reilly 1979), and participants report that they need more interaction than isolates need (Moch 1980). Research sometimes verifies what one would suspect is the case.

One type of node that isn't illustrated in the figure is the person labeled as a **boundary spanner**. The assumption is that any organization under study will have certain boundaries that separate the organization from the environment. Those people who are able to develop cross relations outside the organization are called boundary spanners (earlier research called these people boundary personnel; e.g., Evan 1966; March and Simon 1958; Wilensky 1967). The trick for a boundary spanner is that she or he must have two networks—one internal to the organization and one external (Adams 1976, 1980).

Adams has specifically listed the tasks that a boundary spanner engages in: "(1) transacting the acquisition of organizational inputs and the disposition of outputs, (2) filtering inputs and outputs, (3) searching for and collecting information, (4) representing the organization to its external environments, and (5) protecting the organization and buffering it from external threat and pressure" (1980, 328). Such tasks sound much like those of the public relations professional (Grunig 1976) and other social marketing professionals.

The study of information networks within an organization provides a picture of how information flows within the organization. The formal organizational chart often fails to reflect how information actually flows within an organization and almost never shows how social information travels among people. Understanding how information flow occurs allows those who need to get information to specific groups within the organization to select the optimal route.

Chapter Four

Identifying and Targeting Those You Want to Influence

You are where you live.

—Claritas Corporation

Knowledge of the soul of things is possibly a very new and revolutionary way of discovering the soul of man.

—Ernest Dichter, president, Institute for Motivational Research

IDENTIFYING AND TARGETING PUBLICS

Aristotle (1932) in his book about public speaking, *The Rhetoric,* offered the advice that communicators be concerned about the nature or composition of the audience. The view of Aristotle and of other Greek and Roman communication experts was that "without a thorough understanding of the audience, the likelihood of successful persuasion was deemed very small" (Cooper and Nothstine 1992, 31).

This examination and understanding of the audience is a process that is now called audience analysis or examining publics (Crable and Vibbert 1986). From the audience analysis, the clever communicator finds those arguments that most resonate, or are most acceptable, with the majority of those in the audience. In this way, adaptation to the audience's interests and concerns makes the message more persuasive. The ability to construct persuasive messages is the sign of an effective communicator.

Just as Aristotle instructed 2,300 years ago, social marketers work to understand their audiences. While under certain repetitive circumstances social marketers simply use their past experience or gut instinct, other social marketers use specialized audience analysis techniques such as demographics, psychographics, and geo-demographics to better understand who the receivers of the messages are. Once one knows who the audience is, it is relatively easy to tailor the message to appeal to the specific target public.

In order to tailor and deliver a message with greater precision, a number of different targeting schemes have been developed. Each of these methods of audience analysis—demographics, geo-demographics, and psychographics—represents an increasing sophistication in understanding various publics. This sophistication is based on social science research that attempts to find increasingly finer ways in which to divide, or to segment, groups of people. Thus, communication is divided at segments—the more specific the segmentation the greater the opportunity for persuasion.

Social marketers usually do not refer to those people who will be receiving their messages as the audience. **Audience** is conceptualized by many in social marketing as being a passive group of people with little relationship with the producer or sponsor of the message. The social marketing professional instead sees the receivers of its messages as being active and enduring, and ultimately sustaining relationships with the communicating organization. Within this view, the public is interacting with the organization that is sponsoring the public relations program. They may be interacting as customers, suppliers, or employees.

Many social marketing professionals prefer the term *publics* rather than audience. A public will be interactive with the environment. Members of the public will purchase products, talk to their neighbors, or write their congressional representative. Publics are viewed as being attentive to what is happening around them, their environment. This attentiveness extends to mass-mediated messages (Albig 1956). Publics are sensitive to, and aware of, those issues that concern them. Publics are often defined by those issues or interests that are held in common among a group of people (Weissberg 1976).

These publics are not hypothetical targets of the message but exist prior to any communication effort that is targeted toward them, and these publics continue after the communications activities cease. Carl Botan and Francisco Soto have explained that "a single communicative event such as a speech, movie, or television program may have an audience while an organization, social body or individual has a longer term and more complex relationship with a public" (1998, 24). While this seems to be the majority view, there are those (e.g., Moffitt 1994) who disagree with this distinction.

There are several ways in which one can view how publics come to be. The most popular view in social marketing is one adapted from the United States' most influential and most widely known philosopher, John Dewey (Haworth

1960). It was Dewey's view that people were able to achieve their best only when they were part of a community. Adapting Dewey's approach produced varying classifications of publics. These classifications usually focus on divisions useful to the organization. He defines *public* as consisting "of all those who are affected by the indirect consequences of transactions" (16) such that their concerns become known and will be acted upon by people in power.

The qualification that publics are active can be traced to Dewey. Dewey said "We take . . . the objective fact that human acts have consequences upon others, [sic] that some of these consequences are perceived, and their perceptions lead to subsequent effort to control action so as to secure some consequences and avoid others" (1927, 12). For Dewey, human activity has effects/consequences on the individual and effects/consequences on other people. His definition of public is merely an extension of his view of the interdependency of people.

For instance, the organization may seek to divide publics based on specific situations or issues. The organization's environment then "at any point in time will be composed of an overlapping complex of specific and general publics that may or may not become relevant" (Cobb and Elder 1983, 104). The key issue to whether a public exists is relevancy or saliency of the organization's message. The issue that is placed before the population must be one that is relevant to the group in order for a public to form. Issues don't exist for those who are uninterested. For one to be interested, one has to be knowledgeable about an issue to the extent that one is at least aware of the issue and made a judgment as to saliency.

The awareness level of people defines which type of public the person falls into. The types of publics will be different depending as noted above on the interest level that people have in that particular issue. For every campaign, there will be those people who are "actively engaged at the center and . . . irresistibly attracted to the scene" (Schattschneider 1960, 1). Thus, there are people who are attracted to some issues in varying degrees based on their interest. Some people may be vitally interested, such as those living next to the proposed site of a toxic waste dump. Other people may be only moderately interested, such as people living far away from the proposed site.

Botan and Soto (1998) propose a language-centered approach to our understanding of publics called semiotics. Semiotics is the study of the production and interpretation of meaning through the use of signs.

There are two fundamental semiotics theorists. One was a Swiss linguist named Ferdinand de Saussure and the other was the American Charles S. Peirce (pronounced "purse"; 1960). While they differed in their emphases, both looked at how we create and share meaning. Saussure called his version semiology, and Peirce's work came to be known as semiotics. Others have also talked about language and meaning, but the primary thinkers are Saussure and Peirce.

Publics share commonalities. In some unusual cases, the public may be a single significant individual, for instance a chair of a Senate committee. People who live in California may be one commonality, while movie-going parents of young children may be another. The other trait of a public is that their actions have at least the potential for creating consequences for the entity communicating with them. People in California can vote for or against the governor, affecting his reelection. The movie-going family with young children can decide to either go or not go to a movie, which will directly impact the amount of money that the movie will make. A lawyer for a prisoner on death row may make an appeal to the governor to stay the execution. The lawyer's public is a single person, the governor who can either stop the execution or let it proceed. Clearly, the governor can create consequences for the person on death row.

How many publics are there? At least potentially millions of different publics could be hypothesized as existing. The actual number of publics for a particular social marketing program will vary with how finely the leader of the social marketing effort wants to segment people. People may exist in several different definable publics simultaneously. If this seems nebulous, it is. Publics are constructed or defined based on the needs of those people requiring useful market information.

Publics are constructed by the social marketing planners. In program planning, the planners determine those individuals, groups, or organizations that might be affected by the program or might affect the program. These individuals, groups, and organizations are the publics who must be conceptualized and envisioned for planning a social marketing campaign to create the appropriate communication strategies to use and to select for the appropriate implementation of strategic communication. Social marketing experts develop a type of public map, often called "stakeholders map" (Grunig and Repper 1992) that links "thinking through the consequences an organization has on people and they have on an organization" (Grunig and Repper 1992, 126). Publics that will appear on this map will include stockholders, board of directors, employees, customers, community members, suppliers, competitors, the media, special interest groups, and government regulators (Freeman 1984).

Publics are a necessary concept, and with the exception of a few high-profile individuals, such as the president of the United States or the chair of the Federal Reserve Board, and lobbyists, social marketing activities are not conducted by a single individual utilizing a person-to-person perspective.

Social marketing appeals usually are directed at an aggregate of individuals because individuals can't be uniquely targeted.

SEGMENTATION

If there are multiple publics the question then arises, How do we identify those publics so that as communicators we can adapt our message for maximum effect? There is the seat-of-the-pants approach by which the public relations professional divines the publics through The Force. Some public relations communicators believe that they already know about the publics and how to segment them. The other method is to use research to discover who their publics are and what defining or individuating demographical, sociological, psychological, or geographical characteristics exist within them.

Market Segmentation

This is a process of consumer segmentation. The possible audience for a commercial message is divided into segments, each with a specified likelihood of purchasing a product. "In the communication jungle out there, the only hope to score big is to be selective, to concentrate on narrow targets, to practice segmentation. In a word 'positioning' [sic]" (Reis and Trout 1986, 6). Products must be sold in a "package" structure developed based on the targeted public's preferred product position. Take for example the difference between the marketing of the Chevrolet Corvette and the Mazda Miata. Both cars are two-passenger vehicles and both come with removable tops. However, the cars are targeted to different markets. Corvettes are high-performance "muscle" cars with high-power engines and tuned suspension systems and beg the driver to unwind and travel faster than the speed limit. Power and speed are key selling points of one of the few U.S.-produced two-seater sports cars. Corvettes are targeted heavily toward men and particularly those who fancy themselves as pushing the edge. Corvettes were a favorite among the 1960s astronaut corps.

Miatas are less masculine-centric than Corvettes. These are "fun" cars for younger people in their twenties and thirties—both men and women. While the Corvette emphasizes performance, a Miata stresses "freedom." The Corvette price tag is about twice that of the Miata's low to mid $20,000s, suggesting that the Miata is more easily affordable by younger people who have less income.

Grunig and Repper (1992) make a distinction between market segmentation and public segmentation. They argue that the distinction between the two is important, because marketing organizations can choose at whom they wish to aim their marketing messages. Market segmentations are the groups to whom the organization wishes to attract their product or service. Publics would include those to whom the organization is marketing, but it would also include any number of other potential publics. The creation of publics is a dynamic process. New publics may be created while other publics disappear. These publics located by social marketers may be created specifically out of some activity by an organization. As such, social marketers may have to deal with a new unexpected public. These publics may be supportive and cooperative with the organization or antithetical and opposed to the organization. While marketers can decide to ignore a segment of the market as far as their product or service goes, the social marketers, they argue, must pay attention to all significant publics.

While Grunig and Repper note the difference between public and market segmentation, they do go on to say that the process of segmentation is roughly the same. That is, the communicator must find some method to divide a population (market) into smaller groups. Group members will share some characteristic(s). William Smith provides a concise definition of segmentation as "the process of finding out how to best group people by the similarities that are important to their behavioral choices" (1997, 24).

PUBLICS AND CONSUMER BEHAVIOR

Public segmentation is needed because many people view the marketing of products within a sociological framework. Those who ascribe to this view see such typical sociological factors as reference groups, social conformity, and group membership as important in explaining and predicting what products people will purchase.

Cultural environment and its subcomponents (subcultures) influence the types of products we purchase. The Amish are the almost exclusive purchasers of horse-drawn buggies in the United States. Collard greens are a popular food item among those raised in the South but are not a big seller in New England states. Often the culture is defined by issues of economic status, ethnic identity, social values, religion, geographical location, and other influences.

Within the sociological view of consumer behavior products have not only a utilitarian value, for example a car for transportation, a chair in which to sit, a hotel in which to stay when away from home, but also make a social statement. The selection of a Rolls Royce rather than a Saturn; a Louis XIV chair rather than a white molded plastic chair; or the Ritz Carlton Hotel rather than Motel 6 makes a statement about who the person perceives him- or herself to be or at least how they wish to be perceived by others.

A Louis XIV chair in your living room is a sign of what Thorstein Veblen (1948) called conspicuous consumption. In other words, we are defined by those around us in terms of the types of goods that we purchase for use. Veblen finds that the purchase of those things that are not essential provides the social gratification of being able to waste money.

Common objects can take on sociological significance as indicators of the wealth of a society. Many people from Europe and Asia view Americans as being rich because, in their view, we tend to be wasteful. For example, it is common in European countries to own a shopping bag or basket. This bag is taken whenever it is time to go to the market. The grocery purchases are placed in the bag and taken home. The shopping bag is put away until the next trip to the store. The use of plastic and paper bags in grocery stores in the United States is a perceived waste as these bags will be placed into the trash upon arrival at home. This conspicuous consumption on the part of Americans serves as an indicator that our society is sufficiently rich enough that we can "waste" plastic or paper grocery bags.

Reference groups also influence the purchasing behaviors of members. Similar to emulation but from a group rather than individual viewpoint, reference groups provide a measuring stick for what one should have in order to become a member of the reference group. Social class directly influences many of the products and services that are purchased. A given product may be purchased by different social classes, but the product will have a different significance for each class. Different types of a product may be purchased by different social classes, and some products may be purchased by only one social class. Yachts, for example, are the exclusive products of the rich.

The ability to divide people based on any of these five sociological factors should provide some predictive information for those who know how to read it. This information can help a marketer better focus the introduction and continuing sales of products and services. Segmentation provides the means necessary to break people into different groups that can be targeted with more specific information.

Joseph Scott and Dan O'Hair break down the information that will be of crucial importance to marketers; they believe that there are three fundamental characteristics:

(a) an accurate description of the demographic make-up of the audience in question, (b) using psychographic information to focus on the individual's values and lifestyle, and (c) determining the emotional reaction of the audience members. Upon fulfillment of these assessment criteria a complete audience profile can be determined. (1989, 205)

Let's turn our attention to some of the more popular means of segmentation. These methods are designed to find similarities and differences among people and exploit them. As Scott and O'Hair suggest, let's begin with demographics.

DEMOGRAPHICS

The first set of marketing tools was the introduction of **demographics.** Demographic literally means "people writing," although the root *demos* may be a derivative of *damos*, which means a "division of the people" (*Webster's New World College Dictionary*). Division-of-people-writing is exactly what demographics is all about. It is the study of dividing people along certain traits such as age, race, sex, ethnic background, income, and/or occupation. Demographics serve as the primary basis for most decisions in advertising (Alwitt 1985).

One of the commonly used demographic variables is age. If you were to look at a page from an Arbitron radio ratings book, you would see that the listenership is divided into age groups. This age group data is useful for radio station programmers and the advertising sales personnel who sell advertising on the station. For example, the age of the radio audience will influence the types of concerns that will likely advertise on the radio station. There are other typical demographic categories such as sex, income, education, and occupation. Demographic categories are usually measured as self-perception categories; that is, the data for these categories are usually based on what the individual respondent says. If asked for hair color and the response is blonde, it doesn't matter that without help it naturally would be brown and gray, the person is a blonde.

The use of multiple traits yields a better picture of a radio station's audience or of the people for whom advertising is crafted. For example, the owner of a men's clothing store wants to reach primarily a male public with information about his clothing line. However, women cannot be ignored. Wives particularly may influence the clothing choices that a spouse makes. Primarily, the owner is looking for males eighteen years of age and older. Because he has a specialty store, he may also be focusing on males, eighteen years or older, who have above average disposable income. Each of these demographic variables—age, income, gender—could be considered an individual public. Or, the public could be defined as those people who have each of the desired elements: male, eighteen or older, and above average disposable income.

When he advertises in the college newspaper, the clothing store owner often features "interview" suits, that is, suits that men may wear to a job interview. Here the haberdasher is adapting his message to a specific public—college-educated males who will soon be going on job interviews and who will need to present an appropriate "business" appearance.

Although the use of demographics in public relations is a relatively recent phenomenon, the use of demographics by public relations practitioners is readily accepted. In marketing research, the use of demographics is considered a matter of routine. For instance, examine the case of cigarette marketing.

Michael Basil and colleagues (1991) demonstrated how cigarette manufacturers use demographic segmentation to better adapt their advertising to their targeted audiences. They found that the content of cigarette ads differed based on the orientation of the magazine in which it appeared. The study examined magazines for general audiences as well as those directed to specific audiences, such as those marketed to men, women, youth, and African Americans. Basil and his colleagues found that "women, Blacks, youth and less-affluent readers seem to be targeted with more overtly sexual appeals than men or general audiences" (1991, 88–89), leading them to conclude that "content differences show how cigarette advertisers market the same product to different audiences" (89).

Simmons Market Research Bureau (SMRB), a subsidiary of Symmetrical Global Information Services, specializes in providing information about several demographic markets. This specialized research data is usually called target market research. For instance, SMRB provides information about youth with two of their products. Their Kids Study "reveals the marketplace power of children 6 to 11 years of age. It examines the demographics, print and broadcast media exposure, and the personalities that influence children and their buying decisions" (www.symmetrical.com/smrb_serv.html, accessed 12/27/1999). And, STARS (Simmons TeenAge Reseach Studies) "provides an in-depth look into the world of teens ages 12 to 19. . . . STARS details the buying habits, media usage, beliefs and attitudes of teens. Advertisers use this information to pinpoint critical target markets and develop strategies to reach them" (www.symmetrical.com/smrb_serv.html, 12/27/1999). Simmons also produces a Hispanic Study that "provides a complete picture of the Hispanic market on a national, regional and local level in terms of product and media usage, including details on what Hispanics view, listen to and read, as well as their habits and preferences. . . . The study represents adults in Spanish-dominant, English-dominant and bilingual households" (www.symmetrical.com/smrb_serv.html, 12/27/1999). Simmons has also examined sexual orientation as a demographic group with their Gay and Lesbian Market Study, which "is the only research currently available that details the pur-

chase habits, media usage, attitudes and opinions of this market"
(www.symmetrical.com/smrb_serv.html, 12/27/1999).

While it is routine among marketers, demographic profiling has been criticized for more than a quarter of a century for its inherent limitations. Ruth
Ziff warned of four problems associated with demographic information
usage. The first problem she called the Facetious Average. She says this is the
problem of having a profile that mathematically finds fractions of children,
cars, bathrooms, and so on. For example, the typical family consists of 2.3
children. Such mathematical artifacts, Ziff says, "provide little guidance for
the development of an advertising strategy—and would continue to provide
little, even were the figures rounded off so that the dog, the automobile, the
room, etc. were more recognizable" (1974, 131).

Ziff (1974) has found that profiles provide a second problem she termed
the Minority Skew. Often, important demographic differences are not found
within a particular product class. For instance, she points to research at the
advertising firm of Benson & Bowles that showed that only one-third of the
advertised products demonstrated an age difference and only one product in
eight showed a difference on income.

In addition, demographic profiles may simply be a problem of Insightless
Numbers. This problem speaks to the difficulty that demographic analysis
has in answering the "why" question. Even in those situations where a demographic difference is detected, the numbers don't tell why the differences
exist among the various groups. As Ziff notes, "there is rarely one reason but
rather several why a particular group buys a certain brand or product" (1974,
132).

The final problem she calls the Homogeneity Myth, which is the assumption that all blue collar workers or all eighteen- to thirty-six-year-olds will be
alike. She argues that these segments should not be viewed as having a single
set of needs and values. One must recognize that there are differences among
any demographic group.

PSYCHOGRAPHICS AND
LIFESTYLE SURVEYS

Such differences led consumer researchers to determine that demographics
do not tell the whole story for someone wishing to understand consumer
purchasing decisions. For example, the outlook, interests, and buying habits
of a twenty-year-old woman from New York City may not resemble those of
a twenty-year-old woman from the Jicarilla Apache reservation in New Mexico, despite the similarity in their age and sex. What was needed was a more

comprehensive measure, one that would allow the communicator to carefully categorize audience lifestyles. This knowledge would lead to the sharpened and more persuasive appeals used within the message or consumer message.

As a result, two different approaches were taken. One was to use standardized psychological personality inventories. J. Walter Thompson Company, one of the largest international advertising firms in 1956, made the first attempt, followed by other agencies and researchers in associating a person's score on some personality test with consumer behavior. The results of these attempts were not, to be charitable, entirely successful (e.g., Cravens 1987; Harrell 1986; Kassarjian 1971; Stanton 1978). The J. Walter Thompson Company would conclude "the influence of these [psychological] factors is relatively small" (Koponen 1960, 12).

Procter & Gamble undertook a three-year effort to link personality classifications with product preferences. After three years of trying, P&G abandoned the effort, because what results they were able to obtain were not usable by the advertising and brand managers (J. T. Plummer 1985). Sidney Levy succinctly summarized the problem as far back as 1966: "we encounter the problem of the refusal of so many people to be consistent" (156).

However, personality studies have not been completely abandoned, because there have been some limited successes (e.g., Ackoff and Emshoff 1975; Evans 1959; Horton 1979). Enough at least, for Carolyn Cline and her associates to claim "personality remains a valid realm of investigation for persuaders" (1989, 225). However, most researchers now view personality factors as only one piece of a much more complex picture than was originally conceived. These personality factors interact and manifest themselves within the individual's environment.

The second psychological approach was begun by either Ernest Dichter, president of Institute for Motivation Research Inc., or Louis Cheskin, director of the Color Research Institute of America, (both claim paternity). This second approach would earn a special place in Vance Packard's (1957) expose of manipulative advertising *The Hidden Persuaders*. Both Dichter and Cheskin claim to have begun what came to be called **motivational research** and depth interviews in the 1930s. Dichter defined motivational research as "the branch of market research which concentrates on the "why" of buying. It is interpretive rather than descriptive. Many of its techniques are borrowed from the field of the social sciences" (1964, 436). Motivational research would come to prominence in the 1950s. Motivational studies were meant to elicit what motivates people to purchase one item rather than another. Cheskin and Ward defined the areas of interest to the motivational researchers:

Some of these have to do with the abstract qualities of the article bought: color, brightness, visual pattern, three dimensional shape and form, feel or texture, odor and so forth. Other, such as brand name, have to do with common meanings, interpretations, and attitudes which are aroused by some selected feature of the article. (Cheskin and Ward 1948)

Or as Dichter put it, "In modern communication we have to penetrate to the deeper meaning which products, services, and objects that surround us have for an individual" (1964, vi).

Thanks to the miracle of motivational research, Dr. Dichter was able to explain the meaning that everyday items have for people. For example, Dichter wrote about bras, constipation, and iced tea:

The Bra
   Motivation studies showed that women expected three major services from well-fitting bras: a. To be made sexually more attractive b. To become eligible for compliments c. To be able to translate and manifest personality through them.
   Women felt that the bra should be both noticeable and unnoticeable, that it should accentuate flirtation qualities but not the deeper meanings of the female breast such as passion or motherhood that it should "communicate" with the man but remain strictly in the feminine domain. Women want a bra to fit their personality. In a special test, the concept of a tailor of bras, a "wizard of bras," was examined and it was found that he would have to be a nonsexual male, whimsical and make-believe, neither man nor woman but symbolic of sexual attraction. (1964, 81)

Constipation
   In a psychological sense, irregular elimination is disturbing because the body is not functioning; control has been lost over it. It is not illness, but it is disquieting; it resembles impotence. On the other hand, bowel movements are accompanied by essentially pleasant feelings that ally it to sexual gratification. There is in elimination, as in sex, a relationship of tension and relief. However, as with sex, there are also feelings of inhibition, guilt, sin, and embarrassment.
   There are powerful words in the vocabulary of constipation—purge, catharsis, elimination, irregularity—words with a connotation of violence. And the first important battle that confronts a child at the beginning of his life is for bowel and bladder control. It is in this field that he wins early approval or reprimand, success or failure. Unconsciously, one of the child's earliest weapons against outside authority is, besides soiling, retention. A child may learn to use retention and, eventually, constipation as a tool to express antagonism. Retention is often an expression of the need for love—not expecting love from others, one holds on to what he has, to a part of himself. (1964, 202–3)

Iced Tea
   In a study of iced tea usage it became necessary to investigate the psychology, of thirst. We found that physical thirst and psychological thirst are distinct from each other, and even gallons of liquid which clearly had quenched physical thirst left Psy-

chical thirst untouched. Iced tea has the ability for many consumers to "split" thirst into the physical and psychical components. The first glass serves to quench physical thirst; the second, operating to transform the hot dusty world into a cool haven, then serves to quench the psychic craving for liquid which gallons of water would not alleviate.

Research has indicated iced tea to be the drink with the unique quality of removing vague and bottomless restlessness and of restoring psychic balance. (1964, 353–54)

These early studies used projective tests and long, depth interviews. What these motivational researchers were attempting to discover were all the layers of the mind. Critic Packard summarized how people such as Dichter or Cheskin view the human mind:

The first level is the conscious, rational level, where people know what is going on, and are able to tell why. The second and lower level is called, variously, preconscious and subconscious but involves that area where a person may know in a vague way what is going on within his own feelings, sensations, and attitudes but would not be willing to tell why. This is the level of prejudices, assumptions, fears, emotional promptings and so on. Finally, the third level is where we not only are not aware of our true attitudes and feelings but would not discuss them if we could. Exploring our attitudes toward products at these second and third levels became known as the new science of motivational analysis or research or just plain M. R. (1957, 25)

Thus, these researchers would "focus on the emotional aspects of the products and the fantasies that products could arouse and/or fulfill" (Hirschman and Holbrook 1982, 93).

A classic example of the way motivational analysts found merchandising possibilities in our deeper sexual yearnings was a study Dr. Dichter made for Chrysler Corporation in the early days of M.R. His study is now known as "Mistress versus Wife." Vance Packard described it as follows:

Dr. Dichter was called upon to explain a fact puzzling marketers of the auto. While most men bought sedans and rarely bought convertibles, they evidently were more attracted to convertibles. Dealers had found that they could draw more males into their showrooms by putting convertibles in the window. After exploring the situation Dr. Dichter concluded that men saw the convertible as a possible symbolic mistress. It set them daydreaming of youth, romance, adventure just as they dream of a mistress. The man knows he is not going to gratify his wish for a mistress, but it's a pleasant daydream. This daydream drew the man into the auto salesroom. Once there, he finally chooses a four-door sedan just as he once married a plain girl who, he knew, would make a fine wife and mother. "Symbolically, he marries the sedan," a spokesman for Dr. Dichter explained. . . . The spokesman went on to explain Dr. Dichter's line of thinking: "If we get a union between the wife and mistress—all we sought in a wife plus the romance, youth, and adventure we want in a mistress—we would have . . . lo and behold, the hardtop!" (1957, 87)

The advantage of motivational research over demographic research was that it provided a tangible description of the targeted public. As William Wells and Douglas Tigert aptly explained, "For the first time, research brought the marketing manager and the copywriter face to face with an audience or a group of customers instead of a bunch of decimals" (1971, 27).

Motivation research provided an audience's face for the copywriter. An audience that might be previously described as "32.4 years old, 12.62 years of schooling, 90 per cent married with 2.1 children" were now supplanted by "fretful wives who didn't know how to make a good pie crust, fathers who felt guilty about watching television when they should be painting the porch and skinny kids who secretively, but sincerely, believed that The Breakfast of Champions had something to do with their batting average" (Wells and Tigert 1971, 27).

The 1970s saw a decline in these motivational studies because, in part, motivational research was amalgamated with personality research. Also, motivational research declined because of researchers' responses to what appeared to be the "excesses of motivation research era" (Hirschman and Holbrook 1982, 92). During the mid-1960s some researchers began to amalgamate these two approaches into a new method, taking the rigorous quantifiable measures of standardized personality inventories and meshing them with the more qualitatively oriented motivational research in order to create what is called psychographic and lifestyles research. Some researchers endorsed the notion that psychographic and lifestyle research presented a more complete picture of the audience. A discussion of psychographics and lifestyles will be provided later in this chapter.

More recently researchers such as Elizabeth Hirschman and Morris Holbrook have returned to the motivational type of research, but this time they are calling it **hedonic consumption.** Another way of expressing hedonic consumption would be to call it **emotional consumption.** An individual selects a product because of its "multi-sensory, fantasy and emotive aspects of one's experience with the products" (Hirschman and Holbrook 1982, 92).

The introduction of psychographics was not universally greeted as a breakthrough technique among some professionals. John Revett reported, in *Advertising Age* in an article subtitled "Is It 'Vogueish' or Is It Piercing Scrutiny That Gets to Fiber?" that many advertising professionals were calling this new approach "'vogueish' and impractical" (1968, 16). Oscar Lubow, president at the time of Daniel Starch & Staff, a research organization that produced readership studies of newspapers and magazines, didn't see the need for such research. He was quoted as saying that when one "gets right down to it, creative people apply their own psychographics" (Revett 1968, 16) when using demographic information. Even one supporter of psychographics was quoted as "doubting that mass product advertisers will ever spend much time on studying 'what makes consumers tick'" (Revett 1968, 16). Much as those who suggested "It will never fly, Orville," the doubters of the worth and the future use of psychographics were wrong.

The terms *psychographics* and *lifestyle* are sometimes used interchangeably; however, there is a difference between the two. Psychographics emphasizes generalized personality traits, attitudes, and interests (Wells 1975). Lifestyles emphasize needs and values that are associated with consumer behavior and have emphasized both broad cultural trends (Alpert 1972; Wells 1975) and more specific, personal behaviors (Hustad and Pessemier 1974; J. Plummer 1971–1972) reflecting needs and values that are closely linked with consumer behavior.

Abraham Maslow (1970), the founder of humanistic psychology, began with a basic question: "I was awfully curious to find out why I didn't go insane" (www.pbs.org/wgbh/aso/databank/entries/bhmasl.html, 8/16/00). Part of the journey to answer that question led him to explicate the fundamental needs of people in what is usually referred to as Maslow's Hierarchy of Needs. It is a hierarchy that suggests that in order for a specific level need to be salient to an individual, all the lower ordered needs on the hierarchy must have been met. Lynn Kahle and her associates explain the workings as "values become salient in a sequential order that progresses from primitive . . . to advanced. . . . These levels are based on deficits in that people tend to value what they lack at the next highest level. In order for a higher level to become salient, each lower-order level must be at least partially satisfied" (1997, 111). Maslow's needs are motivational in that they elicit action in order to fulfill the needs.

The most fundamental of Maslow's needs he called **physiological needs,** forming the first step in the hierarchy. These include the need for food, water, and shelter. The second step contained the needs for safety and security. People will strive to attain a sense of safety for themselves. The increasing mania for the installation of home security systems is one example of peoples' need for a sense of security. The worry about keeping one's job is another aspect of this need.

The next step contains the needs for **belonging** and love. People seek associations and affectionate relationships. Meaningful contact with others is something that most humans desire.

Next up the hierarchy is a need for **esteem,** both to be held in esteem by others and to hold one's self in esteem. The liking of one's self, or self-esteem, and the esteem of others are created by people's need for recognition or attention. However, there are occasions when the need for esteem cannot be acquired through positive behaviors. Recognition may be obtained through both positive and negative means. A child who is being ignored may find it the easiest course to gain attention by throwing a temper tantrum.

Self-actualization is the need of a person to be the best at whatever he or she feels is true to their nature. The striving for self-actualization is the need to realize what a person believes is her or his destiny. This destiny might be to be a good father, an Olympic athlete, or a gardener. The army's advertising slogan is a good synopsis of self-actualization, "Be all you can be." The self-actualizing goal may change as time progresses. The person who desired to be a good father may change his self-actualization goal after the children have left home and have families of their own.

Finally Maslow speaks of the **aesthetic need.** This is the need for beauty and a desire to avoid ugliness. This need was the one that received the least amount of interest by subsequent scholars.

While Maslow's original conceptualization was that these needs were fixed in a sequential order, other research on the hierarchy of needs has questioned whether this is true. William Graham and Joe Balloun's (1973) research generally supported Maslow's ordering of human needs in a hierarchy but found evidence that the hierarchy isn't as rigidly fixed as Maslow's work would suggest. Kahle and her colleagues (1997) found less support for the necessity of fulfilling a lower order need prior to seeking to fulfill the next need in the hierarchy. They concluded from their study that the needs within the hierarchy are "adaptive," meaning that some people may be driven more strongly by some needs than others. Thus, they respond based on their orientations rather than on a purely hierarchal response.

A police officer may risk her life to capture an armed perpetrator even when she knows that the chance of survival may be low. The officer is doing what she thinks is important in contrast to her need for life, safety, or more fundamental needs. The officer has self-actualized what an officer is to do and has acted upon it.

Maslow uses the terms *needs* and *values* interchangeably, but some theorists differentiate between the two. According to the leading researcher of values, Milton Rokeach (1973), **values** guide attitudes, judgments, and actions. Values are ideals that people hold about how one should conduct oneself and the types of goals that one should honor. Values are not tied to a particular object or thing; rather, they are beliefs about how one should act and the judgments one should make.

Clawson and Vinson had great hopes for values research and the use of values in predicting individual behavior. They predicted in 1978 that values "can perhaps equal or surpass the contributions of other major constructs including attitudes, product attributes, degrees of deliberation, product classifications, and life styles" (1978, 400).

Attitudes are different from values in that attitudes are a predisposition to respond to an object or situation. Values provide the foundation upon which our attitudes are constructed. From attitudes come behaviors (Kluckhorn 1951), Pamela Homer and Lynn Kahle (1988) call this sequential relationship the **value–attitude–behavior hierarchy.** The study of values is "relevant to virtually any human problem one might think of" (Rokeach 1973, 52).

Both values and attitudes affect behavior. How we act is a combination of the values we hold and our attitude toward either the object or the situation. Boris Becker and Patrick Connor summarize the values–attitude–behavior hierarchy:

> In brief, then, *values* may be conceived as global beliefs about desirable end states that underlie attitudinal and behavioral processes. *Attitudes* are cognitive and affective orientations toward specific objects and situations. *Behavior*, finally, is a manifestation of one's fundamental values and consequent attitudes. (1979, 37)

Public relations and marketing research has examined how values influence people's behavior in terms of products purchased and their organizational orientations. Knowing how values influence people's behavior whether in the consumer or political environment would allow creators of persuasive messages to more effectively construct their appeals.

Research has demonstrated links between values and a number of consumer products. These products include automobiles purchases (Henry 1976; Kennedy, Best, and Kahle 1989; Vinson, Scott, and Lamont 1977), cigarette smoking (Grube, Weir, Getzlaf, and Rokeach 1984), health foods (Homer and Kahle 1988), and computers (McQuarrie and Langmeyer 1985). Values are also linked to other types of behaviors such as religious observance (Feather 1984; Rokeach 1960), cheating on tests (Hensehl 1971), the preferred leisure activity (Beatty, Kahle, Homer, and Misra 1985; G. Jackson 1973), choice of friends (Williams 1959), job choice (Rosenberg 1957), television viewing (Rokeach and Ball-Rokeach 1984), and general consumer decision making and behavior (Pitts and Woodside 1983).

Values allow people to establish goals and to determine the rules by which the individual will be guided in seeking the fulfillment of those goals. Values are learned from our environment; that is, we internalize values from our family, friends, clergy, teachers, and other significant people. While theoretically there is a link between values and behaviors, it is a tenuous one. David Prensky and Christine Wright-Isak (1997) have argued that behaviors and attitudes are influenced by the various subcultures within a society. In this view, values are shared by people on the national level with some subcultural variations. This is also the view of Rokeach, who believed that values were universal, "all men everywhere possess the same values to different degrees" (3). How one would act upon those values or how one's attitudes would be formed as a result of those values would be influenced by the culture in which the person is raised. Thus, an individual's behaviors are rooted more in the individual's shared community than they are in an individual's private behavior. The result is that as the community in which a person lives changes, so too do the values (Kahle, Poulos, and Sukhdial 1988). Values are still fundamental, but the actions based on those values will vary according to the culture in which the person is enmeshed.

Also complicating this relationship is the role of beliefs. John Murry and his associates have defined beliefs as "interpretations of the environment that people learn, store, and process in order to guide their behaviors" (1997, 47). People form beliefs by their experiences with institutions or products. From these experiences, people correlate attributes and consequences of the inter-action. When experiences with the organization change, then individual beliefs and subsequent behaviors will also change. It is possible to change a behavior, if one understands and manipulates the beliefs that are guiding the behavior (Ajzen and Fishbein 1980).

Thus, one can look at the motivations for people's behaviors as an interest-ing interplay of needs, values, and beliefs. Though each of these terms is related to one another, they also have qualities that are specific to each term.

The scientific study of values has been underway for about three-quarters of a century (e.g., Cantril and Allport 1933). The study of values gained momentum when methods for the measurement of people's value systems were developed. Within the world of consumer marketing and public rela-tions, a practical measure of values means that people could be aggregated with other consumers with similar values. Messages could be tailored to spe-cifically take into account the values that were most important to these groups. The Rokeach Value Scale (RVS) is a major step toward using values as a segmentation device.

ROKEACH VALUE SCALE

The leader in values research has long been Milton Rokeach. He developed the Rokeach Value Scale (RVS) (1973), which is used to assess the values that a person holds. The Rokeach scale distinguishes two sets of values. The first set is what he called **terminal values,** meaning the desired goals that people wish to reach. This consists of eighteen values such as exciting life, sense of accomplishment, inner harmony, and so on. The second set addresses **instrumental values.** These eighteen items deal with preferred forms of behaviors. Some of the behaviors included are ambition, imaginativeness, independence, obedience, and so on. People rank order the various values, constructing a personal values hierarchy. The RVS has been used to study products and services in terms of values; for example, the RVS has been able to reveal how values relate to the automobile (Vinson and Munson 1976), deodorants, vacations (Pitts and Woodside 1983), and charities (Manzer and Miller 1978 as cited in Beatty et al. 1985).

A number of researchers have adapted the RVS to more fully meet the needs of marketers, advertisers, and public relations professionals. Some have adapted the scale by changing the way people respond to the items on the RVS. Instead of rank ordering the items, people provide a rating for all items (Alwin and Krosnick 1985; Miethe 1985; M. Moore 1975; Munson and McIntyre 1979; Rankin and Grube 1980). The substitution of ratings for rankings has shown mixed results as to which is a better system (Kamakura and Mazzon 1991). Some have shortened the scale. The List of Values (LOV) and Values Instrumentality Inventory (VII) are two such attempts at finding a more parsimonious list.

LOV. The List of Values was developed at the University of Michigan (Beatty et al. 1985), shortening the RVS to make the scale more amenable to industry and consumer based research. It is a technique for consumer value's segmentation measurement.

The LOV survey includes a list of nine values. The values include self-respect, security, warm relationships with others, sense of accomplishment, self-fulfillment, sense of belonging, being respected, and fun, joy, and excitement in life. Just as with the RVS, the LOV produces a hierarchy of values for each respondent. Unlike some psychographic measures, that is, values and lifestyles, to be discussed in a moment, LOV has no demographic elements built into it (Novack and MacEvoy 1990).

LOV is often compared to the values and lifestyles measurement device to demonstrate that it provides similar results. The claim of superiority of one of these systems over the other is still up for some debate (cf., Novack and MacEvoy 1990; Kahle, Beatty, and Homer 1986); neither one has proven useful in cross-cultural environments (Grunert, Grunert, and Kristensen 1991). One very real advantage of the LOV tool is that it is not proprietary, and consequently, it may be used without having to pay a fee.

LOV has proven to be a values scale that has been popular as a research tool though there are still those adapting the items to create their own unique scale (e.g. Kennedy, Best, and Kahle 1989). In values segmentation, all you need is LOV.

VII. Another attempt to shorten the RVS is Michael Munson and Edward McQuarrie's (1988) Values Instrumentality Inventory (VII). This scale prunes the RVS down to what Munson and McQuarrie have found to be the values most associated with product consumption. While the VII followed the introduction of LOV, it has not proven to be as popular with researchers as LOV.

PSYCHOGRAPHICS

The most popular approach to segmentation in current use is psychographics. Begun in the 1960s, the interest in better understanding publics led to the examination of psychographics and lifestyle surveys. The originator of the term *psychographics* was Emanuel Demby. He explained the role of this new area of segmentation when he wrote that the use of

> Psychographics seeks to describe the human characteristics of consumers that may have a bearing on their response to products, packaging, advertising, and public relations efforts. Such variables may span a spectrum from self-concept and life style to attitudes, interests, and opinions, as well as perceptions of product attributes. (1974, 13)

Some care should be taken about accepting *this* definition as *the* definition. The definition for psychographics is not fixed. There continues to be some controversy about the specific meaning of psychographics but the general concept is widely accepted (Wells 1975, 196).

The first national psychographics was conducted for a magazine publisher that printed several popular and well known magazines at the time, such as *Saturday Evening Post* and *Holiday*. The magazine paid for a six-month study of *Holiday* readers in 1968. The publishers wanted to find out what types and brands of products their readers used. The practical value of doing this type of research was evident to the director of the study, Emanuel Demby. He found that while people may be similar on demographic characteristics, their product purchasing habits showed much more variability (Revett 1968). The study indicated that self-concept and how readers conducted their lives, or as it more commonly called, **lifestyle,** was more important in understanding the readers (Demby 1974, 15).

Demby defines lifestyles as "a sociological concept which deals with time and energy (and money) allocations where the individual has a choice of one activity or another" (1974, 21). Lifestyle "refers to a distinctive or characteristic mode of living, in its aggregative and broadest sense, of a whole society or segment thereof. . . . Life style, therefore, is the result of such forces as culture, values, resources, symbols, license, and sanction" (Lazar 1963, 130).

Psychographic research has been very beneficial to those in social marketing who utilize this measurement technique. It allows for greater precision in predicting the behavior of groups of people in what seems to be an increasingly fragmented culture (Zotti 1985).

Psychographic variables are measures of such personality traits as leadership, sociability, independence, conformity, and compulsiveness. Psychographic data are collected by asking audience members to rate themselves on a long list of adjectives such as "refined," "tense," "organized," "romantic," using a five-point scale that ranges from "Agree a lot" to "Disagree a lot."

If the viewers of a particular TV show are psychographically similar, this information would be useful in producing commercials to run in that show. For example, if a psychographic survey noted that regular viewers of *Malcolm in the Middle* scored high on independence, ads that stress such themes as "break free from the crowd" or "go your own way" would strike a resonant chord with viewers and might be the right themes to feature in advertising during this program.

Psychographic measures provide "the qualities of the audience" to supplement the "quantity of the audience" measurement that traditional ratings provide. Segmentation of individuals into various types is a way to classify people with similar attitudes, wants, and interests together. People within a lifestyle group will typically share similar behaviors in their selection of goods and services. This is not to say that the people in these various segments are identical. People are all different. However, their commonality within lifestyle groups provides a higher descriptive predictive capability as well as designing guidelines to the construction of effective appeals. These segmentation systems are designed to group people according to these similarities. Segmentation also allows for a prediction as to what type of goods and services members of the segmentation are most likely to choose and their preference in mass-mediated channels of communication.

Those targeting a message to a specific group will utilize those channels that will deliver the desired public, even if the total number of those who attend to that channel is relatively small. For example, organizers of a "fat tire" mountain bike race would do well to promote the race in *Dirt Rag* or *Mountain Bike,* which have relatively low circulation, versus putting an ad in *TV Guide,* which has a very high circulation. The quality of the readers, that is, the targeted audience, is far higher in *Dirt Rag* or *Mountain Bike* because the readers of these magazines are almost exclusively mountain-bikers. Even though *TV Guide* has many more readers, relatively few will be interested in dirt-bike racing.

Related to psychographic surveys are *lifestyle surveys,* which measure the way a person perceives himself or herself in terms of job aspirations, leisure activities, enduring values, and buying habits. There are several ways to classify audience lifestyles, but the one that is best known is VALS™ developed at the Stanford Research Institute, now SRI, Inc. (www.sric-bi.com/) by Arnold Mitchell, who was assisted by Marie Spengler. The original three-year VALS project was begun in May 1978 with thirty-nine corporate sponsors that eventually grew to a total of seventy-three sponsors by the end of the project. SRI conducted a mail survey of 1,635 people in March and April of 1980 which covered such diverse areas as attitudes about life in general, personal goals, media habits, activities, financial issues, and product and service consumption patterns (A. Mitchell 1983). A new VALS system was released in 1989 that placed less emphasis on evolving social values while concentrating on the psychological motivations that drive product usage.

The VALS project is based on three beliefs about consumer choices. First, consumer attitudes are linked to product and service choices and may be used to predict what people want and use. Second, demographics alone are insufficient to make good decisions. And third, VALS provides information the company calls "the key attitudes that motivate consumer behavior."

How does VALS do all these things? VALS is based on a thirty-nine-statement questionnaire. The questions cover a person's like and dislikes, attitudes about the world, and attitudes about oneself. This questionnaire asks about motivations and demographic characteristics that have been shown to be strong predictors of many consumer preferences in products, services, and media. You can take the VALS test yourself at SRI Consulting Business Intelligence's website (www.sric-bi.com/vals). Find out into what type of pyschographic group you fall.

The original VALS was comprised of four comprehensive groups that were subdivided into nine lifestyles. The need-driven group was comprised of Survivors and Sustainers. Outer-directed groups were made up of the lifestyles of Belonger, Emulator, and Achiever. Inner-directed groups included the lifestyles of I-Am-Me, Experiential, and Societally Conscious. The final group was a Combined Outer- and Inner-Directed group with a lifestyle they called Integrated.

The titles as well as orientations have changed in the current VALS system (Novack and MacEvoy 1990). Today, people are divided into eight consumer segments for people eighteen or older. There are two basic categories or dimensions that are measured, self-orientation and resources. The combination of these two dimensions creates eight distinctive segments, as can be seen in figure 4.1.

Starting from the bottom of the pyramid are the people with the least resources. VALS uses the term *resources* to mean the "full range of psychological, physical, demographic, and material means and capacities people have to draw upon. It encompasses education, income, self-confidence, health, eagerness to buy things, intelligence, and energy level. It is a continuum from minimal to abundant" (future.sri.com/vals/VALS.segs.html, accessed 8/17/1999). The self-orientation and resource information combine to create eight

Figure 4.1   VALS

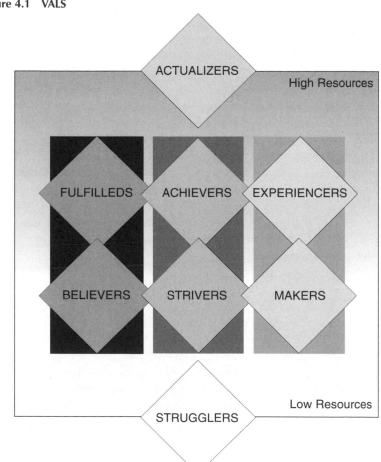

Source: SRI Consulting Business Intelligence. Reprinted with permission.

subcategories: resources ranges from Actualizers (high) to Strugglers (low); those that are principle-oriented are broken down into Fulfilleds and Believers; those who are status-oriented are segmented into the subcategories of Achievers and Strivers; Experiencers and Makers are action-oriented.

The people who occupy the bottom segment are called the strugglers. They are usually the poor and poorly educated, whose chief concerns are for their own survival. These are at the base of VALS, operating similarly to those people who would be on the first level of Maslow's Hierarchy of Needs. Strugglers have few or no resources.

On the next resource level are three basic categories: the Believers, the Strivers, and the Makers, those viewed as principle-oriented, status-oriented, or action-oriented respectively. Believers have more resources than Strugglers, but they are the least physically active of the following three types. Believers have adequate incomes and education, though not extensive. They are traditional people who believe in family, church, community, and the nation. Most of their interactions center on home and church.

Strivers have the same level of resources that Believers have but are status oriented. As the name implies, these are people who are seeking a secure place in society. Members of this group are worried about the approval of others and about the opinions that others have about them. Success equates to money, and money is something that these people haven't acquired.

Makers are the third group at this level. While the resources for members of this group are low but sufficient, they are the most physically active group at this level. As you might guess from the name, Makers are people who enjoy physical activity. Painting the house, fixing the lawn mower, baking bread are the types of activities that would appeal to this group. Makers tend to resent intrusion by the government into what they consider a person's rights, though they are respectful of the authority of government. The possessions they value are those that are functional or practical.

We now move up to the higher level of resources. There are three types on this level. In order of least activity to the most activity there are the Fulfilleds, the Achievers, and Experiencers.

Fulfilleds are well educated and generally are in the professions or retired from them and are still interested in learning more. These people are interested in world and national events and pay attention to the news. These are comfortable people who are satisfied with their career, families, and position in life. Members of this group are mature, satisfied, comfortable, reflective people who value order, knowledge, and responsibility. Most are well educated and in (or recently retired from) professional occupations. They are well informed about world and national events and are alert to opportunities to broaden their knowledge. Content with their career, families, and station in life, their leisure activities tend to center around the home. These people are not afraid of social change or new ideas. As consumers, Fulfilleds usually buy products that are functional, durable, and a value.

Achievers are successful people who feel that they have control in their lives. Generally, this group views work as a means of making money and a source of prestige. Achievers are strongly committed to work and to the family. Even their free time tends to be centered around family and work as well as church. Such people prefer the status quo and respect authority. In consumer items they prefer those items that show that they are successful to those around them. They choose products for their prestige value more than for their utility.

The final group on this resource level is the most expressive of this group. These are the Experiencers. Unlike any other category mentioned, these are people who look for excitement and variety in their lives. Being young, Experiencers are often impulsive or rebellious. Not surprising, then, that these people are interested in exercise, sports, and other forms of outdoor recreation. Not strongly committed to any political view, the Experiencers are usually uninformed about current events and politics. They admire other people's perceived prestige and wealth. They are big consumers of entertainment, clothing, and recreation.

The final group sits atop the pile. These are people who have a high level of resources. This group VALS calls the Actualizers. People of high self-esteem are "take charge" individuals who are successful and active. Actualizers are leaders in business and government. They prefer the better things in life, and the products they purchase are designed to indicate that preference. Actualizers are concerned about social issues and are not fearful of changes. In fact, Actualizers often desire to be responsible for creating changes.

Individuals are not permanently placed within a VALS category. People may move from one psychographic group to another based on their changing attitudes and circumstances. However, these categories are relatively stable, lasting on the order of fifteen years or more. Mitchell (1980) identifies age, generational cohort, "unresolved childhood and other experiences," reshaping of cultural beliefs, progression to maturity, and evolution as being principle reasons for a shift in categorization.

HOW PSYCHOGRAPHICS
MAKES A DIFFERENCE

Researchers have used VALS and other lifestyle measurements in developing advertising and public relations campaigns; positioning or repositioning a product, service, or organization; and segmenting the audience. Lifestyle measurements help an advertiser select a compatible medium for the client's advertising or a compatible program within a specific medium. Television and radio stations have only recently started to use lifestyle measurements to differentiate audiences and their various program preferences (Dominick, Sherman, and Copeland 1996).

The use of psychographics for developing marketing strategies has a number of advantages over demographics. William Wells summarized the benefits:

> Pyschographic methods have offered a way of describing consumers that has many advantages over alternative methods. . . . Psychographic methods have offered new ways of looking at old problems, new dimensions for charting trends, and a new vocabulary in which consumer typologies may be described. (1975, 209)

Audience segmentation systems using psychographic and lifestyle variables provide users with a better understanding of the consumption and media behaviors of targeted publics. Systems like VALS II claim to identify "why" people select the goods and services they do, what media they prefer to use, and even the favorite types of recreation of those in the group. For the social marketer, these systems are invaluable for profiling the potential audience, for only when one knows the audience can one effectively craft a resonating persuasive appeal. Dozier and Repper agree that this type of measures may help a social marketer "humanize publics that might otherwise seem to be statistical aggregates" (1992, 206). In other words, it provides human characteristics rather than simple numbers and gives the social marketer greater guidance in constructing an effective social marketing campaign.

Although researchers have found psychographics invaluable in designing professional persuasive communications in interviewing the largest U.S. advertisers, the majority believed that segmentation and psychographics had limited utility. Gould concluded:

> First, some people such as creatives may be more positive about psychographic use, but even they have some problems with them and perhaps as often as not tend to rely on their own intuitive insights. Second, psychographics seem to be more knowledge-enhancing than action-oriented, thus resulting in low affectivity in terms of overall satisfaction for those advertising agency people who use them. (1997, 223–24)

SRI is keeping VALS current by creating iVALS, which is a psychographic description of Internet users. As of August 1999, iVALS has ten segmentations ranging from Wizards to Immigrants (future.sri.com/vals/ivals.segs

.html, 7/19/1999). Their accompanying generalizations may then be used by people who need to reach these segments with optimally effective appeals.

Mediamark Research, Inc., has developed its own proprietary, syndicated lifestyles system. Their LeisureStyles (www.mediamark.com/, 12/27/1999) segments people in the contiguous forty-eight states into eight categories: Outdoor Energetics, Collectors, General Actives, Nesters, Party People, Golfers, Hunters & Fishers, and Passives. According to Mediamark Research, the use of these categories enables marketers to "pinpoint target markets, develop new products, reposition existing products, formulate marketing plans, and increase the efficiency of media buys" (www.mediamark.com/, 12/27/1999).

Mediamark Research has identified various segments based primarily on their lifestyle. For example, one of their segmentations is Consumer Innovators. These are people who adopted a new service or product early in its availability. Mediamark provides information about early adopters in electronics, finance, home appliance, leisure, and food.

For instance, according to Mediamark Research, food innovators are people who use "'breakfast/snack/nutri bars'; Brie or low calorie Gruyere cheeses; peanut, canola or sunflower oils; frozen main courses; 'natural' cold cereals; pita or sour dough bread; salt, butter, or egg substitutes; Low Sodium Spaghetti Sauce, refrigerated fresh packaged pasta; rice cakes; whole coffee beans or an electric coffee grinder; cook with a convection oven; a pasta machine; electric wok and an espresso/cappuccino maker among others" (www.mediamark.com/, 12/27/1999).

GEO-DEMOGRAPHICS

People who live in different places exhibit different values and lifestyles. Joel Garreau (1981) suggested that the countries that constitute North America, including the United States, should be subdivided and viewed as nine nations. These nations were created based on their inhabitants' worldviews. His nine nations include: New England, Dixie, The Islands, Empty Quarter, Breadbasket, The Foundry, MexAmerica, Ecotopia, and Quebec. This illustrates that geography may influence values and attitudes.

These values then translate into different consumer-oriented choices. For example, southern college students value social recognition—that is to be noticed as being in the proper socioeconomic class. When compared to students from Los Angeles, these southerners wanted larger, more prestigious cars and stylish, more attractive clothing. Their value of social recognition is mirrored in their consumer behavior (Vinson, Scott, and Lamont 1977).

While Garreau's hypothesized that eight nations didn't hold up well when tested with a secondary analysis of survey data (Kahle 1986), these subdivisions are suggestive of another way that the population may be segmented.

Persuasive communicators are seeking means to more effectively target key audiences and publics. Because the United States is so large, the cost of reaching consumers, those most likely to purchase a product or a service or adopt a new idea, may be prohibitive. Research acts as a means to reach a quality audience/public. According to Claritas, a major research firm, "there are more than 270 million people living in more than 100 million households located in over 260,000 neighborhoods, or Census block groups, across the country" (yawyl.claritas.com/faq.asp). It is possible to segment this large group of households into much smaller groups. If one may assume that people who live next door to one another usually have certain things in common, that is, they share income, education, and buying habits, then it would be possible to break the United States down into smaller groups based on where a person lives.

This is exactly what PRIZM (Potential Rating Index for Zip Markets), a proprietary segmentation system owned by Claritas Corporation, does (www.claritas.com/index.htm, 8/19/1999). Claritas Corporation was begun by the originator of PRIZM, Jonathan Robbin. Robbin, "King of the Zip Codes," created the system in 1974 (Weiss 1988). The PRIZM system originally began by assigning every ZIP code to one of forty lifestyle categories. This may be done at the ZIP code level, which usually includes 2,500 to 7,500 households, or it may be more specific by using the ZIP code + 4 number, which will narrow the geographic area down to six to twelve homes (yawyl .claritas.com/faq.asp, 8/19/1999). Since its introduction, the number of segments has now increased to sixty-two "clusters," reflecting the changes in neighborhoods and lifestyles in the past quarter century. The sixty-two clusters subsume fifteen social groups. Today, PRIZM provides the main competition to VALS.

These clusters were built with the help of U.S. census data and consumer data drawn from many diverse sources, including both consumer and media databases. The assignment of homes to a lifestyle cluster is based on the neighborhood's demographics and on lifestyle measures, including products and services used, media channel favorites, and activities. This is a geographic segmentation system; that is, it makes generalizations about the goods and services purchased and the types of media used based on where a person lives.

PRIZM offers the social marketing professional another mechanism to help target specific messages designed for specific publics. By using PRIZM to find where actual and potential customers are located, one can then expect that others within the same cluster are also potential customers of the product or service and need to be included in the planned public relations program. PRIZM is particularly useful in media planning, specifically for direct-mail solicitation campaigns.

Each of the sixty-two clusters is given a name. The top cluster is called "Blue Blood Estates Elite Super-Rich Families." Claritas defines this group as living in luxury in the wealthiest areas. Members are business executives or professionals. They may also be heirs to family fortunes. People in this group often have servants. Only 1.18 percent of the U.S. population falls into this category. Claritas says that these people are the most likely to watch *Wall Street Week* and buy classical music (yawyl.claritas.com/clusterlookup.asp? cluster = 1&zipcode = 48230, 8/19/99).

The bottom cluster, number sixty-two, is called "Hard Scrabble Older Families in Poor Isolated Areas." These are the poorest people who live in rural areas of the country. As the label "hard scrabble" suggests, these are people who struggle to make a living. Claritas notes that this group contains the highest level of Native Americans. Household income averages $18,100. Hard Scrabble makes up 1.99 percent of the U.S. population. People within this cluster watch auto racing on television and enter sweepstakes (yawyl .claritas.com/clusterlookup.asp?cluster = 62&zipcode = 87571, 8/19/99).

Middle clusters have such names as "Big Fish Small Pond Small Town Executive Families," "Mid-City Mix African-American Singles & Families," and "Shotguns and Pickups Rural Blue-Collar Workers & Families." If you are interested in seeing what kind of neighborhood you live in, go to Claritas's web site at yawyl.claritas.com/ and enter your zip code. It will provide you with the top five clusters for your neighborhood.

The PRIZM database links to dozens of syndicated product-use surveys, direct-mail lists, audience measurement, and other key databases in the United States. These links allow the use of PRIZM for a wide variety of marketing applications including direct mail, media-planning, site analysis, and product positioning. The utility of this type of system has been illustrated by Weiss:

> Those five digits [Zip code] can indicate the types of magazines you read, the meals you serve at dinner, whether you're a liberal, Republican or an apathetic Democrat. Retailers use zips to decide everything from where to locate a designer boutique to what kind of actor to use in their TV commercials—be it Mean Joe Green, Morris the Cat or Spuds McKenzie. College and military recruiters rely on a city's zip codes to target their efforts to attract promising high school graduates. (1988, xi)

Robbin, the creator of PRIZM, claims, "tell me someone's zip code, and I can predict what they eat, drink, drive—even think" (as quoted by Weiss

1988, 1). A derivative of VALS called GeoVALS is a direct competitor of PRIZM (future.sri.com/vals/geovals.index.html, 7/19/1999). However, Geo-VALS challenges some of PRIZM's assumptions. As the owners of GeoVALS argue, "Geodemos assume that people in the same neighborhood think, behave, and buy alike. GeoVALS shows that they don't" (future.sri.com/vals/geovals.index.html, 7/19/1999).

LADDERING

VALS, PRIZM, and other segmentation methods have been labeled by Thomas Reynolds and Jonathan Gutman (1988) as **macro approaches.** They view macro approaches as being sociological. Micro-segmentation studies are those that Reynolds and Gutman view as being psychological. The work of motivational researchers would be viewed by these two as operating at the micro/psychological level. The technique may be used to link values with a product or a service (see for example, Reynolds and Craddock 1988).

Reynolds and Gutman's preferred style of **micro-segmentation** utilizes a technique they call **laddering.** Laddering is an attempt to move from attributes to values, a means–end chain that links behavior with values (cf., Gutman 1982; Howard 1977; Young and Feigin 1975). Gutman's conceptualization of the elements in the chain may be seen in figure 4.2. The chain predicts that "consumption is most likely when the values associated with a product mesh with those which are central to the consumer" (McQuarrie and Langmeyer 1985, 242). The question is how to discover how product and values "mesh."

Laddering explores the meshing through its use of in-depth interviews to investigate how people imbue products with attributes that are in turn associated with values. To investigate such meshing, Reynolds and Gutman (1988) have suggested three possible methodological approaches. They first suggest using **triadic sorting.** This approach gives the interviewee three like products and asks him or her to find ways two of the three items are the same, thereby making the third one different. Second, they suggest **preference-consumption differentials.** This technique asks the interviewee, after ranking products, to explain in an open-ended format why top-ranked items are preferable to the ones not as highly ranked. Finally, Reynolds and Gutman suggest creating differences by occasion in that the products are placed within some social context and the interviewee is then asked to make a distinction between the products based upon the given situation. The depth interviews used in these procedures make heavy use of **probes.** The typical probe in this kind of segmentation study is "Why is that important to you?"

Figure 4.2   Gutman's Conceptual Model of Means–End Chain

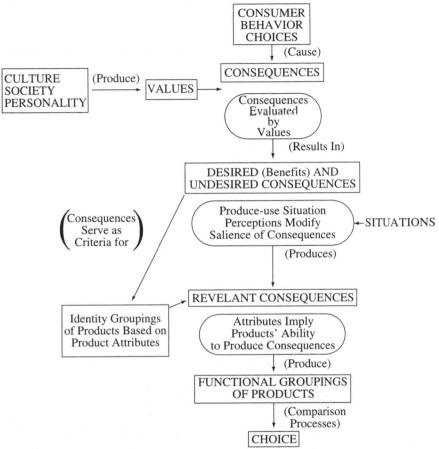

Reprinted with permission from J. Gutman, *Journal of Marketing* [published by the American Marketing Association] 46 (1982): 63.

(Reynolds and Gutman 1988, 12). Probes are used in order to understand how a product characteristic may be important to a person.

Reynolds and Gutman list three steps for deducing values from product preferences. Inquiring about product perception usually begins with the attributes (A) of a product. From these attributes, the researchers attempt to discover what consequences (C) these attributes have for the consumer. It is from these consequences that values (V) are ultimately derived. The laddering effect is shown on page 106. Starting at the bottom rung of the ladder is the attribute of a type of potato chip in that it is a "flavored chip" (an attribute A). From the use of a probe (question) the researchers discover that respondent believes the flavored attribute is important because of the strong taste (A). The strong taste is important, because the person believes he or she will need to eat fewer of those chips to be satisfied (C). That is important because it will help prevent the person from getting fat (C). Not getting fat is of significance to the person, because the person would like a better figure (C). Finally, a better figure is important to the person, because it will increase the individual's self-esteem (V). For example, Reynolds and Gutman suggest:

(Value) self-esteem
(Consequence) better figure
(Consequence) don't get fat
(Consequence) eat less
(Attribute) flavored chip   <⇒>   (Attribute) strong taste
(1988, 12)

However, obtaining the necessary details to make the deduction from product preference to value is not always easy. The two primary problems in getting the necessary details Reynolds and Gutman have identified as (1) the respondent doesn't know the answer, and (2) the issue is too sensitive for the respondent to discuss accurately. For the first problem, they suggest that the interviewer ask the respondent the question in a negative fashion; that is, "what would happen if the attribute or the consequence was not delivered?" (1988, 15) or the researcher might contextualize the problems, for example, "how is the attribute important in your daily shopping?"

Reynolds and Gutman (1988) suggest three ways of handling sensitive issues. First, they suggest that the discussion between the respondent and researcher be done in the third person. A second approach is to note the problem area and come back to it near the conclusion of the interview; this allows the interviewer to collect as much information as possible before returning to the possibly interview-stopping sensitive question. Reynolds and Gutman also suggest that the interviewer reveal some aspect about the interviewer's life that is relevant to the sensitive area. Finally, they note that the interviewer's personal anecdote is usually a lie told only to make the interviewee more willing to discuss the sensitive area.

Reynolds and Gutman believe that understanding the steps that begin with attributes that lead to consequences, from which flow values, is one way to understand how people distinguish between various products even within the same product classification. This is accomplished through the use of a hierarchical value map (HVM) that demonstrates the links between the various attributes. These HVM represent "dominant perceptual orientations, or 'ways of thinking,' with respect to the product or service category" (1988, 13).

Why is the segmentation information produced by this procedure needed by social marketers? The practical reason for doing all this segmentation is to do a better job of constructing effective messages that resonate with the desired target audience or public.

While such laddering is useful in product research, it is also useful in analyzing public policy issues. Phillip Tichenor and his colleagues (1977) have suggested that there are three fundamental variables that must be addressed when analyzing segmentation information relevant to a public issue analysis. One should examine the social conflict process, the structure of the community, and the structure of the communication channels. Such analyses will provide the social marketing professional with a number of clues as to what type of messages distributed through which channels will be most effective with a particular public.

In conclusion, many companies have developed ways to better segment publics so that persuasive communicators may more finely hone their appeals to produce more efficient and effective persuasive communication, ultimately saving both time and money. Audience analysis, the identification and profiling of publics, is the keystone to producing effective persuasive messages. Aristotle's suggestion from more than 2,300 years ago still holds true today. One needs to understand and fit one's message to the target audience. The greater the adaptation the more influential and effective the communicator will be. After all, the reason for the segmentation research is to increase communication effectiveness.

Chapter Five

The Individual in a Mass-Mediated World

The mass [sic] do not now take their opinions from dignitaries in Church or State, from ostensible leaders, or from books. Their thinking is done for them by men much like themselves, addressing or speaking in their name, on the spur of the moment.

—John Stuart Mill, *On Liberty*

All too often, social marketers focus on the power and the glitz of mass communication, that is, the persuasive potential of mass-communicated messages rather than considering how interpersonal communication might increase the salience or persuasive power of those messages. For this reason, we will explore the power of mass communication while at the same time examining the potential uses of interpersonal communication to enhance the effect of such messages in the practice of social marketing. Initially, much of the research analyzing mass communication effects was in the area of political communication effects and opinion leadership studies. We will examine these classic studies as well as later commercial opinion leader, market helper, and market maven research. Furthermore, we will review a new area of interpersonal interface research involving "the influentials."

CLASSICAL STUDIES

Direct Effects Paradigm

During the first part of this century, the mass media were considered to be all powerful. Indeed, most researchers subscribed to what has become known as the **"magic bullet theory"** or **"hypodermic needle theory"** of media effects (Rogers 1973b). (In this instance when we talk about theory, we are using a loose conceptualization of the term. In many mass communication texts, the terms *theory* and *model* are used almost interchangeably when discussing the various paradigmatic shifts.) The mass media was viewed as having "direct, immediate and powerful effects on a mass audience" (Rogers 1973b, 292). This view may be characterized as endorsing a stimulus-response model of mass media effects.

Closely linked to the magic bullet theory was a corresponding belief in **mass society theories** (Kornhauser 1953; Rogers 1973b). Mass society theorists viewed industrialized societies as being made of isolated or atomized individuals who shared little commonalities. The increased mobility of workers, the rapid growth of urban life, and the weakening of traditional bonds such as religion and extended family structures were all viewed as creating a mass audience open and receptive to mass-mediated messages. Together these theories came to be known as the direct effects paradigm (Roberts and Maccoby 1985).

In addition to mass communication effects, the power of interpersonal communication had also long been recognized. For instance, Knower (1935) found that face-to-face conversations are far more persuasive than situations involving a speaker and an audience. Similarly, researchers have long known that interpersonal communication is far more persuasive than mass-mediated communication (Katz and Lazarsfeld 1955; E. Katz 1957; Lazarsfeld, Berelson, and Gaudet 1948; Lenart 1994; Rogers 1973b). Interpersonal communication provides two-way communication designed for a specific communication setting. This allows for high levels of feedback and communication adjustment. And research has shown that interpersonal communication has a greater ability to overcome the selective processes (selective exposure, perception, and retention)—particularly selective exposure (Rogers 1973b). While mass communication is particularly effective in information or knowledge gain, interpersonal communication is far more effective in bringing about attitude change (Rogers 1973b). It should be noted that during this same time frame, other communication researchers did not share either the mass communication effects or interpersonal orientations, most notably the propaganda researchers who chose to analyze the role of institutions in crafting group and public communications.

For this reason, social marketers often include planned interpersonal communication strategies and tactics in their campaign plans. Such use of interpersonal communication works to reinforce mass-mediated messages and to promote attitude formation or attitude change. In some situations, more formal media/interpersonal structures are used by public information campaigns to bring about behavioral change. Indeed much research indicates that "although mass media can be independently successful, greater and longer lasting effects typically follow from interpersonal communication support" (Rice and Atkin 1994, 379). The social context arguably exerts strong influences on individual behaviors, providing either supportive or constraining influences on an individual. We will now consider types of media/interpersonal structures and the means by which they interface.

Early Studies on Opinion Leadership

Assuming that the mass media had direct and powerful effects on individuals, researchers during the 1940s went into the field to discover and analyze how and in what ways the mass media influenced voting decisions. A group of researchers conducted a panel study in Elmira County, Ohio, during the course of the 1940 presidential election. Yet after the data was analyzed, the results depicted an alternative view of mass media effects. First, the published study *The People's Choice* (Lazarsfeld, Berelson, and Gaudet 1948) suggested that the mass media's influence on voters was far less direct and far less powerful than it had previously been depicted. Second, the researchers observed that certain individuals within society were exhibiting greater interest in the political process and were very influential in helping shape other voters' views. They called these involved and influential voters "opinion leaders." And the study indicated that these opinion leaders were heavy consumers of the mass media as compared to other voters.

Two-Step Flow Theory of Media Effects. *The People's Choice* concluded that "ideas often flow from radio and print to opinion leaders and from them to the less active sections of the population" (Lazarsfeld, Berelson, and Gaudet 1948, 51). In other words, these opinion leaders were active information seekers who then disseminated that information to others.

Unlike the Elmira study, the fictional Rovere study assumed that personal influences were important in making decisions about all types of matters. A pilot case study with only eighty-six participants was conducted in the small town. These individuals were asked whom they thought were influential in their own lives. Hundreds of names were collected, and if a name was mentioned more than four times, then that person was interviewed by the research team (Merton 1949). Thus the case study focused on those viewed as being "actively" influential. After analyzing the results of these interviews, Merton (1949) then proposed several classifications of opinion leaders: localites vs. cosmopolites and monomorphs vs. polymorphs.

Localites and Cosmopolites. Localites are opinion leaders dedicated to their communities. Their interests are parochial in that the focus of their attention is directed at the local community and little attention is given to those issues, events, or items outside of the local community. These local opinion leaders pride themselves on knowing as many people in their community as possible and frequently interact with them. Indeed, these local opinion leaders employ an elaborate network of contacts to maintain influence in the community. It might be said that one could look upon them as local notables or celebrities in that people turn to them for advice not because of what they know, but whom they know, and who knows them. Social recognition and perceived influence are key components to understanding the power of localites. Localites are perceived as being empathetic with close personal relationships with a wide variety of people. Localites consume more mass-mediated messages than those they lead, but they rely on local media and interpersonal sources for most of their information. They prefer straight news reports to the more analytical pieces (see Merton 1949; Weimann 1994).

Cosmopolites are opinion leaders who do not focus their personal identity on living in a local community. Indeed, they consider themselves highly mobile, and their orientation is toward the world outside their community. Cosmopolites have some interest in the local community, and they maintain a small, select group of friends and acquaintances. The cosmopolite's influence is based on his or her prestige and recognized knowledge base. Often when exerting their influence, there is a perceived social distance between the cosmopolite and those they influence. Cosmopolites frequently turn to mass media sources from outside the community, such as national magazines and journals. They prefer analytical sources to straight news reports (see Merton 1949; Weimann 1994).

Monomorphs and Polymorphs. Merton (1949) also typed opinion leaders in terms of the number of **spheres of influence** in which they operated. Spheres of influence may be considered to be domains or areas of influence. Monomorphs are opinion leaders who only operate in one area (such as in fashion, cars, food, or politics) and are not perceived as being influential in other areas. Polymorphs are influential in a wide variety of areas.

After World War II, Katz and Lazarsfeld (1955) conducted what became known as the Decatur, Illinois, project, evaluating the two-step flow model of mass media effects. The resulting book was *Personal Influence,* a thorough analysis of opinion leadership. Because the research was funded by McFadden Publications, the study focused on the opinion leadership concept's implications for professional advertisers and marketers (Weimann 1994). Female respondents participated in two in-depth interviews concerning everyday decision making. Researchers had isolated what they termed "decision-making fields" or related or interrelated product, issue, or behavioral decision domains. Specifically, these decision-making fields were domains addressing marketing, fashion, public affairs, and movies. For example, in the marketing area, respondents were questioned about what foods they routinely purchased or what household cleaning products they bought. If responses were observed to have changed from one interview time to the next, researchers then probed the respondents as to why these changes had occurred (Katz and Lazarsfeld 1955).

The Social Dimensions of Influence. The *Personal Influence*'s findings were quite illuminating. Social dimensions were found to influence the position and functioning of opinion leaders within society. Katz and Lazarsfeld (1955) found that opinion leaders came from all walks of life, appearing in high, medium, and low social status groups. And most importantly, opinion leaders influenced those most like themselves. In other words, a horizontal influence relationship was observed. This was particularly true in the marketing decision-making field. However, although public affairs leaders were observed in all social levels, the number of functioning opinion leaders appeared to increase as one climbed the social status ladder. Roughly three times as many opinion leaders in public affairs were found to be of high social status. Thus, when respondents wanted to make purchasing decisions, they turned to people most like themselves—"seeking out a woman with similar budgetary problems and limitations" (Katz and Lazarsfeld 1955, 236). But when making judgments about public affairs, respondents turned to those more educated and more politically active, which typically means higher social status. Opinion leaders tended to be gregarious, having more friends and belonging to more clubs and organizations (Katz and Lazarsfeld 1955).

Although social marketers do not need to conduct opinion leadership research, it is insightful to understand how opinion leaders are identified in order to judge the validity of contemporary research findings concerning public opinion. We recommend Rogers's *Diffusion of Innovations* (1995), which provides a thorough review of the four methods of assessing opinion leadership.

LIMITED-EFFECTS PARADIGM

After nearly two decades of research, researchers now viewed interpersonal communication as being far more powerful than mass-mediated communication. In 1960 Joseph Klapper wrote that the mass media were not the usual cause of attitudinal or behavioral change but rather served to *reinforce* preexisting dispositions. Klapper believed, for example, that if a person were conservative, the media could reinforce that conservatism or even accentuate it, but the media by themselves could not usually cause a liberal to become a conservative. Klapper maintained that the media operated within a nexus of influences and that most of these influences—for example, family, religion, friends, education—were far more important in creating attitudes, beliefs, and behaviors than were the media. Klapper's classic work *The Effects of Mass Communication* (1960) became the battle-flag for what came to be known as the limited-effects paradigm of mass communication influence (see Gitlin 1978; Roberts and Maccoby 1985; Rogers 1973a).

Contemporary Research on Opinion Leaders

Levels of Activism. Kingdon (1970) found that political opinion leaders are far more knowledgeable than nonleaders. However, he also found political opinion leaders differ as to the amount of knowledge they have. **Activists** who engage in political activities have the most information and are asked more frequently about their opinions. Other opinion leaders who Kingdon calls **"talkers"** enjoy talking about politics with others but have less information, yet still advise others. And finally there are those who do not seek to influence others by introducing politics into personal conversations but nevertheless are asked their opinions. Kingdon calls these individuals **"passive leaders."**

Booth and Babchuk (1972) found that opinion leaders could be characterized as active opinion leaders or passive opinion leaders. **Active opinion leaders** tend to be well-read, knowledgeable, gregarious, polymorphic, and of a higher social status. **Occasional opinion leaders** only influence those within their families. They are usually monomorphic and occur equally in all three social status levels (low, medium, high).

Their Role in the Adoption or Rejection of Innovations. Research has shown that opinion leaders are particularly important in influencing others when it comes to the adoption or rejection of new products and new ideas (Leonard-Barton 1985; Rao and Rogers 1980; Rogers and Svenning 1969). Typically the cultural norms of the community determine whether opinion leaders will promote innovations or reject and fight innovations. If community norms supported change, then the opinion leaders were innovative. If the community norms were traditional, then the opinion leaders worked to maintain the status quo and were non-innovative. Interestingly, Leonard-Barton (1985) discovered that different personality types follow different types of leaders. Followers expressing positive attitudes about their work were more likely to be influenced by innovators. And followers expressing negative attitudes about their work were more likely to be influenced by non-innovators.

Clusters of Interest Domains. Myers and Robertson (1972, 45) investigated possible overlaps of interest/opinion leadership, constructing what they saw to be possible clusters of issue domain. They reported two principle interest clusters (which represent both interest domains and personal influence): **endogenous** (home) interest clusters (home upkeep, personal care, women's clothing, household appliances, household furnishings, cooking, and foods) and **exogenous** (outside-the-home) interest clusters (politics, automobiles, recreation, and travel). Although this classification may lead one to think that there are "female interest domains" and "female competencies" versus "male interest domains" and "male competencies," recent research indicates that this was no longer the case by 1988 (Johnson-Cartee and Copeland 1997a; Johnson [aka Johnson-Cartee], Copeland, and Huttenstine 1988; Johnston and White 1994).

Nature of the Community and Opinion Leaders' Spheres of Influence. In traditional societies or in modern societies where relatively cohesive, homogeneous, and closed systems occur (e.g., company towns, religious communes, fraternities, and single-industry towns), polymorphism is more likely to characterize opinion leaders (see Richmond 1980; Rogers and Shoemaker 1971). Indeed in highly traditional societies, there is more likely to be only one opinion leader advising on all matters, such as a shaman or chieftain (Dodd 1973; Ho 1969). In modern, complex societies with more specialization of labor and greater heterogeneity, opinion leaders are more likely to be monomorphic (see Richmond 1980; Rogers and Shoemaker 1971).

Opinion Leadership Characteristics. Katz and Lazarsfeld warned us not to confuse opinion leadership with Leadership with a capital "L":

> What we shall call opinion leadership, if we may call it leadership at all, is leadership at its simplest: it is casually exercised, sometimes unwitting and unbeknown, within the smallest groupings of friends, family members, and neighbors. It is not leadership on the high level of Churchill, nor of a local politico; it is the almost invisible, certainly inconspicuous form of leadership at the person-to-person level of ordinary, intimate, informal, everyday contact. (1955, 138)

An opinion leader "must be *interested, involved, informed,* and updated about his or her area of expertise" (Weimann 1994; emphasis added), more so than their followers. However, opinion leaders must be *roughly similar* to their followers *in terms of intelligence;* opinion leaders must also be similar in that they *must share a common language* (level of sophistication) *and have similar interests and values* (Weimann 1994).

When opinion leaders are innovators they tend "to be more venturesome, less dogmatic, and more innovative" (Weimann 1994) than their followers, but when opinion leaders are non-innovators, they serve as mediators and do not exhibit these personality traits. In traditional societies, it is very rare for opinion leaders to serve as innovators, for if they are, their followers may well reject them (Rogers 1983, 231).

Opinion leaders are also more confident or willing to follow their own judgments than those of others. This is called **"public individuation"** or the ability to be different without fearing ostracism or rejection (Chan and Misra 1990). Not only do opinion leaders obtain information from the mass media, but they also are more *gregarious* and *socially accessible* (number of interactions, number of different contacts) (Coleman, Katz, and Menzel 1966; Saunders, Davis, and Monsees 1974).

Culture and Opinion Leadership. Weimann (1994) warns that *opinion leadership characteristics cannot be generalized across cultures.* Indeed, significant differences exist across societies in not only leadership characteristics but also in interest domains.

Goldsmith, Stith, and White found that "differences among blacks based on income, education, occupation, sex, life style, and personality seem to be greater and of more use to marketers than global generalizations about black/white differences" (1987, 423). In terms of fashion attitudes, middle-class whites and blacks were highly similar; however, black males are far more likely to be fashion opinion leaders than white males. And white and black females are roughly equal in incidence of fashion opinion leadership (Goldsmith, Stith, and White 1987).

Information Exposure and Information Processing. It is safe to say that opinion leaders engage in significantly more information gathering from all sources (media, interpersonal, and other sources) than do non-opinion leaders. The choice and utilization of various channels is dependent on both their cultural setting and expertise subject area (see Heath and Bekker 1986; Robinson 1976; Weimann 1994).

And the more professional the opinion leader and the more specialized the expertise, the more likely to be exposed to professional and trade publications; programming; specialized sections/segments of traditional media, other like-professional opinion leaders, and non-opinion leader like-professionals (Chan and Misra 1990; Schiffman and Gaccione 1974).

And most importantly, Richmond found that "under either voluntary or forced exposure conditions, individuals reporting high opinion leadership acquire more information than people reporting either moderate or low opinion leadership" (1977, 42). In other words, individuals with high opinion leadership have better information-processing skills in that they attend to, acquire, and retain more information.

Horizontal Sources of Influence on Opinion Leaders. Troldahl and Van Dam (1965) found that opinion leaders interact with each other, thus they engage in **opinion-sharing.** Wright and Cantor (1967) and Robinson (1976) suggest that one may often observe the horizontal flow of influence between opinion leaders. In addition, opinion leaders who are usually **centrally located** in social networks because of high social accessibility will come in contact with those less centrally located or marginals. These **marginals** have weak ties to the social network, but they often make the centrally located opinion leader aware of new information from external sources (other social networks). But it is the centrally located opinion leader that ultimately disseminates the information to his or her social network (Weimann 1982). Therefore, the two-step flow model is found wanting, in that as Weimann (1982) suggests, opinion leaders may seek information on a horizontal level from personal sources who are not necessarily opinion leaders. In later research, Weimann characterized such influence flow as "upward" influence (1994, 250). From these studies, one must conclude that influence flows bidirectionally (see also Robinson 1976; Rogers and Svenning 1969).

The Resulting Criticism of the Two-Step Flow. The vertical two-step flow quickly came under attack. While it was a good initial step at explaining the observed data, continuing research soon demonstrated the inadequacy of the simple two-step flow concept in explaining subsequent observations. To provide a feel for the difficulties, presented is a brief outline of some of the major objections to the two-step flow theory and the research associated with that difficulty that took place in a four-decade span.

1. Ignored Evidence of Direct Flow (Media Directly to the People)
   a. Knowledge of major news events and/or controversial events diffuse to a majority of the public (Allen and Colfax 1968; Deutschmann and Danielson 1960; Hill and Bonjean 1964; Westley 1971).
   b. Television may have direct influences on people.
      • Children learn aggressive behavior (Bandura 1969; 1977).
      • Electoral instability may result and the inability to predict voting behavior based on social demographics occurs (Nie, Verba, and Petrocik 1976; 1979).
   c. Under certain conditions, print media may have direct influences on people.
      • Newspaper endorsements of candidates influence voter choice (Robinson 1974).
   d. Direct flow failed to distinguish between information flow (news diffusion) and influence flow (persuasion, role in making choices) in research measurements (Weimann 1982). Treating diffusion as

the same thing as influence flow ignores the dynamics of social/ political behavior (Chaffee and Hochheimer 1982; Weimann 1982).

2. Incorrectly Characterized Opinion Leadership Influence

   a. Opinion leaders may provide mostly supplemental relaying of information (Allen and Colfax 1968; Deutschmann and Danielson 1960; Greenberg 1964a; Greenberg 1964b; Hill and Bonjean 1964).

   b. Few Americans report hearing news from other people (Robinson 1976; Roper 1975). Robinson found less than 10 percent of people received their news from others (1976).

   c. The two-step flow model ignored the horizontal flow of influence (Robinson 1976; Troldahl and Van Dam 1965; Wright and Cantor 1967).

   d. Multiple steps in the influence chain were ignored (Mentzel and Katz 1955). Weimann identified a number of additional potential steps: "the leader-to-leader flow, the follower-to-follower flow, the upward flow from follower to leader, the more active leader to a less active leader, from the media directly to the public, and other options" (1994, 245).

   e. Opinion leadership cannot be depicted by a crude dichotomy between leaders and nonleaders but should be expressed as a *leadership continuum* (Weimann 1994, 246).

   f. Interpersonal communication serves as an important supplementary source when there is maximum attention (e.g., the Clinton and Lewinsky sex scandal) or minimum attention (an obituary in the newspaper) paid to an event by the population (Greenberg 1964a; 1964b).

Eventually, the two-step flow model was replaced by the multistep flow model (Mentzel and Katz 1955; Robinson 1976).

Multistep Flow Model. As researchers rejected the two-step flow model, the multistep flow model emerged, taking into consideration the criticisms aimed at the two-step flow model. The multistep flow model

> suggests that there are a variable number of relays [links] in the communication flow from a source to a large audience. Some members will obtain the message directly though channels from the source, while others may be several times removed from the message's origin. The exact number of steps in this process depends on the intent of the source, the availability of mass media and the extent of their exposure, the nature of the message, and its salience to the receiving audience. (Rogers 1973b, 296)

In addition, the multistep flow model allows for optional directions of flow. It also presents opinion leadership as being on a continuum of influence.

Weimann has summarized the differences between the two-step and multi-step flow models:

> *Horizontal Flow* (among leaders, among followers) and *vertical* (leaders to followers, active to inactive);
>
> *Direct* (linking two actors directly) and *indirect* (linking actors through a third party or a chain of intermediaries);
>
> *Downward* (leaders to followers, media to public) and *upward* (from opinion leaders to media, followers to influentials, marginals to centrals) (1994, 250).

The multistep flow model of mass communication effects was the dominant perspective for more than a decade. However, by the early 1970s, advances in both theoretical and methodological approaches saw a growing acceptance of the power of the mass media and a "return to the concept of a powerful mass media" (Noelle-Neumann 1973; 1981).

While much of the research involving opinion leaders has been conducted in the political arena, specifically in political news diffusion and influence studies, additional work has also been conducted in the commercial arena as well. Consumer behavior research examining market opinion leadership has had a significant impact on marketing, advertising, and public relations strategic planning. We turn now to a discussion of these important studies.

CONSUMER BEHAVIOR AND MARKET OPINION LEADERS

Repeatedly, research has found that while consumers are more likely to first learn of a new product from advertising, they are more likely to rely on the opinions of respected acquaintances when they are making a purchasing decision. Weimann summarizes the research in this area, "The media are effective in early stages of the consumer's decision-making process (i.e., creating awareness and interest, and informing), while personal sources appear to be more influential at the later stages (of evaluation, trial, and final decision)" (1994, 112).

Personal influence is important not only in an individual's decision making, concerning say a household purchase, but it is also important in the industrial market where thousands upon thousands of purchase decisions are made each day (Martilla 1971). In the industrial adoption process, purchasing agents more often turn to people within their own company and/or people like themselves in other firms for product information during the introduction, consideration, and post-purchase evaluation phase of decision making. However, personal influence is much greater during the actual active consideration of whether to purchase and the post-purchase evaluation phase (Martilla 1971).

Weimann (1994) has summarized research findings that indicate under what circumstances personal influence is most likely to have an impact on consumer decision making. In brief, personal influence will have far more impact where products are personally involving (like clothes, cars), highly visible in terms of consumption (clothing, houses, cars), highly complex and difficult to adequately and comfortably evaluate (computers, cars), and considered risky (whether in terms of lost expenditures, social gaffes, or physical dangers) (Weimann 1994, 119). In addition, consumers will turn to other individuals who have experience with products when products cannot be easily tested, and the purchase is of sufficient importance that such "testing" is highly desirable (Weimann 1994, 119).

A market opinion leader tends to be more gregarious, self-confident, innovative, socially active, and willing to individuate himself or herself (Weimann 1994, 128–30). Robertson, Zielinski, and Ward suggest "to affect personal influence, the most logical strategy is to reach opinion leaders and to let them influence their followers" (1984, 412). Yet, the use of market opinion leaders involves the process of locating or identifying them, which in commercial applications may well be cost prohibitive. But innovative researchers have suggested that companies just create their own market opinion leaders (Mancuso 1969; Rieken and Yavas 1986). Mancuso (1969), for example, selected social leaders among area high schools, exposed the select group to new rock and roll recordings, allowed them to discuss their preferences, and then urged them to discuss their rock and roll preferences with their friends outside of the group. The result was quite remarkable; records selected by the groups reached the top ten charts in the studied cities; and, these same records in other cities where groups were not functioning did not make it to the charts. Mancuso explained the keys to such a successful market opinion leader program:

> The underlying belief about the process of creating opinion leaders is basically simple. First, select a subject already possessing to the greatest degree possible the variables that the creation techniques are least able to strengthen. Second, to the degree possible, strengthen the remaining variables, so that the subject receives as high a rating as possible in the areas of mobility, status, and confidence. (1969, 25)

In other words, choose someone who is easily identified as gregarious, provide her with attractive information, encourage her product involvement, and build her confidence in not only evaluation decisions but in influencing others. Or a company might want to discover highly confident individuals who needed their status and mobility boosted. The key is recognizing which combinations of variables need to be heightened.

Market Opinion Leader Activation. For many years, the banking industry failed to capitalize on many positive relationships they had in their community (Stern and Gould 1988). For example, real estate brokers and agents are important financial opinion leaders to not only newcomers to a community but to established residents as well. Yet until quite recently, banks did not capitalize on their natural partnership with the real estate community. Today, however, innovative banks provide community information packets to real estate firms that not only feature real estate investments and the bank's own financial services but also detail important shopping, medical, legal, dental, accounting, and educational services in the community. Historical articles and cultural events are showcased. Messages from political and civic leaders are also included. Local government and state regulations such as property taxes and driver's license and car tag requirements are explained. And local businesses frequently provide coupons for discounted or free merchandise to introduce themselves to potential customers. Local companies may provide magnetized telephone reference lists or sports schedules for the new homeowner.

It should have become obvious by now that the banking institution is doing a large part of the real estate agent's job for him and at no cost to the real estate agent. In short, real estate agents love the bank for providing them with such informational packets for their own clients. The packets spread good will in the community not only through the agent's initial distribution of the packets to their customers, but also by the real estate agent's verbal positive assessment of the financial institution, and by the retained and frequently utilized promotional materials within the packet that provide additional value to the consumer (independent of the sponsoring institution), for example, a magnetized emergency telephone list that is placed on the refrigerator door.

Indeed, marketers today find that often mass media campaigns are not necessary to reach their ultimate audience. A more specialized advertising approach involving seminars directed at market opinion leaders may well prove more effective and less costly. Munson and Spivey (1981) argue that persuasive messages should be developed for market opinion leaders that are consistent with their values, lifestyles, and needs. In the case of the real estate brokers, the innovative bank perceived their need and determined it was to the bank's advantage to fill that need.

Information, given free to the opinion leader, can become a revenue item rather than a cost item. The financial firm that gives away information, albeit at considerable cost, probably receives a high return in terms of satisfied customers who spread positive word-of-mouth messages and attract new users. (Stern and Gould 1988, 51)

In addition, Corey has suggested that market opinion leaders provide a ready-made quality test market in terms of product development, copy testing, and attitude research (1971, 5). Weimann indicates that market opinion leaders' evaluations

> are more crucial as they indicate the likelihood of acceptance and credibility among the leaders themselves and consequently, among the general public. . . . The . . . [market opinion leaders] who are both reflecting and shaping public attitudes, can serve as valuable sources of information on what determines consumers' choices, images, and considerations. Moreover, they will provide the marketers with the attitudes that opinion leaders "pass on" to their circle of influence. (1994, 136–37)

Market Mavens. Recently a new approach to identifying marketplace opinion leaders has been proposed. Researchers for some time have known that some individuals exhibit what has been termed high **purchasing involvement;** in other words, some people, for whatever reason, are more interested in and are more involved in marketplace activities, such as reading advertisements, cross-comparing of products for features and price, and window-shopping (Slama and Tashchian 1985). Such purchasing involvement has long been measured by the "extent of interest in and enjoyment of shopping, use of coupons, and interest in and attention to advertising" (Feick and Price 1987, 86; Guiltinan and Monroe 1980; Kassarjian 1981). Such individuals may use shopping as a form of entertainment (Kassarjian 1981). They may weigh purchase decisions more carefully than others, and for this reason, they study where to shop for certain goods, what stores have the best prices on certain goods, and what stores are likely to have sales on those same goods (Slama and Tashchian 1985; Thorelli and Thorelli 1977). Kassarjian (1981) suggests that some individuals perceive it to be their duty or obligation to be wise consumers (Thorelli, Becker, and Engledow 1975; Thorelli and Thorelli 1977). They enjoy talking about shopping and providing information to others concerning the marketplace (Feick and Price 1987). Feick and Price (1987) characterize such people as **market mavens.** During a pilot study, they noted that respondents used the Yiddish term "maven" to describe "individuals who have information about a variety of products and like to share this information with others," or more succinctly, "a neighborhood expert" (1987, 85). Feick and Price went on to operationalize market mavens as "Individuals who have information about many kinds of products, places to shop, and other facets of markets, and initiate discussions with consumers and respond to requests from consumers for market information"

(1987, 85). Just as with market opinion leaders, market mavens' influence is based on knowledge and expertise; however, that perceived knowledge and expertise is not product specific but is triggered by more general marketplace information. You might say that market mavens specialize in market outlets, comparison pricing, and sales. To identify market mavens, Feick and Price developed six items to be evaluated on a seven-point scale.

1. I like introducing new brands and products to my friends.
2. I like helping people by providing them with information about many kinds of products.
3. People ask me for information about products, places to shop, or sales.
4. If someone asked where to get the best buy on several types of products, I could tell him or her where to shop.
5. My friends think of me as a good source of information when it comes to new products or sales.
6. Think about a person who has information about a variety of products and likes to share this information with others. This person knows about new products, sales, stores, and so on, but does not necessarily feel he or she is an expert on one particular product. How well would you say that this description fits you? (1987, 95)

Feick and Price provide evidence that market mavens are "aware of new products earlier, provide information to other consumers across product categories, engage in general market information seeking, and exhibit general market interest and attentiveness" (1987, 93). Among those identified as market mavens, both white women and African Americans are heavily represented. No clearer demographic profile emerged from the Feick and Price study, which makes specifically targeting market mavens most problematic. But the research did reveal that market mavens read more magazines and watch more television than non–market mavens. Indeed, general media usage is higher among market mavens. In addition, market mavens are more likely to read not only direct-mail advertising but also local direct-mail classified newspapers than non–market mavens (Feick and Price 1987; Higie, Feick, and Price 1987).

Price, Feick, and Guskey-Federouch found that market mavens are "'smart shoppers'. They budget their expenditures, use lists, and plan their purchases using advertising. In addition, they are heavy coupon users and are very active in providing coupons to others" (1988, 354). In fact, their study found that market mavens give away four times as many coupons to their friends and acquaintances as non-mavens do. Price and Feick (1995) found that market involvement is the key to understanding market maven behaviors. Thus, they recommend that companies design marketing, advertising, and product information programs with the information-sensitive consumer segment (i.e., market mavens) in mind, for it is the market maven that assists other consumers in making purchasing decisions (Price and Feick 1995).

Most importantly, Feick and Price were able to demonstrate that market mavens exist independently of monomorphic product-based opinion leaders in that "consumers are able to identify market mavens, use them in making consumption decisions, and distinguish them from individuals with product-based expertise" (1987, 94). Market mavens are of importance to marketing, advertising, and public relations professionals because they provide an important opportunity for consumer influence. We have known, for example, that monomorphic product-based opinion leaders are more likely to function in situations where products serve as a means of personal expression or the demonstration of perceived self-identity (Bloch 1986). For such products as automobiles or electronic equipment, which are self-identity statements for the owner, monomorphic product-based opinion leaders would serve as an ideal means to influence opinion. However, for those products where no emotional attachment exists, such as dehumidifiers or trash compactors, monomorphic product-based opinion leaders are not likely to function. The market maven might prove to be a far better means of influencing consumers.

Feick and Price suggest that "market mavens appear to be good targets for general messages about marketing mix changes, messages spanning multiple product classes, and messages about products that may not have much inherent consumer interest" (1987, 95). And market mavens might be particularly important for retail department stores offering a wide variety of goods and services, inasmuch as market mavens routinely provide people with information concerning the marketplace.

Recently a group of researchers have taken a new look at interpersonal influence and have developed a rich area of research dealing with what they term "the influentials." We will now turn to a review of this literature.

A NEW TAKE ON THE INTERPERSONAL INTERFACE: THE INFLUENTIALS

The Allensbach Institut für Demoskopie (Allensbach Survey Center) was challenged by *Der Spiegel,* a German news magazine, to discover a means to identify "the active consumers who set standards in their community" (Weimann 1994, 255). The institute's director, Elisabeth Noelle-Neumann, was charged with identifying what she called "the influentials." After years of pre-testing, refining, testing, refining, and retesting, she developed the Strength of Personality Scale (Personlichkeitsstärke) (PS) (Weimann 1994; 1991). Researchers compared respondent scale ratings with the interviewer's impressions of the individual. Strong correlations were observed. This study was then replicated in Israel, a very different social and cultural setting, and the results were then compared with those found in Germany. The findings indicate that PS is "related to various social characteristics, and these relationships are very similar for both populations" (Weimann 1994, 258; 1991). Two distinct factors emerged: a measure of *internal sources* of influencing others (scale items: 1, 2, 3, 4, 5, 7, and 10), which accounted for 75 percent of the variance in the German study and 72 percent in the Israeli study, and a measure of *comparative external origins* of influencing others (scale items: 6, 8, and 9). At this point, the institute chose to apply the scale to an Israeli kibbutz community. By mapping the social network of communication links, personal positions, flows of information, and influence and comparing the results with an administered PS scale, the institute was able to conclude that the scale was valid in that it was able "to predict communicative and influential behavior" (Weimann 1994, 261; 1991; see figure 5.1 on page 131). Noelle-Neumann had found her "influentials."

The concept of influentials, however, is not interchangeable with that of market opinion leadership. Weimann has detailed how they differ: (1) the concept of influencing others is a continuous variable; (2) influentials differ from market opinion leaders in media consumption, for the influentials rely more heavily on "quality" of media exposure rather than quantity, which is more typical for market opinion leaders; (3) influentials make greater use of personal sources for both information dissemination and acquisition than do market opinion leaders; (4) influentials unlike market opinion leaders were concentrated in higher socioeconomic status levels; and (5) influentials unlike market opinion leaders were found to operate in several interest domains with a high degree of overlap (1994, 263–64; see appendix A).

Weimann (1994) argues that the PS scale is more helpful in discovering those that influence others in purchasing than the market opinion leader research. Indeed, he notes that the PS scale is really a combination of social (external) and internal (psychological) sources of influenceability, and for that reason more closely recognizes what Katz noted many years ago—that influenceability is an interaction of: who one is, what one knows, and whom one knows (1957, 73–75; see appendix A). This theoretical linkage of social (network positioning) and psychological (personal traits) in terms of "influence" has tremendous potential for "practical-minded scholars of politics, marketing, advertising, and public opinion in general. The identification of influentials and the study of their sources of information and decision-making processes may have substantive value to those who combine social research with persuasive communication" (Weimann 1991, 277).

Identifying Influentials. Findings indicate that *PS is related to socioeconomic status, age, and gender* (Weimann 1994). The higher the socioeconomic status (SES) level, the higher the PS score; the lower the SES level, the lower the PS score. Males score higher than women on the PS scale. And the highest PS scores were observed in the thirty to thirty-nine age group, while people over sixty years of age scored the lowest (Weimann 1994). Influentials with higher PS scores exhibit a great deal of *social connectivity/activity* in that they belong to more social, civic, charitable, and political organizations; are more likely to hold offices in those groups; and report having more friends and acquaintances (Weimann 1994). And individuals with high PS scores differentiated themselves from lower PS scores by *life style values (VALS)* (Weimann 1994). And Weimann found that high PS individuals "more frequently endorse certain goals" (1994, 267) and "rate more frequently goals relevant to their influential status, such as 'to keep learning new things,' or 'to be there for others,' and 'to have many good friends'" (268), and rate more frequently values pertaining to work or professional accomplishments such as "'to succeed professionally,' 'to discover my abilities,' and 'to be happy with my work/job'" (268). It would appear that those with high scores on the PS were likely to engage more highly in reading books and newspapers, participating in sports and athletics, traveling, attending cultural events such as theatre and concerts, entertaining, and being with friends. Those who scored low on the scale were more likely to prefer to stay home, do nothing, listen to the radio or watch television.

Germans and Israelis did differ in some understandable cultural preferences. Israelis are far more outdoor oriented and place greater emphasis on their country and its national independence and security (Weimann 1994, 267–68). But in terms of media consumption, German and Israeli behaviors were highly similar in that "the influentials prefer the quality papers . . . , the quality weeklies, and the economic and political publications. . . . [A] readership is, on average, as high as five times more than the weak PS" level individuals (Weimann 1994, 272). And the influentials watch far less television than low PS individuals; but, when they do watch, the programs were far more likely to be "news, documentaries, discussion panels, and political debates" (Weimann 1994, 274). From Weimann's analysis, it appears that influentials have an important role in the public agenda-setting process:

(a) they are more exposed to media contents that focus on public issues; (b) their personal agendas correlate strongly with media agendas, moving in accordance with media's changing agenda thus affected by recent changes in issues' prominence; (c) they are more active in discussing these issues with others; and (d) their willingness to discuss issues is affected by the issue's prominence in the media thus declines with media's decreasing attention and coverage. (1994, 285)

THE MASS MEDIA AND
SOCIAL INFLUENCE

As early as 1935, Lasswell observed that "Everywhere the labyrinth of modern living ensnares specialist and layman in the common necessity of acting without knowledge" (187). Such actions create anxiety in that people feel uncomfortable when dealing with ambiguity, and thus most people are compelled to understand the uncertainties around them. And this often means turning to the mass media for information and guidance. People want to be seen by others as being able to function effectively in their world. Whether it is being able to recall last year's baseball World Series events or being able to discuss the latest political scandal, most people want to appear informed. And as leisure time has become more precious, people turn to the mass media for entertainment rather than to friends or group sports.

Thus as society has become increasingly specialized, complex, and conflictual, time has become even more precious, and for this reason, people rely on the mass media system to provide them with essential information that is deemed necessary to conduct their daily lives (see Ball-Rokeach and DeFleur 1976, 6–7). The character or nature of this reliance on the mass media is determined by the individual's perceived interests and needs; thus, for those interested in politics, political news becomes essential or more centralized in the individual's information-seeking behaviors than for someone who is primarily interested in gardening.

In 1976, Ball-Rokeach and DeFleur proposed the dependency model of mass media effects. According to them, the audience is "dependent" on the mass media to satisfy a variety of important needs in contemporary society. People look to the mass media to help them

(1) to understand the world in which they live;
(2) to function meaningfully and effectively in that social, political, and economic arena;
(3) to escape the cares and travails of contemporary life through a presentation of fantasy and escape. (Ball-Rokeach and DeFleur 1976)

Media dependency occurs because societal members need to efficiently utilize time to maximize their effectiveness in goal attainment. However, it should be noted that media dependency in no way eliminates the significance of social group influence. Unlike the previously described hypodermic needle model, the dependency model recognizes the public's reliance on media-supplied information as well as the process by which that information is then talked about and altered by individuals who function within societal groups. Ball-Rokeach and DeFleur explain:

> As the social structure becomes more complex, people have less and less contact with the social system as a whole. In other words, they begin to be less aware of what is going on in their society beyond their own position in the structure. The mass media enter as not only economic systems engaged in deliberate attempts to persuade and entertain, but also as information systems vitally involved in maintenance, change, and conflict processes at the societal as well as the group and individual levels of social action. (1976, 4–5)

To reiterate, as societies have grown more complex and technologically advanced, the media have taken on more and more **societal functions**—the many tasks performed in traditional societies by individuals. Denis McQuail has outlined the major social functions of the mass media:

Information
- providing information about events and conditions in society and the world;
- indicating relations of power;
- facilitating innovation, adaptation and progress.

Correlation
- explaining, interpreting and commenting on the meaning of events and information;
- providing support for established authority and norms;
- socializing;
- co-coordinating separate activities;
- consensus building;
- setting orders of priority and signalling [sic] relative status.

Continuity
- expressing the dominant culture and recognizing subcultures and new cultural developments;
- forging and maintaining commonality of values.

Entertainment
- providing amusement, diversion and the means of relaxation;
- reducing social tension.

Mobilization
- campaigning for societal objectives in the sphere of politics, war, economic development, work and sometimes religion. (1994, 79)

Potential Power of the Mass Media. In a society with great social change or conflict, we will expect the mass media to play a more central role in helping people cope with their world. And as information sources become more highly specialized, providing very specific information to highly select audiences, the centrality of that experience for those select audiences becomes ever more important. And with that, the potential power of the mass media for influencing people's lives increases dramatically.

Levels of Effects. Traditionally, the mass media have been viewed as having two potential levels of effects or analysis. micro-effects and macro-effects. Micro-effects usually are those effects related to an individual. These effects may be cognitive—influences on what an individual knows or of what the individual is aware, affective effects—influences on how an individual emotionally responds to what is known, and behavioral effects—influences on how an individual acts on what is known and felt. Macro-effects examine how the media affects the society at large. Broadly, media's macro-effects may either provide influences that maintain existing structures and behaviors (status quo capacity) or provide influences that allow society to change or evolve (catalyst capacity).

For example, in recent years, an increasing amount of attention by both the medical profession and the mass media has focused on the amount of fat in the typical American's diet. Indeed, we have been inundated with information about fat grams, dietary restrictions, low-fat or no-fat products, and nutrition fact panels. As a result most Americans recognize that it is important to limit the amount of fat in their diets. Public health information campaigns, then, may change what we know, what we feel about what we know, and how we act on what we both know and feel.

A Tripartite Audience–Media–Societal Structured Relationship. Within U.S. culture one can easily identify that social institutions are affected by the media and people. People are affected by the social institutions through which they function and the mass media that informs and amuses. The media are influenced by social institutions in terms of their control and through economic forces and through people who may or may not use the particular medium or a channel within a particular medium. This tripartite interrelationship is at the heart of Ball-Rokeach and DeFleur's (1976) dependency theory (figure 5.1 presents a model illustrating dependency theory). They hold that each of these three has become to a greater or lesser degree based on circumstances dependent on the other two.

The dependency model takes a systems perspective, with audiences, media, and societal structures as three transactional elements. Dependency theory posits that for any one of the three elements (audiences, the media, society) to attain its goals, it must depend upon the other two. As a result, researchers examine how all three parties—audiences, media, and society—influence each other (see figure 5.1).

Such a systems perspective is meant to indicate an approach that views a whole as an interrelated group of objects (see P. Monge 1977). An understanding of these relationships and the resulting systemic analysis is difficult. Rather than looking at potential influences as one-to-one or each with equal influence, it must be understood that the influences that each party yields should be described as ratios of power that change given the culture and other environmental influences through time. For example, people's dependency on the mass media, particularly radio and television, increased on September 11, 2001. Depending on their location, people turned to the radio if driving, to television if at home or work, and to a lesser extent to the Internet to understand what was happening.

One of the advantages of the dependency theory is that it allows examination of both micro- and macro-effects within the framework of a single model. Thus, individual and societal effects are considered at the same time. This is particularly useful in highly complex societal situations where interactions and the flow of influence are not necessarily easily ascertained.

Recently dependency theory has been revised by combining it with a body of knowledge long known as uses and gratifications theory (see Rubin and Windahl 1986) from which dependency theory draws much of its foundation. We will first briefly turn to the legacy of uses and gratifications research before returning to the revised theory of uses and dependency theory (see Rubin and Windahl 1986). Uses and gratifications research has long investigated an individual's use of the mass media and the gratifications received from the medium use. From watching soap operas for clues dealing with coping with marital difficulties to watching the *Late Show with David Letterman* for a natural, nonaddictive sleeping pill, Americans seek out various types of mass media to satisfy perceived needs. In other words, uses and gratifications researchers investigate the functions the mass media serve by gratifying the perceived needs in an individual's life; thus, uses and gratifications is often characterized as a functionalist approach (e.g., Katz, Blumer, and Gurevitch 1974). However, after more than sixty years of uses and gratifications research, uses and gratifications is now presented as a much less mechanistic, functional approach. McQuail has summarized contemporary uses and gratifications research in the following manner:

(1) Personal social circumstances and psychological dispositions together influence both (2) general habits of media use and also (3) beliefs and expectations about the benefits offered by media, which shape (4) specific acts of media choice and consumption, followed by (5) assessments of the value of the experience (with

Figure 5.1   An Explicated Version of the Ball-Rokeach and DeFleur (1976) Dependency Model of Mass Media Effects

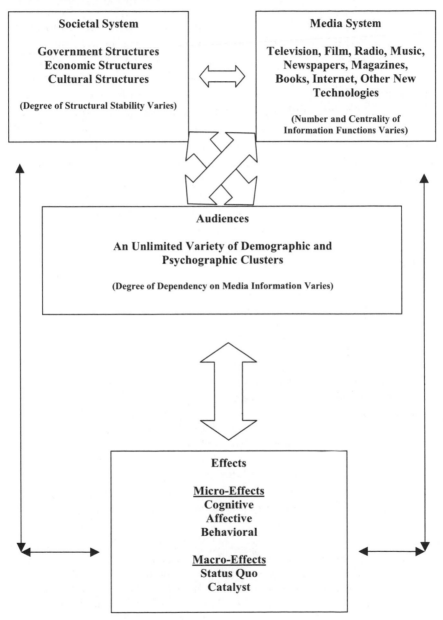

consequences for further media use) and, possibly (6) applications of benefits
acquired in other areas of experience and social activity. (1994, 319)

Of particular importance in the transformation of uses and gratifications
theory is the refinement of the concept of expectation, now clarified as an
"expectancy-value approach" (Palmgreen and Rayburn 1985b). Individuals
attend to the mass media based on their beliefs that certain types of media
and media content will satisfy a felt need. The ability of the selected mediated
experience to actually fulfill the expectation is the expectancy value approach.
People judge not only what mediated content will likely fulfill their needs,
but also how well it is likely to so. Thus, we can observe a three-stage linked
process of attending to the media: audience expectations of attributes (gratifications sought), media consumption, and gratifications obtained (Rayburn
and Palmgreen 1984). McQuail has identified a number of motives for
attending to the mass media (gratifications sought) and a number of satisfac-
tions received from media use (gratifications obtained):

- Getting information and advice
- Reducing personal insecurity
- Learning about society and the world
- Finding support for one's own values
- Gaining insight into one's own life
- Experiencing empathy with problems of others
- Having a basis for social contact
- Feeling connected with others
- Escaping from problems and worries
- Gaining entry into an imaginary world
- Filling time
- Experiencing emotional release
- Acquiring a structure for daily routine. (1994, 320)

However, Palmgreen, Wenner, and Rosengren maintained that uses and gratifications theory is far more complicated than identifying gratifications
sought and obtained, when they proposed a model of media gratifications
that

[w]hile taking into account the feedback from gratifications obtained to those
sought, also considers (among other things) the social psychological origins of
needs, values, and beliefs, which give rise to motives for behavior, which may in
turn be guided by beliefs, values, and social circumstances into seeking various gratifications through media consumption and other nonmedia behaviors. The gratification processes are seen as taking place within a field of interaction between
societal structures and individual characteristics, an interaction calling forward spe-

cific realization of the potentials and restrictions inherent in those structures and characteristics. (1985, 16)

Because so much of social marketing activity focuses on influencing various publics through influencing the news media and the resulting news coverage, it is important to understand news gratifications in particular. An analysis of these news gratifications indicate how and in what ways social marketing experts should craft messages and provide information to the news media. Crafted messages that appeal to need-states are more powerful than those that do not. Wenner (1985) prepared a transactional map that explains how individuals are gratified not only from news media content but also through the process of attending to the media. According to Wenner, there are two media news content gratifications or gratifications experienced as a result of the substance of the news messages such as orientational gratifications or "message uses for information that provide for the reference and reassurance of self in relation to society" and social gratifications or "message uses that link information about society derived from news to the individual's interpersonal network" (1985, 175).

Wenner (1985) also divides the news process gratifications or the gratifications received from the process of attending to the news media into two groups: para-social gratifications and para-orientational gratifications. Para-social gratifications are the result of the "para-social interaction" (see Horton and Wohl 1956; Rubin and McHugh 1987) of experiencing the news media as if you are a fellow news reporter, a participant in the news, or a physical observer to the news event. Such gratifications "provide for personal identity and reference through ritualized social relationships with media 'actors' who coexist with news content" (Wenner 1985, 175). And para-orientational gratifications occur through play-acting or role-playing during the course of the news attendance. Such expressive activities allow for tension reduction or ego-defense. After a particularly frustrating day on an industry-line with an abusive supervisor, an individual might reduce tension by enjoying a news broadcast showing police subduing an armed fugitive through the use of nightsticks and high-powered karate moves (Copeland and Slater 1985). And at times such activities might turn us away from information gain to information avoidance or simply reinforcement or the reaffirming of one's own beliefs. Such expressive activities allow us to **counterargue** or play at arguing back against the source of the message. Such counterarguing often causes reinforcement of existing beliefs and attitudes. For example, negative political television advertising attacking an individual's chosen candidate may allow the viewer to counterargue each attack point with prior knowledge, and the experience of that counterarguing reinforces the individual's choice for office.

Uses and Dependency Theory. Building upon the theoretically rich areas of dependency theory and uses and gratifications, Rubin and Windahl (1986) have proposed a merger of uses and gratifications theory and the dependency model of mass media effects, resulting in a uses and dependency theory. As with any hybrid, they view their new theory as having strengths not found in the theories from which it spawned and as having fewer weaknesses. They assert that "Uses and gratifications, then, adds a voluntaristic element to dependency, just as dependency adds a more deterministic flavor to uses and gratifications" (1986, 279). Although uses and dependency theory is more complex, it broadens our understanding of human behavior in a contemporary media society.

NOELLE-NEUMANN'S RETURN TO THE CONCEPT OF A POWERFUL MASS MEDIA

From her research in Germany, Noelle-Neumann (1973; 1981) also envisions the power of the media to be a product of peoples' need to know. As the world becomes more complex, people's need for news, information, and entertainment finds succor in the media. Though Noelle-Neumann never says so explicitly, her reasoning over the renewed power of the media comes from the media's ability to provide the information that people want. The increase in television penetration into homes that were then in West Germany has been accompanied by an increased interest by the population in politics (1981). Noelle-Neumann views this increased interest as a result of the focus of television on political issues.

In addition, Noelle-Neumann (1973) provides us with clues as to how to make mass-communicated messages more powerful. She says that under certain conditions the mass media have real and powerful effects. These conditions—ubiquity, consonance, and cumulation of mass-communicated messages—are met in a modern industrialized society. Ubiquity means that the mass-mediated messages give the appearance of being uniform throughout all the mass media channels (Noelle-Neumann 1973). Consonance, as Noelle-Neumann uses the term, means that the messages from mass media news sources provide a similar picture of the world, and cumulation speaks to the repetition of similar messages over an extended period of time. She views the conditions of ubiquity, consonance, and cumulation as "unanimous illumination, unanimous argumentation with regard to events, people, and problems" (Noelle-Neumann 1981, 138). Such uniformity overshadows if not overwhelms potentially competing messages, and the result is media influence.

McQuail has identified certain areas where the mass media have the greatest potential for powerful societal effects:

- Attracting and directing public attention
- Persuasion in matters of opinion and belief
- Influencing behavior
- Structuring definitions of reality
- Conferring status and legitimacy
- Informing quickly and extensively (1994, 69).

SOCIAL CONSTRUCTION OF REALITY

The Austrian-born phenomenologist Alfred Schutz wrote:

> The world of my daily life is by no means my private world but is from the outset an intersubjective one, shared with my fellow men, experienced and interpreted by others: in brief, it is a world common to all of us. The unique biographical situation in which I find myself within the world at any moment of my existence is only to a very small extent of my own making. (1967, 163)

For Schutz, man operating in the world engages in situations that call for a "reciprocity of perspectives" (1962, 315–16). In other words, man explores "we-relationships" in which he constructs "ideal-types" of behavior patterns, ascertaining appropriate social behaviors. People then imagine action and the consequences of the action. When considering action, man assesses his past, present, and future expectations for his personal conduct as well as that for others, and it is through this assessment that he constructs his own social reality. Berger and Luckmann's (1966) work has drawn attention to Schutz's notion of the social construction of reality.

Reality, then, is created through the social process of communication (cf., Berger and Luckmann 1966; Schutz 1970; Watzlawick 1967). What one knows and what one thinks one knows are both shaped by the communication process. Thus what one responds to is a subjective reality, created through the process of social interaction. And because language is so fundamental to the communication process, the culture's language itself determines to a large extent what can be known and what can be achieved (Whorf 1956). This linguistic relativity is known as the Sapir–Whorf hypothesis. As Whorf notes:

> It is quite an illusion to imagine that one adjusts to reality essentially without the use of language and that language is merely an incidental means of solving specific problems of communication or reflection. The fact of the matter is that the "real

world" is to a large extent unconsciously built up on the language habits of the group (1956, 134).

Nimmo and Combs have interpreted the work of Watzlawick, Sapir, and Whorf, and others who view reality as being created through communication to mean:

(1) our everyday, taken-for-granted reality is a delusion; (2) reality is created, constructed, through communication not expressed by it; (3) for any situation there is no single reality, no one objective truth, but multiple subjectively derived realities. (1983, 3)

However, in recent years, the emphasis has been placed not only on social interactions but also on mediated interactions in an individual's construction of his or her social reality. Lippmann (1965) has argued that the "pictures in our heads" or the images that we hold in modern society are primarily created through an individual's contact with the media rather than through direct experience. For most people, political knowledge is constructed through the mass media. Many people have never met their city council member or mayor in person but don't doubt they exist, because the media have told them they do. Even lands far away and cultures outside of our own personal experience suddenly become real as we attend to the mass media. And we behave toward what we have learned as if it were real (real in the sense of personal validation of existence). Most Americans have never set foot on the continent of Africa; yet, when famines occur on that continent, thousands upon thousands of Americans will send money, medical supplies, and food to help those in need. Clearly, then, the mass media provide us with the mosaics from which we build our own personal reality (Kraus and Davis 1976; Brody and Page 1975). Individuals attend to the mediated mosaics, filter them through their own perceptual screens, and discuss them with others. The end result of this process is what Nimmo and Combs (1983) have called a mass-mediated reality. Thus, meaning has been socially constructed through a process often dominated by the mass media. Because of this, research analyzing the images found in mass-mediated messages reveal important social indicators.

As suggested by the dependency model and uses and gratifications, the individual and the mass media (which some see as a societal institution) are linked together. However, one cannot understand the actions of one without having an understanding of the other, as both are at least codependent and at most transactional with each other. The power of the media in terms of the individual is much like trying to find the starting point on a bunched-up strand of Christmas lights. One knows that it is there, but much patience is required to tease out the starting point and unravel the strand.

Chapter Six

Propaganda Strategies

The psychological power of the curse and the benediction, of the creed, the cross, or the flag, all show the effect of emotional transfer between symbol and reality. The persistence with which creed has been mistaken for substance only emphasizes the importance of the transfer and its possibilities for propaganda.

—Dodge (1920, 249)

To be effective, propaganda must constantly short circuit all thought and decision. It must operate on the individual at the level of the unconscious. He must not know that he is being shaped by outside forces (this is one of the conditions for the success of propaganda), but some central core in him must be reached in order to release the mechanism in the unconscious which will provide the appropriate and expected—action.

—J. Ellul (1965)

In his speeches he [English Prime Minister David Lloyd George] found that form and that expression which opened to him the heart of his people and in the end made this people serve his will completely. Precisely in the primitiveness of his language, the primordiality of its forms of expression, and the use of easily intelligible examples of the simplest sort lies the proof of the towering political ability of this Englishman. *For I must not measure* the speech of a statesman to this people by the impression which it leaves in a university professor, but by the effect it exerts on the people. *And this alone* gives the standard for the speaker's *genius*.

——Adolf Hitler (1943; emphasis in original)

CONTEMPORARY PROPAGANDA

In contemporary society, propaganda is pervasive (Sproule 1991). MacDonald has observed that in democratic societies, competing propaganda sources are often "locked in competition for social acceptance, political loyalty, or customer approval; but such situations may be no less calculated in their intent than mass communication in an autocratic regime where reality is often shaped to fit a monolithic party line" (1989, 24). As early as 1920, Dodge noted that "There seems to be no essential differences between religious, political, and business propaganda, except the ends it serves, and the license under which it operates" (1920, 241). And he went on to observe:

> The main point seems to be that the tremendous forces of propaganda are now common property. They are available for the unscrupulous and the destructive as well as for the constructive and the moral. Any agency with enough cash and brains can develop a formidable propaganda for any purpose under the sun. (1920, 241; Bernays 1928)

Thomson's (1977) work illustrates not only the wide range of propaganda operating within modern societies, but also the scholarly and professional interest in those various manifestations of propaganda. Scholars and professional communicators study propaganda in order to understand how best to exercise influence in contemporary society. A professional communicator may need to improve a company's reputation among a given target population before the company can expand their facilities and increase their use of local governmental services. Or it may mean a marketing director utilizing social marketing to tap a neglected target market to sell a particular luxury good that seems to have lost its growth potential. Whatever the situation, professional communicators analyze the use of propaganda in historical and contemporary situations in order to better understand for their own purposes how to wield influence in today's world. We will now turn to the means by which such analysts investigate propaganda.

Thomson (1977) has provided seven domains within modern society where propaganda serves as the dominant means of influence. A brief descriptive outline of these domains follows:

Political Propaganda—used in the regulation of social conflict, the negotiation of political power, and the social allocation and distribution of scarce resources within society (see Banfield 1961; Easton 1953; Lasswell 1958; Nimmo 1978).

Potential Sources: Governments, political parties, interest groups, pressure groups.

Likely Manifestations: Appeals to patriotism; appeals to loyalty.

Symbols: National anthems, tombs, flags, parades, monuments.

Economic Propaganda—used to sustain the capitalist equilibrium by either encouraging consumption or encouraging conservation; to manipulate market forces for organized interests whether governmental, industrial, corporate, or fiscal concerns; and to create and/or maintain consumer confidence.

Potential Sources: Governments, Federal Reserve Board, banking industry, manufacturers, builders, retailers, real estate brokers, savings and loans, credit unions, advertising, marketing, public relations.

Likely Manifestations: Raising or lowering of interest rates; timing and release of government crafted economic news and forecasts; presidential speeches.

Symbols: Counterfeit-proof currency, Fort Knox, stock market, sales, bundling, coupons, commodities market, Chicago Mercantile, point-of-purchase displays, product demonstrations.

War/Military—used to maintain the morale of one's military, the unity of one's people, the supportiveness of one's allies, the continued neutralization of those uninvolved, and the undermining of the morale of your enemy, both military and citizenry.

Potential Sources: Government, pro war organizations, the military, veterans' organizations, ethnic support groups, news media, film industry.

Likely Manifestations: Speeches, vilification of the enemy, encouraging but yet urging for continued sacrifices, formal prayers, Congressional Record.

Symbols: War/veteran holidays; World Trade Center flag; military music, for example, army anthem, Marine Corps anthem; yellow ribbons; parades; christening of ships, launching of aircraft carriers.

Diplomatic—used to improve existing relationships with allies, to facilitate favorable relationships with neutrals, and to maintain or increase the desired negative or hostile relationships with one's enemies.

Potential Sources: Secretary of state, president and vice president, national security advisor, joint chiefs of staff, independent roving ambassadors such as Jimmy Carter and Jesse Jackson, congressional resolutions, United Nations ambassador, embassies and embassy personnel around the world, Central Intelligence Agency, Immigration and Naturalization Service, United States Customs, news media, American film industry, radio and television programming, American-based multinational corporations.

Likely Manifestations: Vilifying the enemy, praising our allies, warning and neutralizing our potential enemies, complicating international trade agreements, threatening to boycott importation of products, threatening to use economic embargo, threatening to use blockade, deportation of aliens who are citizens of enemy nation.

Symbols: Embassy residences, flag, Air Force One, receiving lines, peace table, signing of agreements, U.S.A. flags on Afghan food rations.

Didactic—used to educate, indoctrinate, and socialize populations; to promote social or cultural change to meet health and safety goals; to modernize through reeducation.

Potential Sources: Governments, educational organizations, religious organizations, medical and health organizations, interest groups, pressure groups, professional or work organizations.

Likely Manifestations: Rewarding for adopting new behaviors or rewarding for conforming to traditional behaviors; reinforcement of traditional structures, beliefs, and values or promotion of adoption of new structures, beliefs, and values; the teaching of old skills or new skills.

Symbols: earned medals, printed T-shirts, diplomas, graduation exercises, initiation ceremonies, identification pins, flag pins.

Ideological—used to convert, characterized as emotionally violent and physically threatening, often described as terrorism or brainwashing; said to be ideological in that it works to change worldview.

Potential Sources: Governments, revolutionary groups. terrorist groups, military organizations, counterintelligence groups, hostage and prisoners-of-war guards/care givers.

Likely Manifestations: Threats to property, life, liberty; unpredictable and seemingly irrational behavioral manifestations; threats to family, friends, associates; hostage taking; physical acts of violence and repeated accounts of such acts; breakdown of individualism; negative manipulation of food, fuel supply.

Symbols: uniforms for general citizenry; increase in detention, jail, prison facilities; expansion of arrestable offenses; iconization of movement leaders; authority uniforms such as those of the New York Fire Department; the specter of the twin towers of the World Trade Center; the phrase, "Let's Roll!"

Escapist—used for emotional catharsis, to release tensions of modern-day life, to divert emotional energies and hostilities, to provide for an emotional joining.

Potential Sources: Governments, religious orders, revolutionary groups, corporations, industries, film industry, print publications, entertainment industry.

Likely Manifestations: Public festivals, conventions, sporting matches, mass meetings, parades, public executions, ceremonial degradations, May Day celebrations, Octoberfest celebrations, carnivals, circuses, race-car matches.

Symbols: Trophies, costumes, music, rituals, colors, singing, dancing, public flogging, public stocks, masks (see Thomson 1977).

Art. Art works have been used successfully by propagandists, managing their public persona. According to Jowett and O'Donnell:

> Napoleon was among the first of the modern propagandists to understand the need to convince the population that the rights of the individual were less important than the willingness to sacrifice one's life for emperor and nation. In this way he was able to gather large, populist armies even in the worst of times. (1992, 73)

And Napoleon was able to do so, in part, due to the efforts of his loyal court artist and confidant, Jacques Louis David. It was David "who helped design the clothes, hairstyle, and other accoutrements [white horse, imperialistic trappings, and Napoleonic architecture] that have come down to us today as an unmistakable symbol of the diminutive French leader" (Jowett and O'Donnell 1992, 73; see for example David's *Napoleon Crossing the Great St. Bernard Pass, 1800*). Napoleon, always conscious of his public image, created, executed, and staged his public image as a romantic hero. David's *The Coronation of Emperor Napoleon and Empress Josephine, December 2, 1804*, gave witness to the historical event of Napoleon taking the imperial crown from Pope Pius VII's hands and placing it on his own head, "symbolizing that he [read Napoleon] owed allegiance to no one, and that he was a self-made emperor" (Jowett and O'Donnell 1992, 74).

Such artistic etchings, renderings, and/or paintings have long been important propagandistic devices. As young children in America, we are all exposed to Emanuel Gottlieb Leutze's *George Washington Crossing the Delaware*. The painting has both religious and political significance in that it captures for many Americans the bravery of not only Washington but of his men, who, though cold and away from home, were victorious on that Christmas Eve night so many years ago. The painting remains powerful even in our adulthood, despite the fact that as adults, we recognize that it is highly unlikely that Washington would stand up in the boat because of the danger of falling into a turbulent and freezing river and of making himself an easy target for the enemy's muskets.

Francisco de Goya, the noted Spanish artist, produced both etchings and paintings dramatizing man's inhumanity to man. And in his series of etchings called *Disasters of War,* he chronicled "the descent of a nation into universal barbarity" (Craske 1997, 107). As if they are another breed, de Goya shows "a Napoleonic officer engrossed in cheerful debate with some of his well-dressed compatriots whilst a ragged group of Spaniards starve to death before their eyes" (Craske 1997, 107). And de Goya's *The Execution of the Rebels* on May 3, 1808 (1814), remains a powerful testimony to the cruelty and cowardice of organized power over political and social protest.

Pablo Picasso's *Guernica* (1937), a representation of the Spanish Civil War, remains the quintessential modern art statement devoted to peace. Picasso would not allow the painting to be exhibited in Spain until after the Fascist dictator Franco was dead. Picasso's *Massacre in Korea* is also recognized as a brilliant statement against the abuses of totalitarian regimes throughout the world.

Cartoons and Caricatures. Just as Napoleon used great masterpieces to influence his subjects, others have chosen art for the masses, whether cartoons or caricatures. Raymond Dodge (1920) has argued that such items are often very effective in stirring the people.

During the eighteenth century, as ordinary people sought greater access to political freedom, simultaneous advances in printing technology allowed political critics to reach a mass audience for the first time. However, the desire for political freedom and participation was ahead of the ordinary person's ability to read and write. For this reason, many of the early political writers turned to graphic satirists and propagandists to deliver their political statements in a new visual language (Phillipe 1980). **Satire,** according to *Webster's New World Dictionary,* refers to "a literary composition in which follies, vices, stupidities, and abuses in life are held up to ridicule and contempt" (1996, 1193). Graphic satire often came in the form of cartoons or caricatures. A **cartoon** is defined as a "drawing, as in a newspaper, caricaturing or symbolizing, often satirically, some event, situation, or person of topical interest" (*Webster's New World Dictionary,* 1996, 216), and such drawings are often accompanied by a **caption** or "a descriptive title, or legend, as under an illustration" (209). On the other hand, a **caricature,** according to the same dictionary, is "a picture or imitation of a person, literary style, etc. in which certain features or mannerisms are exaggerated for satirical effect" (1996, 212).

Graphic satire proved quite popular, and it quickly became an integral part of propaganda campaigns and the newspapers' daily commentary and today remains a staple in contemporary political and public discourse. The popularity of graphic satire has been attributed to its "universal, direct, immediate, and pithy" nature" (Phillipe 1980, 9). But to understand its partisan effectiveness is more complex; Phillipe writes:

> They espouse causes. Exaggeration is second nature to them. Their methodology is accumulation and synthesis—and hence events, places, moments and people acquire an extraordinary intensity and power. A print [cartoon or caricature] is neither historic evocation nor narrative, but rather a conjunction of symbols and allusions. It enlarges, shrinks, or disguises people, to reveal their many facets at a glance. The synthesizing power of the print [cartoon or caricature] expresses both what is visible and what is concealed.

> To what is, it adds what has been and what will be. The image is thus liberated from the grammar of space and time and the print remains dynamic, aggressive, fertile and creative. (1980, 9)

Music. Music is also a powerful instrument of propaganda. Legend has it that in 1792 during the French Revolution, the French captain Claude-Joseph Rouget of Lisle wrote "La Marseillaise," a battle song for the army of the Rhine during the war with Austria. However, the song met with such popularity that on July 14, 1795, France named "La Marseillaise" its national anthem. Although it was prohibited from being played or sung during the Empire and the Restoration, in 1879, the Republic resurrected "La Marseillaise" and once again made it the French national anthem. The official version of the music and score was accepted in 1887 (see M. G. Mitchell 1970, 8; www.fordham.edu/halsall/mod/marseill.html).

It remains one of the most moving national anthems in the world. According to Mitchell's account, a French general once said, "give me a thousand men and the Marseillaise and I will guarantee victory" (1970, 8). The reverence with which the French people treat their national song is powerfully demonstrated by a scene in Michael Curtiz's film *Casablanca* when French expatriates break into song following a confrontation with German officers in Rick's Nightclub. The words of the first couplet and refrain are known throughout the world:

> Allons enfants de la Patrie,
> Le jour de gloire est arrivé!
> Contre nous de la tyrannie,
> L' étendard sanglant est levé, (bis)
> Entendez-vous dans les campagnes
> Mugir ces féroces soldats?
> Ils viennent jusque dans vos bras
> Egorger vos fils et vos compagnes!
> Aux armes, citoyens,
> Formez vos bataillons,

Marchons, marchons!
Qu'un sang impur
Abruve nos sillons! (www.fordham.edu/halsall//mod/marseill.html)[1]

A similar story is told of Francis Scott Key's penning of "The Star Spangled Banner." During the night of September 14, Key, a young Georgetown lawyer, watched from afar the British siege of Fort McHenry, the sole protector of Baltimore. The exploding American and British munitions lit up the night sky, and Key took solace in the pyrotechnic display, for he knew as long as the explosions continued that Fort McHenry had not surrendered. But a few hours before daylight, the shelling stopped. Key feared the worst; but as morning dawned, the American flag was still there! Key's lyrics recreate his excitement as he realized that Fort McHenry had held:

> O' say can you see by the dawn's early light,
> What so proudly we hailed at the twilight's last gleaming,
> Whose broad stripes and bright stars through the perilous fight,
> O'er the ramparts we watch'd were so gallantly streaming?

At times, music moves a people, uniting them in a common experience that transcends race, religion, ethnicity, class, or social status. The world watched as Elton John performed his tribute to Princess Diana at her funeral, and his rewording of his classic and her favorite Elton John song *Candle in the Wind* remains a fitting tribute to the People's Princess. The words said what millions felt, and in this expression of grief and farewell, Elton John began the healing of the millions affected by Princess Diana's death.

Elton John donated the proceeds of *Candle in the Wind* (1997) to Princess Diana's Trust in order that Diana's charities and causes would continue to receive financial support. Just three months after her death, Elton John handed over thirty-three million dollars to the trust, and more was yet to come (www.usnews.com/usnews/issue/971222/22Xmas.htm).

Propaganda as Orthopraxy

Lasswell reminds us that propaganda is "the technique of influencing human action" (1934, 521–22). Thus the propagandist not only manipulates symbols but seeks to manipulate the public's attitudes and behaviors as well. Successful propaganda, then, has real consequences. Ellul, despite his classification system, does recognize this. He describes modern propaganda as being

> [n]o longer to modify ideas, but to provoke action. It is no longer to change adherence to a doctrine, but to make the individual cling irrationally to a process of

action. It is no longer to lead to a choice, but to loosen the reflexes. It is no longer to transform an opinion, but to arouse an active and mythical belief. (1968, 25)

Thus for Ellul, a propagandist is no longer seeking for the audience to adopt an orthodoxy but to generate an **orthopraxy**—an action that "leads directly to a goal, which for the individual is not a conscious and intentional objective to be attained, but which is considered such by the propagandist" (1968, 27). Much has been written about the misuse of propaganda, particularly that perpetrated on the citizens of the world during the rise and fall of Nazi Germany. While we find the Nazi regime's goals—world domination, the elimination of European Jewry, and the virtual enslavement of millions—to be both abhorrent and repugnant, we may not overlook as scholars the thought processes by which Adolf Hitler and his minister of propaganda Joseph Goebbels came to craft one of the most powerful, some would say *the most* powerful, and influential propaganda organization in the world. While much has been written about this era elsewhere, we will incorporate information as we deem appropriate to our discussion of propagandistic strategies, tactics, and principles in this chapter. In addition, we have included in the appendix, for those wishing a more synthesized and detailed historical review, a brief sketch of Goebbels's propaganda machine (see appendix B).

Propaganda as Desired Outcomes

Ellul (1965) distinguishes between propaganda that creates agitation and that which creates integration. Although other researchers, most notably Szanto (1978), have utilized a very broad-based interpretation of these goal-oriented propagandistic strategies, we have chosen to present narrower explanations for classification purposes and to present additional classifications that should be more readily understood and easily utilized by the reader (see table 6.1).

Propaganda of agitation provokes the audience, asking them to make enormous sacrifices to achieve short-term goals, often repeatedly, with the hope of securing in the distant future some highly regarded prize, usually

Table 6.1 Typing Propaganda by Desired Outcomes

Propaganda	Short Identifications
Agitation	Provokes, encourages sacrifices and other action(s)
Integration	Promotes solidarity and conformity
Disintegrative	Destroys solidarity and emphasizes differences
Facilitative	Encourages and maintains receptivity

the realization of the group's aspirations. For example, during World War II, Goebbels exhorted the German people to make sacrifice after sacrifice for the cause—the "glorious military victory" that would bring about world domination (see Combs and Nimmo 1993). Shortages in food, clothing, fuel, and medical supplies were tolerated by the general population for the good of the Nazi war machine. As citizens made such sacrifices, whether material sacrifices or the deaths of loved ones on the field of battle, they felt a part of the greater good, "the dragon" of the Third Reich. After the crushing defeat by the Russians at Stalingrad, it became apparent to both Goebbels and the German people that losing the war was no longer an impossibility. Goebbels changed the official propaganda line, dismissing the talk of victory and replacing it with a tale of courageous heroism against overwhelming odds on the part of the German soldier and the citizen population. German soldiers continued to fight courageously until the bitter end. And the German people made sacrifice after sacrifice for a losing cause.

Propaganda of integration, on the other hand, unifies the audience by establishing and reinforcing the solidarity of the group. It binds people together through the weaving of shared symbols and myths, crafting a collectivity much greater than the efforts of lone individuals, for it provides a messianic purpose, the achievement of the group's long-term goal, which builds group solidarity and conformity. Such integrative propaganda was used during the Third Reich.

Welch writes that Goebbels's propaganda machine was successful in creating at least passive support from all quarters in German society (obviously not the Jews), and this was possible because Goebbels understood the concept of resonance in that his propaganda "was in tune with the real aspirations of large sections of the German people" (1987, 419).

In summary, propaganda both *provokes* and *unifies* the target audience(s), leaving "the impression that leader and led are joined in a cooperative effort to the mutual benefit of both" (Nimmo 1978, 103). Both the propaganda of agitation and of integration are evident in the propagandistic argumentation stages identified by Rank (1984) and later elaborated on by Combs and Nimmo (1993, 196). Their work suggests that propagandists adhere to a specific propaganda script of agitation and integration.

LOOK OUT!
- identifying the threat (out-groups) with accompanying appeals to senses, emotions, and thoughts
- emphasizing the magnitude and critical significance of the threat to the people personally

GET TOGETHER!
- bonding people together by identifying commonalties
- projecting victory over the threat, if the people remain united and loyal to each other (which builds confidence)
- building self-confidence through the public's acceptance of such claims
- building source credibility through the people's acceptance and agreement with the "truth" and "logic" in the argument

DO GOOD!
- reinforcing the desirability of the victory over the threat
- emphasizing the urgency with which the people must commit to the cause
- emphasizing the overwhelming public approval of committing to the cause
- identifying the sacrifices that must be made for the greater good in the ultimate achievement of the desired "victory"
- outlining the ultimate rewards for the group's compliance to the leaders' requests (e.g., more land, greater prosperity, greater prestige, better economy)

LET'S!
- identifying the specific actions, sacrifices, joint-activities requested (e.g., join the army, buy war bonds, plant victory gardens, accept food and fuel shortages, work longer hours)
- linking the community's shared sacrifices to the victory over the threat

Put more succinctly, the integration propagandist's most basic story line is: "There are the sources of your deprivations, and here are the means for removing them" (Kecskemeti 1973, 864). In addition to the propaganda of integration and agitation as identified by Ellul (1965) and elaborated on by Combs and Nimmo (1993) and Rank (1984), we propose two additional forms of outcome propaganda: the propaganda of disintegration and the propaganda of facilitation.

Disintegrative propaganda is used by the propagandist to destroy or break down internal solidarity among group members. Typically such efforts are directed at external groups that the propagandist wishes to influence. For example, during the Persian Gulf War, the U. S. Fourth Psychological Operations dropped twenty-nine million leaflets on Iraqi soldiers in an effort to encourage defection to the NATO Allies. And the "Voice of the Gulf," a program on the U.S. Voice of America Radio Service, provided Iraqi listeners with the next day's bomb targets as well as testimonials by Iraqi prisoners of war who praised both prison conditions and their treatment by the Allied Forces (Jowett and O'Donnell 1992; Psy-Ops Bonanza 1991, 24).

Facilitative propaganda is communication directed at groups whom the propagandist wants to maintain open channels of communication, fostering if not good will at least neutral will. Often facilitative propaganda appeals are

[d]irected at the rational faculty; they are calm, leisurely and well reasoned, sometimes even dignified, and always idealistic, for they are invariably linked to the general ideology of the society. This is why in our society such propaganda tends to
masquerade under the guise of "education," and the promotion of the general wel-
fare. (Choukas 1965, 231)

And for this reason, such facilitative propaganda appears unthreatening.
This is done in the hopes that one day by repeatedly exposing audience members to friendly or nonthreatening programming or messages the audience
will be more receptive or less hostile to propagandistic appeals. This positive
maintenance of communication between the propagandist and the intended
audience has been called *facilitative communication* by Martin (1971). Similarly, Doob (1948) uses the term *subpropaganda* to indicate the exposure of
audiences to unfamiliar messages over a long period of time in order to
decrease potential hostility and increase potential acceptance of the message
in the long run. The broadcasting of American rock music to the rather
closed religious societies of Iraq and Iran may be viewed as cultural imperial-
ism on the part of the United States. But for the United States, the presentation of up-beat, catchy tempos during musical programming is an attempt
to weaken aversion to American culture and thus to ultimately weaken resistance to American-based messages that often contradict those provided by
Islamic governments.

In another example of facilitative propaganda, Altheide and Johnson
(1980) have argued that organizations ranging from electrical utilities to uni-
versities to paper manufacturers will use what they call bureaucratic propaganda to maintain their legitimacy in the eyes of powerful decision makers
such as congressional subcommittees. **Bureaucratic propaganda** is *"Any
report produced by an organization for evaluation and other practical purposes
that is targeted for individuals, committees, or publics who are unaware of its
promotive character and the editing processes that shaped the report"* (Altheide
and Johnson 1980, 5; italics in original). From official reports to congressional
testimony, organizational officers work to maintain their favored status among
the congressional elite. In such situations, organizations will not have specific
objectives to meet; instead, the officers want to continue to be viewed as
"the good guys." For example, Bogart quotes one United States Information
Agency's operative who lamented, "So much of our program is geared to
gaining Congressional favor that we aim more than 50 percent of it on what
effect it is going to have on Congress and less than 50 percent on what effect
it is going to have on people overseas" (1976, 27).

Doob (1950) notes that propaganda is far more effective, internally consistent, and persuasive if it is produced by a single bureaucracy or authority.

Goebbels's preference for the centralization is acknowledged by Doob in his description of the Reichsministerium für Volksaufklärung und Propaganda:

> Every bit of propaganda had to implement policy, and policy was made clear in directives. These directives referred to all phases of the war and to all events occurring inside and outside of Germany. They indicated when specific propaganda campaigns should be begun, augmented, diminished, and terminated. They suggested how an item should be interpreted and featured, or whether it should be ignored completely. (1950, 423)

In addition to centralizing authority, Goebbels believed that for propaganda to be effective it had to permeate the organization. Or more specifically, those people who are policy makers and policy implementers must be thoroughly grounded in propaganda strategies. "Goebbels sought to reveal the rationale of his propaganda to these subordinates and to improve their morale by taking them, ostensibly, into his confidence" (Doob 1950, 423). And Goebbels believed that any governmental or military actions that could have propaganda consequences should be reviewed by the centralized authority, and propaganda considerations should be taken into account as part of the planning of the proposed action (Doob 1950). Goebbels often argued that propaganda was mightier than the sword when it came to achieving objectives. And most notably, Goebbels convinced Hitler to commit to an air warfare strategy against England that was primarily based on psychological principles rather than military ones (Doob 1950, 424).

In today's increasingly complex and interdependent world, bureaucratic propaganda has become far more complicated. Altheide and Johnson (1980, 26) and Presthus (1978, 44–84) have argued that bureaucratic propaganda is by far the major form of deception in the Western world, for people do not see that what is produced and presented to them as governmental decisions or policies are the products of unidentified bureaucracies interacting within the governmental sphere. Altheide and Johnson (1980, 25) maintain that rapid social, political, economic, and technological upheaval has blurred the traditional lines between government(s), industries, corporations, and banking concerns. In other words, it is difficult to determine what and where "interests" actually rest and which governmental activities are merely governmental or a combination of banking, industrial, or commercial and governmental concerns. In effect, public interests, government interests, and corporate/monetary interests are so intertwined as to be indistinguishable. And as people have become better educated with greater access to mass communication channels, governments compete with other governments, industries, corporations, etc., for the public's attention. With an increasing economically interdependent world, governments form partnerships or allegiances with large corporate and industrial concerns to produce favorable international markets and to correct balance-of-trade problems. Indeed, such concerns often help construct foreign policy. And as government red tape and government regulation have come under even greater public criticism, governments have relinquished the reins that once regulated a variety of industries and commercial concerns. "In short, the power of government has increased substantially, but the dependence on extragovernmental organizations for ideas, support, and legitimacy has also grown. Such significant structural interdependencies are another reason that traditional notions of propaganda must be updated" (Altheide and Johnson 1980, 26). Thus what we might once have characterized as "governmental propaganda" may well be an amalgamation of propagandistic information from a wide variety of anonymous sources whose messages have been structured into a policy or public debate and then released by governmental actors.

Accidental Suasion. In some instances, persuaders or propagandists may have an impact on individuals without having any intent to do so; they weren't motivated to influence nor did they strategically design communication to influence; thus such effects are said to be examples of accidental suasion. As we have said previously, sociation is the "cultivation of social relationships that help people define, and thereby do, what they want" (Combs and Nimmo 1993, 10). Through the process of sociative communication, individuals engage in social learning or **suasion.** We learn from the world around us. We engage in environment suasion, storing or discarding as the case may be. Our reaction to environmental stimuli and our attendant assignment of significance to it may often not have anything to do with the intention of the source. For example, a young Appalachian couple, recently exposed to television news channels from outside the Blue Ridge Mountains, may, after viewing hour-after-hour of news stories highlighting child abuse, murder, corruption, epidemics, pestilence, hate crimes, natural disasters, contaminated food supplies, chemical spills, etc., decide not to have children. This newly acquired information has convinced them it would be wrong to bring a young life into such a world. We use the term *accidental suasion* to indicate that persuaders and propagandists may contribute to the social learning process in ways that they had never intended, thus, accidental suasion. Doob calls such accidental suasion "unintentional propaganda"; however, we see this term as misleading, in that all propaganda is intentional (deliberate) and organized (systematic); thus, Doob has constructed an oxymoron (1948, 246; for a similar criticism, see Lasswell and Blumsenstock 1939, 10–11, footnote).

Ellul's (1968) distinction between political and sociological propaganda may be viewed as a discussion of accidental suasion. For Ellul, political propaganda is overt in that easily recognized members of the government, political campaigns, interest groups, or political parties address targeted groups to achieve political objectives; it is usually immediate with highly specialized appeals; and most importantly, attendees recognize it as propaganda. Sociological propaganda on the other hand is more ephemeral and more difficult to recognize, and therefore more difficult to combat. Messages contained in films, music, television news and entertainment, and product advertising present messages that help create a "shared reality." For example, magazines promoting skinny, anorexic-looking women as the epitome of female beauty and the presentation of grossly underweight television and movie stars in productions distorts the American woman's version of an ideal body type. Indeed Wallis Simpson's and Helen Gurley Brown's oft-cited dictum "You can never be too rich or too thin" represents, for the most part, the social psyche of Americans. And because most American women fail to achieve this "ideal" in weight, the result is a glorification of the aspired-to ideal and the accompanying negative self-image for having failed to achieve that ideal. Sociological propaganda, in some instances, may be regarded as the unintended consequences of communication produced for reasons other than propagandistic effect.

In the United States, Ellul believed that sociological propaganda was the "natural result of the fundamental elements of American life"—mass immigration and the resulting cultural diversity (1965, 68). In other words, sociological propaganda was an adaptive response to cultural diversity. "The solution was psychological standardization—that is, to use a way of life as the basis of unification and as an instrument of propaganda" (Ellul 1965, 68). Qualter explains: "The sudden throwing together of tens of thousands of immigrants from diverse cultural, linguistic, economic and political traditions created a new role for political persuasion. The 'melting pot' is a primary symbol of American propaganda" (1985, 126). Sociological propaganda may have an intended political agenda, however difficult to recognize. Oliver Stone's *Kennedy* or *Natural Born Killers* are appropriate examples.

IN SUMMARY

"It is impossible to understand the success of propaganda without also understanding how great a part of what men regard as knowledge is in fact no more than a collection of stereotypes" (Qualter 1962, 52). In praising Walter Lippmann's work, Qualter noted that Lippmann "knew that abstract ideas, feelings of national, local or racial pride, glory in ancient traditions, personal wishes, and popular passions are more real to the great mass of the people than are actual realities" (1962, 52). For the propagandist, the weaving of stereotypes into myth is at the heart of what he does. The propagandist recognizes that "because the myth is intangible, it is easier to mold than fact, although it is still as real as life itself to those who believe in it" (Qualter 1962, 52). We turn now to a means by which we can not only analyze the propaganda of others, but also plan for our own propaganda messages.

PROPAGANDA ANALYSIS: OBVIOUS POINTS OF DEPARTURE

In 1958, Harold Lasswell published *Politics: Who Gets What, When, How,* whose title quickly became the abbreviated definition for politics—who gets what, when, and how. Ten years previous, Lasswell had also provided the world with a shorthand explanation for the communicative act: "Who Says What in Which Channel to Whom with What Effects?" (1948, 37). Today, Lasswell's dictum "Who gets what, when, how" is still used, but his shorthand conceptualization of communication was modified in 1978 by Dan Nimmo, who inserted bidirectionality into the definition when he wrote, "who says what in which channel *with* (rather than *to*) whom with what effect(s)?" (11). We find these dictums highly useful in organizing our discussion of propaganda analysis. For whether propaganda is selling a car, instigating a revolution, or promoting an international computer conglomerate, we believe that propaganda is fundamentally political communication. **Political communication** has been defined as "communication (activity) considered political by virtue of its consequences (actual and potential) which regulate human conduct under conditions of conflict [or competition]" (Nimmo 1978, 7). If a car manufacturer uses social marketing to sell a luxury car and that marketing then affects the car-buying experience, whether before or after purchase, by altering how buyers view themselves, their social group, and those outside their social group, then the manufacturer's social marketing had political consequences. When we define social roles, when we place individuals on a hierarchical pyramid of social status or class, we are engaging in political behavior; and the communication of such classifications constitutes political communication and, in this particular incidence, propaganda.

We turn then to a discussion of the various components of propaganda, adopting Lasswell's (1948) dictum, as modified by Nimmo in 1978, for organizational purposes. We begin with the Who of the dictum, or the propaganda sources. A number of scholars have discussed the significance of the propaganda source, frequently integrating their discussion with elaborations concerning the veracity, that is, truthfulness, of the source's messages (Choukas 1965; Doob 1966; Ellul 1965; Jowett and O'Donnell 1992; Lasswell 1927; O'Donnell and Jowett 1989; Smith 1989a). However, rather than present a multitude of often fuzzy conceptualizations, we have endeavored to present an analytical typology that is mutually exclusive and exhaustive. We will begin with propaganda sources.

The Who: Propaganda Sources

Accurate Identification. When the source of the propaganda is accurately and clearly acknowledged within the delivery of the message, the propaganda is considered to be accurately identified. Facilitative propaganda sources provide accurate identification when they are in the process of building credibility for some future endeavor. For example, Crossman determined that the Allied propaganda during World War II was eventually persuasive because it was candidly presented:

> The purpose was achieved by the provision, day in, day out, of a news and information service so authoritative and candid that the listener or reader learned to rely on it and pass it on to his friends. By doing so, he committed an act of spiritual desertion, or confirmed his earlier apostasy from Totalitarianism. And that was the one enduring aim of Allied Psychological Warfare. (1971, 344)

Integrative propaganda, agitational propaganda, and disintegrative propaganda may also provide accurate identification in situations when knowing the source will only increase the power of the message or will likely increase the likelihood of bringing about the desired outcome. A direct address by a respected leader is likely to have greater influence than if the message was presented anonymously.

False Identification. When the source is falsely presented to the audience, the propaganda is considered to be falsely identified. The propagandist may create what is called a **deflective source,** which either may be an invention of the propagandist's imagination called **a shell,** or the propagandist may use a **front group,** a functioning group presenting itself as an independent organization yet secretly sponsored by the propagandist. For example, the Soviet Union during the 1950s sent Russian-written stories to a KGB officer working within Burma, who translated the articles, placing them in local newspapers with Burmese-sounding bylines (Brownfield 1984). Propagandists use popular or credible sounding names when fabricating or creating organizational sources for propaganda; for example, political candidates in the United States often use fancy names to describe their political action committees (PAC). The names of these PACs must be disclosed in all political ads, and for this reason, you might see "A whole lot of good people for Congressman X," or "Your friends and neighbors in X for X." When propagandists use a deflective source, whether imaginary or a secretly sponsored organization, the name or title of the deflective source sounds positive, credible, or likable, and the audience believes the deflective source is an independent originator of the message. For this reason, the propagandist is disassociated with the message, leading to increased credibility for the source as well as the message. In extreme cases, propagandists simply publish a newspaper or a book, falsely identifying both the authorship and/or publication source that are known to the audience and deemed credible.

During the 1956 Hungarian revolt against the Soviet Union, Radio Free Hungary pleaded for the United States to enter the dispute, ensuring the revolutionaries victory. In the vilest of terms, the Soviet Union and the Russian troops were denounced during its programming. Such attacks helped *legitimize* Radio Free Hungary as a source for disgruntled Soviet Bloc activists. In other words, anti-Soviet citizens within the Soviet Satellite Bloc viewed Radio Free Hungary as a valid representation of their views, approving and promoting their struggle for freedom. However, it wasn't until after the Soviets broke the Hungarian revolutionaries that the CIA uncovered that the Soviet Union was behind Radio Free Hungary. Recognizing that the United States would not likely enter what amounted to a civil war within the Soviet Bloc, the Soviet Union used Radio Free Hungary to impress upon the rest of their satellites that the United States and other NATO forces would not come to their aid in any conflict against the Soviet Union (see Jowett and O'Donnell 1992; Knietal 1982).

During the twentieth century, political and religious leaders in the United States have often attributed ideas, writings, or quotations to those venerable gentlemen whom we as a society consider to be our founding fathers. Any time this happens, the listener should be wary. Indeed, much of what is attributed to the founding fathers is outright lies, and so grossly distorts their true philosophical and intellectual perspectives that the fabrications are ludicrous to the extreme. The pro-Nazi movement published and attributed the following "prophecy" to none other than Benjamin Franklin during the Constitutional Convention.

> I warn you, gentlemen, if you do not exclude the Jews for all time, your children will curse you in your graves. Jews, gentlemen, are Asiatics, let them be born where they will, or how many generations they are away from Asia, they never will be otherwise. Their ideas do not conform to an American's, and will not even though they live among us ten generations. A leopard cannot change its spots. Jews are Asi-

atics, a menace to this country if permitted entrance, and should be excluded by this Constitution. (Choukas 1965, 109)

The quotation, of course, is complete fabrication.

In yet another instance of false identification, propaganda is disguised as a **symbolic fiction;** the propagandist simply arranges for a reputable party who is normally not associated with the propagandist to endorse or disseminate an untruth (Smith 1989a, 87). In other words, the reputable source is identified, but the true initiator remains a secret. In 1985, Oxford University Press, a scholarly press respected around the world, allowed the Soviets to change a number of definitions in two of their dictionaries prior to publication. These dictionaries would later be circulated within the Soviet Union still carrying the prestigious and highly credible Oxford University Press imprint. In the altered dictionaries, "capitalism" is defined as "the last antagonistic social and economic system in human history, based on the exploitation of man by man, replacing feudalism and preceding communism" and communism is listed as "a theory revealing the historical necessity for the revolutionary replacement of capitalism by communism" (Smith 1989a, 87). While it may be argued that the Oxford University Press simply published what was "politically correct" within the Soviet Union, the fact remains that rather than translating English into Russian, the publishers chose to rewrite basic definitions.

Says What: Information/Disinformation

Contrary to what many believe, propagandists frequently provide reliable and accurate information to their intended audience. According to Doob (1950), Goebbels was a firm believer in providing accurate intelligence, if it would not jeopardize the security of the propagandist's operation or the objectives of the state or greater organization. Goebbels believed that information that can be verified, what we commonly refer to as facts, is far more credible than empty assertions on the part of a propagandist. And this credibility bleeds over not only to the source but to surrounding messages as well. Propaganda messages that are easily supported by readily available information will work to increase the credibility of the source among audience members. And most importantly, when "factual" bits are pieced together in a carefully crafted news story whose theme ultimately may or may not be factual, these verifiable factual bits lend credibility to the overall news story.

Goebbels was also a strong proponent of using **pseudoevents**—staging of "news events" for the resulting news coverage and consequent propaganda benefits. In one such episode, Goebbels wanted to showcase Germany's humanitarian spirit and its continued support for and friendship with Finland, and he arranged for media coverage of Germany's sponsorship of restorative vacations for ailing Finnish children (Doob 1950, 426).

For Goebbels, the question of whether propaganda should be truthful or false rested on the propagandist's maintenance of the organization's credibility. According to Doob, Goebbels believed that truth "should be used as frequently as possible; otherwise the enemy or the facts themselves might expose falsehood, and the credibility of his own output would suffer" (1950, 428). And consequently, Goebbels only used lies when he believed those lies could not be disproved.

However, often when the propagandist is inexperienced or when faced with desperate situations, untruths or falsehoods are likely to be produced and disseminated. Such untruths, falsehoods, lies, or "incomplete, or misleading information that is passed, fed, or confirmed to a targeted individual, group, or country" is known as **disinformation** (Shultz and Godson 1984, 41).

An example of one type of disinformation is what noted novelist Norman Mailer called a **factoid** (1973, 18). A factoid is "an assertion of fact that is not backed up by evidence, usually because the fact is false or because evidence in support of the assertion cannot be obtained" (Pratkanis and Aronson 1991, 71). Factoids tend to be negative information pertaining to individuals, companies, or products, and for this reason, as negative information theory suggests, they are easily remembered and frequently repeated (Lau 1980, 1982, 1985; Richey, Koenigs, Richey, and Fortin 1975). A variety of factoids exist within the propagandist's repertoire.

Propagandists understand the power and credibility of those appearing as news media figures; often such news reporters or anchors present factoids, and even though the audience may recognize that no evidence exists to support the assertion, the audience is likely to believe that the factoid is true because of what Merton (1949) called the **status conferral function** of the media. Simply put, appearing in the "news" gives people credibility and status, and audience members frequently accept without challenge a media figure's statements. For this reason, propagandists will frequently recruit journalists to serve as their **paid mouthpieces.** These undercover journalists purport to be supportive of one country while in the employ of another, producing stories deliberately intended to deceive and demoralize not only the government but the citizens of the country where they are living and working. Usually such paid mouthpieces are nationals of the country they are betraying, but in some instances, they are carefully trained impostors. Such undercover operations are very tricky in that "care has to be taken to place the sources and messages within a social, cultural, and political framework of the target audience"

(Jowett and O'Donnell 1992, 13). If the source does not adequately "understand" or "empathize" sufficiently with the intended audience, this will be reflected in cultural missteps or inconsistencies within the propaganda, and the audience members will likely discount not only the messages but eventually the source.

During World War II, French journalist Paul Fredonnet, who was a closet Nazi sympathizer, broadcast a radio program from Stuttgart, Germany, telling French soldiers to fight the Nazi invaders, while at the same time warning that the better-paid British soldiers were wining, dining, and seducing their French wives and girlfriends while on leave. By urging the soldiers to bravely defend their homeland, Fredonnet established credibility in the eyes of his audience, thus his disinformation concerning the conduct of French women became credible as well (Jowett and O'Donnell 1992, 9).

When the propagandist identifies a group of people as belonging to a "conspiracy" or secret plot, this is exactly when the targeted audience will easily believe the propagandist's related factoid, because there would be no evidence to support the factoid if there was a "secret" plot. Such **fact-by-conspiracy** reasoning may often be found within the Potomac beltway in our nation's capital. And some researchers have suggested that such factoids are even more persuasive by the very fact that they can't be proven or disproven as they would be if attributed to a credible source. For example, the Nazis during World War II were able to convince large numbers of people of a Jewish conspiracy to take over the world. Pratkanis and Aronson write: "The fact there is no evidence that a Jewish conspiracy exists is just further evidence regarding the cleverness of Jews. The big lie is then supported by many small, but often irrelevant, facts to make the big lie all that more believable— for example, some Jews own banks, and Marx, the founder of communism, was Jewish" (1991, 72). Therefore, for Nazi followers, all Jews are Marxists; all Jews want to own banks to control the world. When presented in this way, such assertions are patently absurd; however, the durability of such an analysis gives testimony to this factoid's propagandistic power. Even today, you will find remnants of this factoid in the speeches of Pan-Christian and Neo-Conservative Pat Buchanan, three-time candidate for the presidency of the United States (Krauthammer 1992, 28).

Innuendoes are another form of factoid. An **innuendo** is a slur against one's name or character. And in common practice, this has by extension come to mean any slur against any entity important to one's self-identification such as an ethnic or religious group, occupational group, or geographical region or country. Recently, the Walt Disney Company has had a number of public relations travails, but one provides us with an interesting yet complicated example of innuendo. After the 1994 release of *The Lion King*, Disney's animated children's cartoon, an article appeared in the respected British news-paper *Manchester Guardian Weekly* discussing the film. The newspaper printed accusations concerning the naming of the film's characters. Disney used Swahili, an African language, to name the animal characters. And the innuendoes dealt with translations of those names. According to the British news article, "Simba" translates as lion, and "Shenzi" is the word for barbarian, which all seems fairly tame until one reads the charge that the name of the little warthog, "Pumba," is Swahili for "excretion from under the fore-skin" (www.urbanlegends.com). Using a Swahili translator provided by Yale University, we found that "Pumba" means foolish or dull-witted (www.yale.edu/swahili/), which most would agree accurately described the little wart-hog. The Walt Disney Company was once again the victim of disinformation.

Similarly, in the 1970s, religious groups inspired media stories that linked Procter & Gamble with satanic cults because of the thirteen stars (identified as a satanic symbol) in the company's logo. Many Americans boycotted the company's products, despite the fact that there was no evidence to back up these absurd accusations (Pratkanis and Aronson 1991, 71). Americans often distrust such large-scale success stories as Procter & Gamble, for they often believe that such success is only the result of taking advantage of the "little guy"; thus, success, for many Americans, is the result of abuses inflicted on the general public, in other words—BIG is BAD (Gans 1979; Johnson-Cartee and Copeland 1997a).

A **rumor** is an unconfirmed story in general circulation. Baus and Ross (1968) have argued that the most effective rumors are those that resonate with cultural truisms or mythologies shared by the community or society. And they argue that rumors provide a psychological reinforcement for the individual sharing the rumor with a friend, because he or she feels that by "being in the know," so to speak, "they are in" with the right group.

In 1991 one particularly bizarre rumor circulated in low-income neighbor-hoods throughout the Northeast. The Brooklyn Bottling Corporation had started producing low-cost soft drinks called Tropical Fantasy. A 20-ounce size of Tropical Fantasy cost only 49¢, and as a result, the soft drink rapidly became quite popular. Company sales projections forecast $15 million for 1991. But leaflets began appearing in minority neighborhoods, warning Afri-can Americans that the Ku Klux Klan was producing Tropical Fantasy, a secret chemical compound containing "stimulants to sterilize the black man" (Storm over Tropical Fantasy 1991, *Newsweek,* April 22, 34). The result was catastrophic for the Brooklyn Bottling Corporation. And as one national newsmagazine reported, angry customers took to the street, threatening "dis-tributors with baseball bats" and pelting "delivery trucks with bottles; some stores even refused shipment. . . . Sales . . . plummeted" (Storm over Tropical Fantasy 1991, *Newsweek,* April 22, 34).

Whatever their form, factoids are very powerful. Indeed, Wegner, Wenzlaff, Kerker, and Beattie (1981) found that even the suggestion of wrongdoing in a newspaper headline affected political candidates' credibility. Directly incriminating headlines were the most powerful in negatively affecting a candidate's credibility. However, denying a candidate has done something wrong or associating a candidate with a questionable or mildly undesirable behavior was also damning. The source of the innuendo or charges made little difference. And even when people are directly told to ignore innuendo or factoids by authority figures, such as by a judge in a court of law, research has found them to still be influential (Carroll, Kerr, Alfini, Weaver, Mac Coun, and Feldman 1986; Kassin, Williams, and Saunders 1990; Sue, Smith, and Caldwell 1973).

Clearly dealing with potentially damaging disinformation is serious business whether your organization is a lone proprietor or a multinational corporation, a political candidate, or a CEO casting about for a better-paying and more prestigious position. Koenig provided a decision-making outline for companies confronted with a rumor; because of the nature of rumors and its sister factoids, the outline may serve as a guide for handling all factoids (1985).

A. ALERT PROCEDURE

1. On first hearing a rumor, note the location and wording of the allegation and target.
2. Keep alert for any other rumors to see if the original report was spurious.
3. If rumors increase to ten or more, send requests to distributors, franchise managers, and whoever else meets the public to find out who told the rumor to the person reporting it. It is important to specify the regional boundaries of the problem and the characteristics of the participating population. Distribute forms that can be filled out for the above information, as well as fact sheets rebutting the rumor.
4. Check with competitors to see if they share the problem. Try to find out if the target has moved from your company to them or from them to yours, or if it has spread throughout the industry.

B. EVALUATION

1. Check for a drop in sales or a slowdown in sales increase.
2. Monitor person-hours required to answer phone calls and mail.
3. Keep tabs on the morale of the company personnel meeting people in the corporation. Do they feel harassed? Do they feel that management is doing enough to help them?
4. Design a marketing survey to find out what percentage of the public believes any part of the rumor.
5. Make an assessment of the threat or potential threat the rumor poses to profits. Is the corporation in danger of appearing to be an inept, impotent, and passive victim of the rumor problem? How much is management's image affected by the way

things are going? The next move is a judgment call. If it seems that something more should be done, then it is time to move to the next square.

C. LAUNCH A MEDIA CAMPAIGN

1. Assemble all facts about the extent of the problem to present to co-workers and superiors. Be prepared for resistance from people who support the myth that "pussyfooting is the best policy."
2. Based on information gathered in the previous phases, decide on the geographical regions for implementing the campaign. If it is a local rumor, treat it locally; if it is a national rumor, treat it nationally.
3. Based on information gathered in the previous phases, decide on the demographic features of the carrying population.
4. Select appropriate media outlets and construct appropriate messages.
5. Decide on what points to refute. (Don't deny more than is in the allegation.) If the allegation is of the contamination variety, be careful not to bring up any offensive association or to trigger potential "residuals" in the refutation.
6. Two important points to make in any campaign are that the allegations are untrue and *unjust*. It should be implied that the company's business is not suffering, but that "what's right is right!" and that people who pass on the rumor are "going against the American sense of fair play!"
7. Line up spokespeople such as scientists, civic and/or religious leaders, rumor experts—whoever you think appropriate—to make statements on the company's behalf.

If all the above is done properly, the problem is well on the way to being solved. (Reproduced with permission of Greenwod Publishing Group, Inc., Westport, Conn. Koenig, F. [1985]. *Rumor in the marketplace: The social psychology of commercial hearsay*, 171–73. Dover, Mass.: Auburn Publishing House.)

With Whom: Internal/External Propaganda

Internal propaganda occurs among members of the group; group leaders use interpersonal and organizational communication as a means of influence within the group. The traditional union meetings during the first half of last century provide concrete examples of internal propaganda. The union's detailed recountings of the working man's suffering at the hands of his oppressors, the industrial barons, polarized the owners and the workers. In effect, this practice of vilifying the owners produced for the workers a hated out-group, thus improving group solidarity to combat the workers' common enemy, the owners. **External propaganda** is the use of mass communication by an organized source to deliver propagandistic appeals to targeted groups within the population whom the source needs to fulfill identified goals. Corporate image advertising that targets various social markets or demographic groups is an example of external propaganda. And every four years, the Democratic and Republican U.S. presidential conventions are fine examples of both internal and external propaganda.

With What Effect(s)

As we have suggested previously, it is not the propagandistic tactic that is moral or immoral, ethical, or unethical; the tactic in and of itself is without moral or ethical values. Rather, it is the effects or end results that should be judged on the grounds of morality and the propagandist's intent that should be judged on ethical grounds.

NOTE

1. A rough English interpretation of these stanzas is as follows:

> Arise children of our Fatherland,
> The day of glory dawns!
> Against us, tyranny's
> Bloody standard rises;
> Do you hear in the fields
> The howling of these fearsome soldiers?
> They come into our midst
> To cut the throats of our sons and consorts!
>
> To arms, citizens,
> Form your battalions,
> March, march!
> Let impure blood
> Water our furrows!

This interpretation is adapted from several translations found at www.marseillaise .org/english/ (maintained by Iain Patterson) and http://ourworld.compuserve.com/ homepages/Thierry_Klien/lamarsee.htm.

Chapter Seven

Propaganda Tactics and Principles

In 1937 President Franklin D. Roosevelt established the Institute for Propaganda Analysis (IPA), which brought together leading scholars from a wide variety of interdisciplinary fields. Ultimately, the IPA published *The Fine Art of Propaganda* (Lee and Lee 1939), which provided readers with the means necessary to detect propagandistic arguments. By providing a simple, highly memorable list of techniques with accompanying examples, the IPA hoped to enable Americans to detect potentially destructive propaganda on their own. According to Doob, an IPA member, these techniques were crafted so high school students and even taxicab drivers could understand them (1966, 289; 1948). However, a number of writers have seriously criticized the IPA's efforts.

Qualter, in his criticism of the IPA's list, contends that propaganda as "Communication acquires meaning only in its context. Propaganda effect [sic] arises from the interaction of a communication and an audience, through a specific medium, in a particular cultural and ideological environment, at a particular time and place. All these variables must be considered as a unit" (1985, 110). Qualter correctly argues that the Lees' list presents merely manipulative devices, ignoring the communication context. Such propagandistic measures work only to the extent that they accurately and effectively tap something within the audience's collective identity operating in a specified context. And it should not be forgotten that the audience takes an active role in constructing meaning from the communicative acts created in the interaction. Qualter's points are well taken; all that he contends is indeed true. But, Qualter's assertions do not mean that the IPA's list is without value. The IPA's list is not a predictor of influence; rather, it serves as a network of guideposts for people trying to identify propagandistic cues in contemporary rhetoric. The identified argument styles or techniques serve as those cues. Perhaps Qualter should consider that if a wolf always presents itself in sheep's clothing, then a wise sheep would be wary, using careful consideration when confronting unfamiliar sheep.

While it is true that the IPA's original seven propagandistic techniques do trivialize the propaganda process, such lists do provide some initial insight for the novice into contemporary propaganda. Therefore, the authors, with full knowledge and forethought, have decided to perpetuate the trivialization of propaganda by presenting a greatly enhanced list of propaganda techniques. We have taken the liberty of editing, adapting, modernizing, and adding to the IPA's list. By utilizing the work of Chase (1956), Smith (1989b), Jowett and O'Donnell (1992), and our own research (Johnson-Cartee and Copeland 1997b), we hope to present a more comprehensive, understandable, and easily applicable guide. Accompanying each propaganda technique is an example, utilizing the highly charged if not inflammatory remarks so characteristic of such propagandistic tactics. Often multiple techniques are used within one missive. Consider the following.

PROPAGANDA TECHNIQUES
IN THE YEAR 2002

Smoke and Mirrors

Name Calling: The condemning of an idea on its face by giving it a bad label regardless of the evidence.

> George Bush, running in the 1980 Republican primaries, labeled Ronald Reagan's so-called "trickle down" economic theory, *voodoo-economics.*

Propaganda Slinging: The labeling of the behavior of others as propagandistic without due consideration of the argument.

> *Don't go to see the film* Saving Private Ryan; *it is nothing but antiwar propaganda put out by the liberal Hollywood elite.*

Asymmetrical Definition: The deliberate use of audience-familiar words that evoke shared meanings but are not shared by the source of the message for the purpose of deception (T. Smith 1989b, 91). Variations in this technique range from being moderately deceptive to being totally dishonest. For example, when the United States dealt with the former Soviet Union, each of the superpowers used the word *peace,* but they each had widely divergent meanings for the word.

Thus "peace," which ordinarily means a state of friendly relations with other countries, is interpreted by Communists to mean the state of affairs within a Communist country since capitalist countries are assumed to be in a state of open class war and of at least potential hostility amongst each other in their competitive struggle for survival. (J. A. C. Brown 1963, 121–22)

And as T. Smith (1989b, 93) has observed, for a Communist a commitment to world peace is a commitment to world communism and the demise of capitalism.

Juxtaposition: The placing of perceived highly unrelated (and therefore totally unexpected) ideas together in order to shock and to influence the argument's evaluation.

I'm a criminal. My 25-year-old daughter was dying of bone cancer. The pain was so great that she couldn't bear to be touched. And drugs didn't help. Judy only had a few weeks to live, and she decided she wanted to end her life. But it wasn't legally possible, so I broke the law and got her the pills necessary. And as she slipped peacefully away, I climbed into her bed and took her in my arms for the first time in months.—Patty Rosen, a registered nurse, appearing in a 1994 Oregon television commercial urging the passage of Proposition 26, which would have legalized euthanasia requested by terminally ill or incapacitated persons (as quoted in Johnson-Cartee and Copeland 1997b, 103).

Glittering Generality: Using a positive or virtuous sounding word to promote an idea.

Rumsfeld's handling of the war is inspirational.

Positive Testimonial: Having an admired person endorse an idea or product.

The right to own and bear arms is the most precious fundamental right awarded to us in the greatest constitutional document ever produced, the Constitution of the United States of America.—Charlton Heston, star of stage and screen, spokesperson and eventually president of the National Rifle Association, at a speech in Tuscaloosa, Alabama, 1997; also see symbolic fiction.

Positive Transfer: Attaching the authority, sanction, and prestige of one idea, object, person, etc., to another.

The Republican Party represents the Jeffersonian ideals in contemporary political debate.

Desirable by Association: Making a complementary association between two people, objects, ideas, or events that share a given label.

Desiree is a highly eligible marriage prospect; after all, Desiree, her mother and three of her grandmothers were Tri-Delts.

Negative Testimonial: Having a normally disrespected person (in general or in a specific context) or a uniformly disliked person endorse an idea or product.

I'm Bill Clinton, and I believe in chastity and self-denial.

Negative Transfer: Attaching the authority, sanction, and disrespect of one idea, object, person, etc., to another unrelated idea, object, person, etc.

The Nazi propaganda film Der Ewige Jude (The Wandering Jew) *presented the foulest of racial stereotypes and compared* Jews *to a plague of rats that needed to be exterminated.* (as described by Jowett and O'Donnell 1992, p. 188)

Guilt by Association: Making a pejorative association between two people, objects, ideas, or events that share a given label.

Siegelman's left wing leanings are no secret to those who keep up with politics, but many of your friends and acquaintances may not know about him or may need reminding. Make sure they know he supported McGovern in 1972 and Dukakis in 1988, worked for liberal Congressman Al Lowenstein, and took a campaign contribution from Jane Fonda.—Anonymous hate letter mailed to Alabama voters during the 1990 gubernatorial campaign (as quoted in Whillock 1995, 51)

Card Stacking: To overwhelm the audience with purported evidence arranged for maximum effect.

The doctrines of Europe were that men in numerous associations cannot be restrained within the limits of order and justice but by forces physical and moral wielded over them by authorities independent of their will—hence their organization of kings, hereditary nobles, and priests. Still further, to constrain the brute by hard labor, poverty, and ignorance; and to take from them as from bees, so much of their earnings as that unremitting labor shall be necessary to obtain a sufficient surplus barely to sustain a scanty and miserable life. And these earnings they apply to maintain their privileged orders in splendor and idleness, to fascinate the eyes of the people, and excite in them a humble adoration and submission, as to an order of superior beings.—Thomas Jefferson in a letter to William Johnson, Monticello, June 12, 1823; as quoted in Dumbauld 1955, 74

Statistical Proof: Research statistics used as the proof of an argument.

Statistical analysis proves that all Americans believe this.

Today's public opinion poll shows that Americans support the national referendum.

Overgeneralizing: Jumping to conclusions from one or two cases.

Phyllis Schlafly and Patrick Buchanan oppose abortion; all Republicans oppose abortion rights.

False Analogies: A, it is argued, is exactly like B—but it isn't.

Abortion is the worst form of child abuse.

Tautological Appeals: Arguing in circles. Using a conclusion to prove itself.

When guns are outlawed only outlaws will have guns.

Polarizing: Forcing an issue with many aspects into just two sides, ignoring the shades of gray.

The gap between us and our opponents is a cultural divide. It is not just a difference between conservative and liberal; it is a difference between fighting for what is right and refusing to see what is wrong.—Vice President Dan Quayle, Republican Presidential Convention, August 20, 1992 (as quoted in Johnson-Cartee, Copeland, Marquez, Buford, and Stephens [1998, 43])

Fallacy of Limited Alternatives: By restricting alternative explanations, leading the audience to a false conclusion.

Soviet Marshal Ogarkov's explanation for the downing of KAL Flight 007 in 1981 by Soviet aircraft and observing that: "'*When it [KAL flight 007] did not react to 120 warning shots, nothing was left for us to do but to react the way we did*'" (as quoted in T. Smith 1989a, 89; emphasis added). And Smith went on to provide a number of more preferable alternatives than Ogarkov had offered; "Obviously, a number of other actions were possible, such as firing more warning shots, firing shots into the aircraft, or, most important, breaking off the engagement" (T. Smith 1989a, 89).

Fallacy of Impossible Certainty: Using emphatic speech to obscure that the issue remains unresolved (T. Smith 1989a, 89).

The copilot of the Egyptian Airline did not commit suicide, taking more than 200 passengers with him into the sea; devout Muslims do not and never would commit suicide.

Implacatures: Using a rhetorical device encouraging the drawing of inferences by audience members who are constructing meaning from communication acts that goes well beyond the explicit words used (Harris 1981, 87). Such inferences are made by audience members when they are cued by implacatures to retrieve stored schemas of beliefs and knowledge and to apply them (Kennamer 1989, 40). Grice acknowledges that people cue or evoke such inferences by how they structure their communicative acts, writing that "implacature is not carried by what is said, but only by the saying of what is said or by 'putting it that way'"(1975, 74–75). Inferences, then, are drawn on what they think you said—rather than what they actually heard.

Or in some circumstances, what they wanted to have heard. Winograd provides the classic example of an implacature:

> *Mother:* Where is your boyfriend going to stay when he visits?
> *Daughter:* We have a couch in the living room (1977, 82).

Building Significance and Credibility through Secret Sources: Using undis-
closed or secret sources as experts to prove the argument true.

> *Conservatives whose positions give them a mantle of credibility have learned to use us*
> *as a megaphone to reach the American public. They speak in the confidence that we*
> *will not disclose their identity or reject their often astounding stories outright two events*
> *they fear from congressional reporters and Washington bureau chiefs. (Only 4% of*
> *whom, by the latest poll, are Republican.)*—James W. Nugent, president, *The Wall*
> *Street Underground,* "Murder in the First Degree"

The Familiar and the Comfortable

Plain Folks: Associating ideas with the common people and their ordinary
ways, customs, and/or language and insinuating that those items are therefore superior.

> *I don't have no [sic] inferiority complex about runnin' [sic] for president . . . because I*
> *represent just as good and refined and cultured people as anybody else. . . . These here*
> *[sic] national politicians like Humphrey and Johnson and Nixon, they don't hang their*
> *britches on the wall and then do a flyin' [sic] jump into 'em [sic] every mornin', [sic]*
> *they put 'em [sic] on one britches [sic] leg at a time, just like the folks in Chilton*
> *County, [Alabama].*—George C. Wallace in a stump speech in 1966 for his wife and
> gubernatorial candidate, Lurleen Wallace (as quoted in Ayers 1986, January 13, 5;
> keep in mind that Wallace held an undergraduate and law degree from the Univer-
> sity of Alabama.)

Bandwagon Appeal: Everyone else is doing it or joining it; therefore, you
should too.

> *Those are the words of George C. Wallace picked first over his opposition in 57 out of*
> *67 counties on May 1st. Let's stand up for Alabama again on May 29th. And make it*
> *67 out of 67. Elect George C. Wallace governor, a real Southerner.*—A narrator on a
> 1962 TV ad for George Wallace's gubernatorial campaign (as quoted in Johnson-
> Cartee, Elebash, and Copeland 1992, 15)

Granfalloon: An informal, nonmembership group created by the propagandist for the sole purpose of producing proud and meaningless associations of
human beings who then perceive great solidarity within the portrayed collectivity; the granfalloon is used by the propagandist to draw dramatic in-group

and out-group distinctions to achieve objectives, whether it is to raise money, encourage boycotting, or vote as the propagandist suggests (see Pratkanis and Aronson 1991, 168; Vonnegut 1963).

> Many of today's televangelists are masters at producing granfalloons. Pratkanis and Aronson suggest that the granfalloon of the electronic church, *"God's chosen people,"* are recruited from the ranks of those "who are already converted to Christianity and those who are lonely and isolated or have recently suffered a loss, such as a personal disability or the death of a loved one" and by "watching, subscribing, donating, and adopting the behaviors suggested by religious programs," they become one of the religious fold (Pratkanis and Aronson 1991, 173; emphasis added). And as members of this in-group, they may be called upon by the propagandist to protect the religious fold from enemies identified by the propagandist.

Superiority Appeals: My arguments are superior, because you and those like you are superior.

> *In the name of the greatest people that have ever trod this earth, I draw the line in the dust and toss the gauntlet before the feet of tyranny and I say, segregation today, segregation tomorrow and segregation forever.*—George Wallace, noted segregationist, in his 1963 Alabama gubernatorial inaugural address (as quoted in Johnson-Cartee, Elebash, and Copeland [1992, 16])

Self-Evident Truths: Everyone knows this; therefore, it must be true.

> *Teddy Roosevelt climbed San Juan Hill in the Spanish American War; everyone knows that.*—A false political myth first propagated by the Hearts and Pulitzers, as discussed in Blum, Morgan, Rose, Schlesinger, Stampp, and Vann Woodward 1973, 502.

Wise Men Can't Be Wrong: Clinching an argument by an appeal to some higher authority as in a revered God or a revered political leader (either in the past or present).

> *Our culture is superior. . . . Our culture is superior because our religion is Christianity and that is the truth that makes men free.*—Pat Buchanan (as quoted in the *New York Times*, Sept. 12, 1993, p. 37)

Emotion Ignitions

Prospective Fear Appeals: If X happens, then Y will happen, and Y is horrific.

> *Harvey Gantt has promised to back mandatory gay rights laws. Including requiring local schools to hire gay teachers. Harvey Gantt is dangerously liberal. Too liberal for*

North Carolina.—Narrator in a 1990 Jesse Helms Senate campaign ad against Democratic challenger Harvey Gantt (as quoted in Johnson-Cartee and Copeland 1997b, 117)

Retrospective Fear Appeals: X and Y happened, and it was horrific, and if Z occurs, it will be the same thing but even worse.

Michael Dukakis will do for America what he has done for Massachusetts.—A tag line in George Bush's political advertising during the 1988 presidential election campaign referring to Dukakis's record on the environment and crime during his gubernatorial years

Absurdity Appeals: Ridiculing or indicating the absurdity of the opposition's position.

According to lawyers, a person should leave an individual pinned in a burning car rather than risking a lawsuit for having aggravated the individual's injuries by moving him; that's some good Samaritan.

Hate Speech: Appeals to mass prejudice, invoking civic hatred.

There is a religious war going on in this country for the soul of Americans. It is a cultural war as critical to the kind of nation we shall be as the Cold War itself, for this war is for the soul of America. And in that struggle for the soul of America, Clinton and Clinton [Bill and Hillary] *are on the other side, George Bush is on our side.*—Pat Buchanan, in his 1992 Republican Presidential Convention speech (as quoted in Lowi [1995, 211])

Personal Attacks: Attacking the personal character, family, religion, marital history, medical history, etc., of an individual on matters of significant importance to the group.

James uses school prayer and his wife's involvement with national religious organizations to appeal to Christian voters, but his real life is anything but Christian. It is no secret that while he was Governor, James was a heavy drinker and maybe even a borderline alcoholic. What is not so well known is that he is a compulsive womanizer.
—Anonymous hate letter mailed to Alabama voters during the 1990 gubernatorial campaign (as quoted in Whillock 1995, 52)

Using Cathartic Identification: The use of a story that individuals can strongly identify with, resulting in either a highly positive or highly negative realization and emotional experience.

I worked hard all my life, saved a few dollars, my wife had to go in the nursing home, and I've about used it all up. There's one candidate that cares for the old folk [sic] and

that is Paul Hubbert. And I'm fer [sic] him a hundred percent.—Elderly farmer in a 1990 Alabama gubernatorial campaign commercial (as quoted in Johnson-Cartee and Copeland, 1997b, 99)

In Summary

Although some propaganda scholars find such listings of propaganda techniques as being too simplistic for meaningful analysis, we beg to differ. As members of a majority group within a culture, we are often unaware of how our language affects others, for it is as if we do not observe ourselves, because we have become so accustomed to our own mode of behaviors. For example, in the United States, we all too often are unaware of how propagandistic hate speech is used to manipulate us. For this reason, we will now consider how hate speech manifests itself in contemporary society.

Hate Speech: The Powerhouse of Propaganda

All propaganda is capitalized prejudice. It rests on some emotional premise which is the motive force of the process. The emotional transfer is worked by some associative process like similarity, [or perceived difference,] use, [read misuse] or the causal relationship [read caused our problem]. The derived antipathy represents the goal.—Psychologist Raymond Dodge (1920)

One noted scholar observed nearly one-half a century ago that "The cult of hatred and xenophobia is the cheapest and surest method of obtaining from the masses the ignorant and savage patriotism which puts the blame for every political folly or social misfortune upon the foreigner" (Woolf 1953, 313). Whether the identified enemy is foreign or domestic, hate speech is one of the most pervasive propagandistic practices in the modern world, today. Whillock (1995) has defined **hate speech** as a stratagem or "an artifice or trick in war for deceiving and outwitting the enemy, a cleverly contrived trick or scheme for gaining an end" (Gove 1986, 225–26). According to Whillock, "hate speech seeks to move an audience by creating a symbolic code for violence. Its goals are to inflame the emotions of followers, denigrate the designated out-class, inflict permanent and irreparable harm to the opposition, and ultimately conquer" (1995, 32). Hate speech is destabilizing to the body politic—doing grievous harm to members of out-groups, and ultimately to the emotional health and well-being of the perpetuators of out-group hatred, the members of the in-group themselves. For hatred is ultimately a destructive force for the human psyche. Clearly, being aware of hate speech use and its destructive capacity is critical in contemporary society. For as Whillock (1995) suggests, there is no antidote to hate speech. Once committed, the damage is done and cannot be fixed. Whillock maintains that out-groups confronted with hate speech who use such tactics as denials, defensive posturing, counterattacks, or even atonements are ultimately defeated.

> Both defensive and avoidance strategies are ineffectual in responding to the outgroup treatment of the hater. The use of response strategies implies that the opposition will respond to a reasoned defense, or at least find an unreceptive climate for future attacks. By contrast, the stratagem of hate is designed to conquer, not to negotiate. The result is that rather than defusing a crisis, victim responses often escalate the problem. They fuel the fires of hate by proving that the message had the harmful effects intended. (1995, 3)

Racist discourse is a form of hate speech, and, in America, such discourse continues to be a significant obstruction to our society's advancement. Discourse "institutional as well as interpersonal text and talk—plays a crucial role in the enactment, expression, legitimation, and acquisition of racism in society" (Van Dijk 1995, 2). Often it is the elites who are

> [t]he ones who initiate, monitor, and control the majority and most influential forms of institutional and public text and talk. They have preferential access to the mass media, may set or change the agenda of public discourse and opinion making, prepare and issue reports, carry out and publish research—thereby controlling academic discourse—and so on. In other words, the power of specific elite groups may be a direct function of the measure of access to, and control over, the means of symbolic reproduction in society, that is over public discourse. This also means that the power of the elites is especially persuasive. . . . Their discursive resources are such that they are better able than other social groups to influence interpretations and social beliefs and to marginalize or suppress alternatives that are against their interests. (Van Dijk 1995, 4–5; Abercrombie, Hill, and Turner 1990)

It should also be noted that in extreme circumstances, the elites' internal organization and mobilization of hatred reaches the level of terrorism.

Often we are unaware, particularly if we are members of a majority group within society that has enjoyed "in-group" status, how universal hate speech is within our own society. We become so secure in our own status as members of the in-group, so inculcated with our own "rightness," that we fail to recognize hate speech and even succumb to its destructive reasoning; thus, our insensitivity ultimately works in favor of the hate propagandist and the eventual securing of his objectives. For this reason, Pratkanis and Aronson have provided five guidelines for interacting with others in order to avoid being unwittingly seduced by hate speech and granfalloon tactics:

1) When speakers or writers engage in the stereotyping or labeling of others, ask yourself, "Why is this being suggested? What purpose does it serve the speaker or writer? How does my acceptance of these stereotypes or characterizations of in-groups and out-groups benefit the speaker or writer?"

2) Anchor your self-esteem with personal achievement—not the self-image associated with group membership.

3) Don't obsess or base your whole ego or self-esteem on one item, one behavior, or one group membership. Such obsession breeds fanaticism or unreasonable behavior. Diversify your interests to help maintain healthy life-behaviors.

4) Seek the commonalties among people and build upon them. Find common goals and common beliefs and emphasize those. Don't build unnecessary walls between people.

5) Do not think of individuals as a representative of an "out-group" or an "in-group." Think of them as individuals—unique, human beings who have something to contribute, something to offer society. (1991, 174)

We must be aware of how our discourse ultimately shapes our society, and as Doob so eloquently warned in 1935:

> If everyone remains gullible and the willing victim of intentional and unintentional propagandists, the task of finding and then establishing new social values becomes almost impossible. More people must simply puncture the truths in the "lies" which they accept, and appreciate the truths in the "lies" which they reject. Only then will they be able to destroy the evil and buncombe of society; only then will they be ready to recognize leaders whose values and whose propaganda are neither deceptive nor illusory; only then will they be immune to a doctrine like Fascism. This should be possible—but is it? (412)

"Terror itself is the oldest form of psychological warfare. It is the inspiration behind the feathers and paint of the warring tribesmen" (Qualter 1962, 117). It is raw, cruel intimidation. Terror has been defined as "a policy of severe and arbitrary coercion or its credible threat" (Dallin and Breslauer 1970, 87). In propaganda studies, political terror is rarely mentioned; because, for political terror to be operational, it has had, at some time in the past, a widely noted physical act or event that made all future threats of terror credible for the audience. Goebbels's invasion propaganda provides a ready example. Prior to the Germans invading Norway in 1940, Goebbels made available to Norwegian governmental officials a film chronicling the 1939 Nazi invasion of Poland. "The film documented the full horror of mechanized war with endless lines of tanks and armored cars, cities erupting under a rain of bombs, dead and injured women and children, all the noise, speed, and shock of modern war" (Qualter 1962, 117). Goebbels's point was easily made. This pre-invasion propaganda strategy continued well into 1942; the Nazi propaganda machine dictated that the terrifying message to potential prey of the Third Reich was simply: "'This is what happened to others, it's now about to happen to you!'" (Qualter 1962, 117).

Ultimately, terror is internally driven in that in order to wield terror on someone, they must be part of group structure that self-identifies as being at risk. We include a discussion of terror within this chapter on propaganda, because it too is a mechanism of social control, albeit one that while originating in an event, ultimately remains effective by the retelling and sharing of the past terrorist activities among group members.

In some societies, terrorism is a routine strategy of government. Alex Inkeles has explained the overwhelming, consuming fear that is the constant companion for those living in terrorist societies:

> The regime seeks to create in every man the nagging fear that he may have done something wrong, that he may have left something undone, that he may have said some impermissible thing. It is an important part of the pattern that he be unable ever to find out exactly what it was that he did wrong. In this light the studied caprice of the terror in its impact on its actual victims may be seen in a new light. The non-victim, looking at the actual victim, can never find out why the victim was victimized, because there are different and contradictory reasons for different victims, or there may have been no reason at all.
>
> The non-victim thus becomes the prisoner of a vague uncertainty which nags him. It is this nagging uncertainty in the non-victim which the terror seeks to create. For it is a powerful force in making every man doubly watch his every step. It is prophylactic in the extreme. It will make the citizen properly compulsive about saying correct things in public and saying them loud for all to hear, or, almost as good, it will teach him to say nothing in public. It will wake him in the middle of the night to go back to his office to do his sums over again, to redraw his blueprint and then redraw it again, to edit and then edit again the article he is writing, to check and then recheck and then check his machine again. Anxiety demands relief and compulsive reiteration of the most common human patterns for handling of anxiety. It is this compulsive conformity which the totalitarian regime wants. It gets it as a derived benefit from the influence of terror on the non-victim, who puzzles over the reasons for the treatment of the victim. Anxiety has been institutionalized. (1954, 106–7)

B. Moore has observed that ultimately the use of terror is self-defeating.

> There comes a point at which the use of terror defeats its purposes. . . . The regime has to walk a thin and not always easily discernible line between using too much terror or too little. Too much can destroy the minimal framework of regularity and legality necessary to maintain the total system upon which the regime's power

depends. Too little terror diminishes control at the center by permitting the growth of independent centers of authority within the bureaucracy. (1954, 175–78)

Thus, as Dallin and Breslauer (1970) have so aptly demonstrated, terror may in the short term promote compliance, but ultimately it produces system-threatening alienation; for this reason, it may be said that terror while temporarily effective is ultimately self-defeating.

Beyond the Propagandist's Tricks of the Trade

Propaganda analysis is far more than identifying propagandistic techniques or the tricks of the trade. Researchers examine not only the structure and function of propagandistic messages, but also the theoretical impetus for those strategic decisions and the resulting effects on the targeted audience. And most interestingly, propaganda analysis has been a fruitful area of inquiry for both those individuals studying how to manage public opinion more effectively and those seeking to discover how better to inoculate individuals from propaganda. Doob suggested that to analyze propaganda effectively, the analyst must thoroughly examine six stages of the propaganda process:

1. The propagandist
2. The content of the propaganda
3. The perception of the propaganda
4. The initial response of the propagandees [sic]
5. The changes produced within the propagandees
6. The actions of the propagandees. (1966, 258)

Doob takes us through his six stages of analysis and provides us a guideline for the process, which he calls his "analytical attitude" process (1966, 546–47). It is clear that Doob would agree with Fisher's view of the importance of analyzing motives when studying human behavior or communication acts:

A communicator perceives a rhetorical situation in terms of a motive, and that an organic relationship exists between his perception and his response to that circumstance; his perception determines the characteristics of his discourse and his presentation. (Fisher 1970, 132)

For Doob's analytical attitude makes use of what Fisher (1970) called "motive analysis" in that Doob recommends examining the *motives of intent* behind propaganda messages. According to Fisher, "Motives are names which essentialize the interrelations of communicator, communication, audience(s), time, and place" (1970, 132). Man does not randomly act; he ponders; he explores alternatives; he projects potential outcomes; and he eventually distinguishes between alternatives and acts. This is minded, reasoned behavior. And our observations of such behavior will yield necessary and critical information about intent. For it will answer the fundamental question, "Why?"

Scholars have distinguished between "because of" motives and "in order to" motives (Schutz 1962; 1967). **Because of motives** are demographic and psychographic variables in life that "cause" or "lead" man to act in a certain way (i.e., personality, race, religion, social class, and so forth); however, an awareness of demographics and psychographics alone is not enough to understand people's behavior. For people are more than just separate sets of demographics and psychographics; each individual is a minded animal. People have objectives or goals, and they choose behaviors that will more likely lead to the achievement of those goals. Individuals, thus, have "in order to" motives. **In order to motives** create goal-seeking and goal-achieving behaviors (see Combs 1973, 54). Determining motivation is a crucial component in Doob's "analytic attitude."

Recently, Jowett and O'Donnell (1992) succinctly presented a ten-step process of propaganda analysis. A comparison of Doob's 1966 analytic attitude (546–47) with Jowett and O'Donnell's ten-step reveals the two are virtually the same in terms of the work product produced once one has followed the steps of analysis. While Jowett and O'Donnell (1992) avoided the more traditional "Who Says What in What Channel with Whom with What Effects" structure, the fundamental areas of analysis are still provided. Therefore, either one provides a sound framework for not only evaluating and responding to propaganda but also for strategically planning and executing propaganda. From either analytical technique, we are able to identify a number of sociologically based impression management strategies. However, for the novice, Doob's (1966) analytic attitude is both easier to apply while analyzing propaganda and while strategically planning propaganda campaigns, for he leaves little to the imagination. Doob spells out the many variables at each critical step of analysis while Jowett and O'Donnell leave such specification up to the individual analyst:

1. the ideology and purpose of the propaganda campaign,
2. the context in which the propaganda occurs,
3. identification of the propagandist,
4. the structure of the propaganda organization,
5. the target audience,
6. media utilization techniques,
7. special various techniques [read tactics],
8. audience reaction to various techniques [read tactics],

9. counterpropaganda, if present, and
10. effects and evaluation. (1992, 213)

PROCESSUAL MODEL OF PROPAGANDA

Jowett and O'Donnell (1992) have also provided a processual model of propaganda that helps take into account the various considerations in analyzing propagandistic messages (see figure 7.1). Jowett and O'Donnell (1992) maintain that propaganda should be viewed as a social influence process operating within a complex social system. A propaganda campaign is the management of communicative acts strategically designed to manage impressions of group members, either securing or helping to secure the propagandist's objectives. Please note that Jowett and O'Donnell emphasize interactional influence within their processual model; as they explain:

> The process of propaganda takes the form of a message flow through a network system, [sic] that includes propaganda agents, various media, and a social network, originating with an institution and ending with the possibility of response from the public or a target audience within the public. The message flow is contained within a cultural rim that is itself placed within a sociohistorical context. The model, therefore, depicts the necessity of examining the process of propagandistic communication within the multitude of features contained within a social-historical-cultural framework. The flow of propaganda from institution to public has several canals that feed into or are fed by the elements of the cultural rim, to and from the institution itself, to and from the media, and to and from the public. This indicates that as propaganda occurs it has a potential impact on the culture at any point during the process, and of course the culture has, in turn, an impact upon the process of propaganda. (1992, 265; see figure 7.1)

THE MODERN PROPAGANDA CAMPAIGN

Strategic Research and Environmental Monitoring

A sound strategic communication plan always begins with one doing his homework or conducting appropriate research. As a strategist, Goebbels showed great appreciation for the place of social scientific research in strategic propaganda management. Goebbels emphasized the significance of ongoing research and continuing intelligence gathering in the analysis of events and public opinion (Choukas 1965). For the successful propagandist is one that is highly knowledgeable about his or her intended audience, and such knowledge comes only through extensive and intensive homework or

Figure 7.1   Jowett and O'Donnell's (1992) Model of the Process of Propaganda

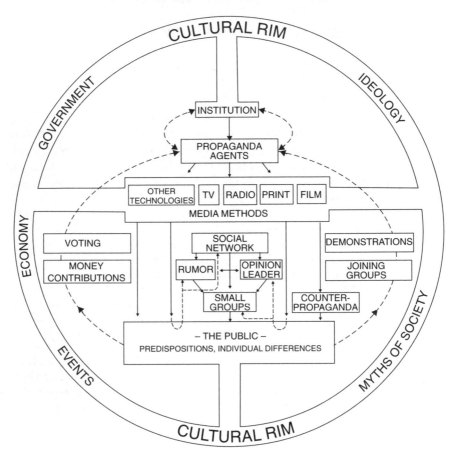

Reprinted with permission of Sage Publications, Inc., from Garth S. Jowett and Victoria O'Donnell (1999), *Propaganda and Persuasion, 3rd ed.* (Thousand Oaks, Calif.: Sage, Publications, Inc.), 371. Figure 8.1: Model of the process of propaganda. Copyright © 1999.

research. Yet as a practitioner, Goebbels, it should be noted, did very little research involving the systematic gathering and analysis of data (Doob 1950, 422). Indeed, Goebbels in his diaries was rather critical of social scientific research methods. One researcher in quoting from Goebbels's diaries wrote:

> Goebbels, moreover, tended to trust his common sense, intuition, or experience more than formal reports. He listened to his mother because, he said, "she knows the sentiments of the people better than most experts who judge from the ivory

tower of scientific inquiry, as in her case the voice of people itself speaks." (Doob 1950, 422; internal quote from p. 56 of *The Goebbels Diaries*, translated and edited by L. P. Lochner, 1948)

Goebbels's diaries and papers illustrate his belief that appropriately researched and analytically devised propaganda messages could strategically affect the enemy's behavior and policies (Doob 1950). For this reason, Goebbels engaged in what many people would describe as *gamesmanship*. In effect, Goebbels psychologically analyzed every potential act or move of his own, projecting likely *reaction scenarios,* making likelihood assessments, and ultimately projecting his own plans based on these assessments. In short, Goebbels designed propaganda as a master poker player plans his hands and rounds. Always for Goebbels, there was more than met the eye. For example, Goebbels would suppress propagandistically desirable material that might prove useful to the enemy's intelligence gathering, for he believed, for instance, that it was better for the English to think they had successfully destroyed munitions depositories than for his own people to know they hadn't. On such occasions, Goebbels played his poker close to the vest; he neither confirmed nor denied; he ignored (Doob 1950). Goebbels also carefully crafted propaganda to project the desired tone and content of what he wanted the enemy to believe. Goebbels consistently produced propaganda to document the patriotic spirit and continued high morale of his people and his warriors and disseminated this to the rest of the world. His spirited profiles of the German people were effective in both his internal and external propaganda campaigns (Doob 1950). Goebbels also believed in flushing the enemy out when it was in hiding; therefore, when intelligence indicated that the enemy was hiding negative information about its own situation, Goebbels goaded or forced his enemy to acknowledge the negative details. Goebbels believed that it was more important for the enemy to appear to be duplicitous to the rest of the world than it was for him to protect his information sources. And when Goebbels saw his opposition doing something self-destructive, he never succumbed to the joys of ridicule. Rather he kept his own pleasure at their self-destructive actions to himself, for he never wanted the other side to read his hand, knowing they would desist if they had (Doob 1950).

Whatever Goebbels's assessment and use of social scientific research methods, human behavioral research is the cornerstone in the successful crafting of modern propaganda; Choukas observes that

[w]hether in a hot war as a psychological warrior, or in the domestic conflicts of interest between organizations and institutions as a public relations counsel or advertiser, the modern propagandist cannot, if he is to be effective, rely on "dumb" instinct or happy inspiration. He must plan. He must fit his plan of attack to the

character of the group or public that is his target; and he must choose or invent the proper devices that his task demands for the occasion. (1965, 230; see also Doob 1950)

This observation brings us to four integral components of propaganda research and environmental monitoring, cultural overcoating, timing, information flow control, and counterpropaganda.

Cultural Overcoating. Perhaps the single most important research task for a propagandist is a thorough grounding in the cultural overcoating of the intended audience. While Choukas acknowledges that propaganda must take into account both the psychological and sociological make-up of the audience, he argues that through social interaction man develops a "cultural overcoating" (1965, 218), which is key to understanding both group and individual behavior. "Though it is true that thinking, feeling, and acting are strictly individual functions, it is equally true that such functions cannot ordinarily be initiated, let alone directed, were the cultural controls to lie dormant" (Choukas 1965, 218). Yet, he acknowledges, group behavior, as universal as we may stereotype it, has its variations; Choukas cautions that "No manifestation of the human mind, either in its raw, undeveloped state, or as it has been cultivated by group assistance, is uniformly distributed within a population" (1965, 221). Such differences within the targeted audience often produce a strategic dilemma for the propagandist; Choukas asks:

> How can he make an appeal general enough to pull into his net as many of those groups as possible, and yet specific enough for each group to be meaningful to it? For it pre-supposes thorough knowledge of each group's interests and traditions, and the discovery of elements that may be common to all of them. (1965, 224)

Therefore, when considering how to best influence the perceptions of an identified target group, the propagandist must recognize the potential complexities within the social system, thoroughly investigating the following variables:

- psychological mechanisms
- general culture
- social structures (and underlying division of labor, specializations)
- fears and problems
- hopes and aspirations
- distribution of variations within the group (the degree to which views are held)
- identification of barriers providing likely immunity to appeals
- identification of significant sub-groups (for the purpose of the influence goal). (Choukas 1965, 218–23)

But for Choukas even the identification and analysis of such variables does not yield the true knowledge necessary for the master propagandist, for the type of knowledge necessitated is **synergistic**—the sum or totality of the "knowledge" of the audience is much greater than the parts. This synergistic understanding is what Choukas calls "the pulse," and he describes it in this manner:

> But he [the propagandist] must know, and know thoroughly, that intangible quality called the "pulse" of a group—national morale, in the case of a nation; group loyalty, in that of lesser groups—a quality involving, since it is a resultant of, all the forces operating within the group; a quality that ultimately determines the manner in which the group might meet the internal or external threats to its existence. (1965, 241)

Thus, as did Goebbels, Choukas prizes the propagandist's acquired instincts.

Once the propagandist has analyzed the targeted group with all of its many complexities, an umbrella-like structure is created, which gives shape to the "ties that bind" (those traditions, interests, beliefs, values that members share); this structure is the propagandist's version of the group's story or **myth.** For it is ultimately sociocultural mythologies that prove to be the most binding, the most fundamentally shared meanings; such myths give meaning to a group's existence. Ellul explains:

> By "myth" we mean an all-encompassing, activating image: a sort of vision of desirable objects that have lost their material, practical character and have become strongly colored, overwhelming, all-encompassing, and which displace from the conscious all that is not related to it. Such an image pushes man to action precisely because it includes all that he feels is good, just and true. (1968, 31)

Once the propagandist determines that the myth represents the agreed-upon reality by the group, then the myth in effect separates the group from the objective world in that the myth serves as a perceptual screen through which members view and interact with the world. Such myths contain psychological and sociological reinforcing agents that work to maintain self and group-esteem and self and group-identity. In addition, propagandists recognize that group members will rigorously fight any external challenges to these myths to maintain group cohesiveness (Bettelheim and Janowitz 1950; Kecskemeti 1973). The next step for the successful propagandist, then, is to surround the target group with a repetitious dissemination of an organized myth "that tries to take hold of the entire person. Through the myth it creates, propaganda imposes a complete range of intuitive knowledge, susceptible of only one interpretation, unique and one sided, and precluding any divergence" (Ellul 1968, 11). Perhaps Qualter expressed the significance of myth best when he wrote, "It is impossible to understand the success of propaganda without also understanding how great a part of what men regard as knowledge is in fact no more than a collection of stereotypes" (Qualter 1962, 52).

Shared mythology contains **primitive patterns** that are the identified symbol systems—the signs, cues, triggers—used within a given group or culture to evoke previously agreed upon mythological meaning. Such primitive symbols or patterns when attached to propagandistic messages become cues that help arrange the subject's behavior (Choukas 1965; Kecskemeti 1973; Keller 1987). In effect, the individuals within a group become "conditioned" to respond to a message in a predictable manner. Ellul writes that "Propaganda tries first of all to create conditioned reflexes in the individual by training him so that certain words, signs or symbols, even certain persons or facts, provoke unfailing reactions" (1968, p. 31). And those conditioned reflexes are evoked both collectively and individually.

In bragging about his strategies and tactics, Goebbels once observed:

> By simplifying the thoughts of the masses and reducing them to primitive patterns, propaganda was able to present the complex process of political and economic life in the simplest terms. . . . We have taken matters previously available only to experts and a small number of specialists [read social scientists and public opinion and public relations specialists], and have carried them into the street and hammered them into the brain of the little man. (Goebbels as quoted in Combs and Nimmo 1993, 72)

For instance, Doob has argued:

> There is a strong tendency for every workman to respect his tools. For without them he would be unable to achieve his objective or at least he would achieve it less efficiently; and with them life is easier and considered better. The respect for tools is sometimes so great that people look on them as an extension of their own bodies: hurt my tools, hurt me.
>
> The tools of the propagandist are of course Ideas and the words which express Ideas. The propagandist's veneration of the Idea has already been suggested. The words themselves are held in similar awe.
>
> Propagandists tend to believe that words can accomplish anything, including miracles. People cannot eat, sleep upon, or have sexual intercourse with words, it is perfectly true, but words can make food taste better, beds appear more comfortable, and sexual intercourse—well, no doubt words can do something about that too. The belief in words leads to a corollary belief: it is merely necessary to find the right verbal combination to make propaganda successful. Somewhere, in someone, there is that right combination—maybe it is a slogan, maybe a new way of saying old things—and, if it can be found, there'll be pie in the sky and the propagandist at any rate will be very, very happy. (1948, 274)

Timing. Doob (1950) has argued that the propagandist's timing in delivering communication products is critical for the ultimate success of the propaganda and the achievement of the propagandist's goals. For this reason, environmental monitoring is essential to sound timing. Doob has identified a number of guidelines for improving timing:

1) Always be the first to name, identify, acknowledge, characterize, describe—whatever. Be first; those who are first are believed.
2) Assess the ripeness of the situation; does the circumstance now most fortuitously demand a communicative act.
3) Repeat as often as necessary for the desired impact but always avoid the annoyance of over-repetition. (Doob 1950, 435)

Propaganda messages are created with timing judgments in mind and may be viewed as working in either the long term or the short term. **Long-term propaganda** is generally facilitative propaganda in that it provides the legalistic, rational, and sometimes idealistic ground upon which later **short-term propaganda** will capitalize. Short-term propaganda usually consists of exaggerated accounts utilizing emotional appeals to action, stressing urgency, and often accompanying forms "of public fashion, or whim, immediately suitable" to the propagandist's objects (Bartlett 1940, 114).

Information Flow Control. The ultimate determination of whether to release information to the public is based on environmental monitoring, for the propagandist must determine what should be made public based on an evaluation of what is environmentally realistic, while still safeguarding the propagandist's objectives. It has been said that the flow and control of information is at the root of power, and for this reason, management of information is a carefully guarded domain within organizational structures and a heavily analyzed process. Since the days of Goebbels, we have known that the news-making process is yet another means by which leaders exercise information flow control, for they simply withhold information from the news media. Goebbels manipulated the news process as he would have another weapon of war. According to Doob (1950), Goebbels used **censorship,** or the deliberate keeping of information from the public, in a number of strategic situations. First, Goebbels would censor even information that was constructive for his cause or that cast his side in a positive light if the final outcome of a news event was yet to be determined. In other words, he would not claim victory in a major battle even though initial reports showed overwhelming numbers of enemy dead. Predictably, Goebbels censored negative information about the German position, and if he anticipated that information could be used negatively in a future context, Goebbels would forbid its dissemination, and this was particularly true for information that might demoralize the German people (see Doob 1950). Today propagandists often practice **omission,** or not giving all the details, when the details would likely hurt the propagandist's cause; but, this is effective only as long as it remains unlikely for the details to be disclosed from another source.

However, it should be recognized that withholding information or secrecy has its costs; its use may be either productive or destructive depending on the situation (Doob 1950). In our country, the secrecy has its benefits and its costs. Ransom writes:

> Because information about defense plans, policies, programs and weapons systems, if prematurely disclosed, can be of great strategic value to a potential enemy, the government has created an elaborate security system for classifying documents according to degrees of secrecy required. Such a system is not without its costs. It can actually endanger security by hampering scientific progress, alienating allies, and making difficult the existence of a well-informed electorate, or, at the very least, a knowledgeable, attentive public. (1964, 197)

Another area that takes substantial environmental monitoring is counterpropaganda, which we will consider next.

Evaluating Potential Counterpropaganda. Doob defines counterpropaganda as a propagandist's efforts seeking "to counteract a competing propaganda which has been previously, is concurrently, or may eventually begin operating" (1948, 253). However, these "efforts" may not be as obvious as one might think. Predictably, Goebbels provides us with some insights into the intricacies of environmental monitoring and counterpropaganda decision making. Goebbels carefully strategized the counterpropaganda of the Third Reich (Doob 1950). For example, the German propaganda minister recognized that the successful propagandist must decide whether to ignore the enemy's propaganda or refute it. And as a result, Goebbels reviewed enemy propaganda, using an analytical framework (see Doob 1950), to ascertain the enemy's motivations behind their own propaganda. If, for example, the enemy's propaganda was intended to provoke a reply, he ignored it. If Goebbels could prove conclusively that enemy propaganda was false, then he would expose and ridicule it. And what enemy propagandistic strategies and tactics he judged ineffective or weak, Goebbels simply ignored (Doob 1950). Always before making a rebuttal or reply, Goebbels would first analyze what potential effect such an act would have on world opinion (Doob 1950), asking himself the question, Would the Third Reich's enemies appear stronger or weaker, depending on the proposed response? And Goebbels restrained from releasing supportive propaganda that might detract from another more important piece of Nazi communication, for he understood not to overload the political news frame of the war.

Clearly, the decision whether to craft and ultimately manage a counterpropaganda campaign is a serious step for the propagandist. But if the decision is to use counterpropaganda, the process of developing and managing a counterpropaganda campaign is even more problematic. Counterpropaganda dictates a delicate balancing act, for it requires the propagandist to juggle a number of diverse fronts. As Qualter explains, it

> requires a painstaking eye for detail . . . [and] it requires efforts to build up unity, to resist the enemy's attempts to incite racial, national, political, or economic conflict within one's own country to demonstrate that victory is certain, but not so certain that effort can be relaxed, to make it clear that the cause is indeed worth the sacrifices demanded, that the leaders have the "good of the people" at heart and to show that one's Allies are worthy of the confidence placed in them. (1962, 120)

Adopting environmental monitoring and an analytical decision-making style will prove invaluable to the social marketer who is faced with a negative propaganda campaign directed at his or her company. Data gathering, environmental monitoring, careful analysis, and ultimately caution are central ingredients in the crafting and management of counterpropaganda.

In Summary. Although current social science research places a premium on the quantification of social data, the social marketing expert recognizes the significant role of quantitative research as well as the importance of experience, learned intuition, and routinized environmental monitoring in the formulation of communication strategies.

The Four Fronts of a Strategic Propaganda Campaign and the Corresponding Strategic Goals

In Lasswell's published dissertation, he implicitly suggested the four fronts a master propagandist should simultaneously tackle or address in a sophisticated propaganda campaign (1927). By analyzing the audiences for each of his explicit strategic goals, we may ascertain that Lasswell saw four fronts or groups to be critical to the propagandist's strategy for success. First, Lasswell emphasized the importance of the **internal front,** or the propagandist's own group members whom the propagandist seeks to provoke to action against a common enemy. Second, Lasswell identifies three separate groups on the external front who are of vital concern: allies, neutrals, and enemies. Lasswell's four strategic principles are

(1) To mobilize hatred against the enemy;
(2) To preserve the friendship of allies;
(3) To preserve the friendship and, if possible, to procure the co-operation of neutrals;
(4) To demoralize the enemy. (1927, 195)

To achieve these four strategic goals, propagandists have had to develop and execute appropriate tactics to fulfill each strategy. A general discussion of tactics, that is, the tactical tools of the propagandist, will follow, and a more specialized tactical discussion leading to the fulfillment of the preceding four strategic aims will be presented.

Propagandistic Tactics

The propagandist's execution of his or her strategy involves a wide repertory of tactics. The tactics of the propagandist are, simply put, communication products. Paul Linebarger once said, "The task of the propagandist is to create something which will arouse attention, will induce attitudes, and will eventually lead to action. It is a task of permanent offense. Its variations are as infinitely diverse as the imagination of mankind can make them" (as cited in Choukas 1965, 218).

We have chosen to catalogue the propagandist's tactics under the corresponding strategic goals first identified by Lasswell (1927; see above). The following tactical outline is a synthesis of the work presented by Doob (1948; 1950), Johnson-Cartee and Copeland (1991; 1997a; 1997b), Jowett and O'Donnell (1992), Lasswell (1927), and Radway (1969) and should prove useful in the execution of a propaganda strategy.

To mobilize hatred against a common enemy.
Characterize enemy as an impediment or obstruction to the group's desired goals and outcomes.
Characterize the enemy as embodying the exact opposite of what is valued.
Characterize the enemy as evil, satanic, without redeeming values.
Characterize the enemy as subhuman or inhuman.
Characterize the enemy's actions as insulting and demeaning to the group.
Characterize the enemy as vulnerable in its own depravity.
Invoke despised symbols, images, music, etc., in connection with the enemy.
Reify a disreputable act as the personification of the enemy.

To preserve the friendship of allies.
Reinforce philosophical and military-based support for the ally.
Reinforce shared commitment to the destruction of the enemy.
Reinforce satanic image of the enemy. Reinforce righteousness of the allied cause (yours and theirs).
Encourage fear of the enemy while negatively assessing their powers and ultimately predicting their destruction.
Demonstrate respect for the ally.

Demonstrate cherished friendship with ally.

Promote positive linkages in war efforts with ally in domestic propaganda.

Give credit to ally's war efforts.

Build positive images, particularly among the military, the young, and the intellectuals (who are normally influential but who are even more powerful in less-developed countries) (see Radway 1969, 146).

To preserve the friendship and, if possible, to procure the cooperation of neutrals.

Identify the neutral's interests with the defeat of the enemy.

Identify the neutral's interests with the furtherance of your interests.

Seek nonmilitary cooperative relationships with the neutral.

Seek nonmilitary cooperative relationships with the neutral that provide tangible rewards for the neutral.

Reinforce the horrors suffered and the sacrifices required in war.

Reinforce the preferred state of pacifism, if at all an option.

Characterize the enemy as militaristic and unwilling to make peace.

Distract a neutral by creating trouble for the neutral with another neutral.

Again, build positive images particularly among the military, the young, and the intellectuals (who are normally influential but who are even more powerful in less-developed countries) (see Radway 1969).

To demoralize the enemy.

Spread discouragement, highlight negative news.

Destroy confidence in things valued.

Encourage negativity and defeatism.

Encourage and cultivate distrust of leaders and allies.

Place blame for existing failures, pain, losses, or other negative conditions on internal forces such as: the governing class or rulers; an identifiable and unpopular national minority; a destructive abundance of competing minorities or interests; or a faithful ally or allies.

Substitute new hates and new enemies for old.

Urge action against new enemies by throwing off the oppressive mantles of the past.

Provide positive propaganda about self.

Associate world condemnation with their cause.

Assign guilt and moral judgment and punishment.

Coexisting Strategic Objectives. Lasswell also identified three other strategic objectives that should give direction and guidance to the propagandist's campaign:

(1) To arouse the interest of specific groups.
(2) To nullify inconvenient ideas.
(3) To avoid untruth that is likely to be contradicted before the achievement of the strategic purpose.

We will now provide a catalogue outline of suggested tactical executions appropriate to these three strategic objectives.

To arouse the interest of specific groups.
Ignore no group whether a membership group or a reference group.
Attend to all groups with the most effective appeal for that group.
Capitalize on cleavages within society by targeting specific appeals geared to further stated goals.
Call upon specialized loyalties/disloyalties within society by invoking meaningful symbols for those specialized loyalties/disloyalties.
Symbols (music, uniforms, flags, medals, photographs, cartoons, colors, art, poetry, etc.) should consistently evoke desired responses previously internalized (from other credible sources and experiences); should be readily recognized and easily learned; should be capable of being repetitively used and reinforced without waning or undesirable effects; should be finally, boomerang-proof (see Doob 1950, 436–37).
Prioritize those groups or publics already approving of the propagandist and those likely to or currently leaning toward supporting the propagandist.
Intensify efforts toward highly prioritized groups.
Take into account differences in education, religion, age, class, or social status.
Take into account subcultural beliefs or biases.
Appreciate subtleties and nuances as well as bold shots across the bow.

To nullify inconvenient ideas.
Limit access to the media.
Exert control over media content.
Deemphasize negative news.
Emphasize positive news.
Display enemies' contradictions, distortions, and hyperbole.
Provide seemingly independent corroboration of your positions.
Repeat your position over and over again in a variety of different ways.
When reporting a negative, compensate by providing a greater positive.
Expose the travails of the enemy.
Provide evidence in refutation of any unfavorable information (if possible) (Johnson-Cartee and Copeland 1991; 1997a; 1997b).

Deny unfavorable intelligence if possible.

If denial is not possible, present a sanctimonious admission (Johnson-Cartee and Copeland 1991; 1997a; 1997b).

If denial is not possible, ignore the accusation and counterattack (Johnson-Cartee and Copeland 1991; 1997a; 1997b).

If denial is not possible, counterimage (Johnson-Cartee and Copeland 1991; 1997a; 1997b).

If denial is not possible, obfuscate (Johnson-Cartee and Copeland 1991; 1997a; 1997b).

Inoculate against anticipated unfavorable characterizations or accusations (Johnson-Cartee and Copeland 1991; 1997a; 1997b)

Inoculate against highly probable losses or against those that have already occurred but have not reached the public's awareness.

Hint at secret weapons or secret plans to reverse negative situations.

Provide piecemeal disclosure of negative news.

Float indirect initiatives through a third party demanding such actions.

Provide distraction for both the media and the public by presenting unrelated but sensational event or events.

To avoid untruth that is likely to be contradicted before the achievement of the strategic purpose.

Strive for the truth.

Strive for the plausible.

Avoid untruths that would inevitably be exposed.

Avoid unnecessary specifications of either past accounts or the projected future.

Avoid self-contradiction within a group.

Avoid self-contradiction among groups likely to overlap.

Avoid self-contradiction in communicative acts likely to be widely reported.

Facilitate positive group interpretations of comments.

Avoid fabrication to achieve positive group interpretations of comments.

Propaganda Caveats

When Propaganda Boomerangs. Dodge in 1920 warned his readers about "three limitations to the processes of propaganda," however, a close reading of his work reveals that his so-called "limitations" are really conditions under which propaganda may well boomerang within the targeted population, working against the propagandist's objectives rather than for them. Dodge writes that the first "boomerang" "is emotional recoil, the second is the exhaustion of available motive force, the third is the development of internal resistance or negativism" (1920, 250–51). Dodge (1920) warns that a propagandist may so overwhelm the audience with repetitively drawn distinctions of good and bad that an emotional recoil occurs. And Dodge provides a telling example; he suggests that if you tell a teenage boy that everything he wants to do, to have, to be is "bad," and everything he doesn't want to do, to have, or be is "good" then the young man may well experience what Dodge calls "an emotional recoil." For, "the moral values may get reversed in the boy's mind. Bad may come to represent the sum-total of the satisfactory and desirable, while good may represent the sum-total of the unsatisfactory and the undesirable" (1920, 251). Second, Dodge warns that a propagandist may simply exhaust the audience by demanding too much from it. A propagandist may appeal too often, creating a situation where appeals go unheeded and may trigger a backlash (1920). For example, a propagandist's urging an audience over and over again to do "their duty," may well result in their vehemently refusing to ever do "their duty" again (Dodge 1920, 251). And Dodge writing immediately after World War I observed:

> There seems to be evidence that in some quarters at least, patriotism, philanthropy, and civic duty have been exploited as far as the present systems will carry. It is possible to exhaust our floating capital of social motive forces. When that occurs we face a kind of moral bankruptcy. (1920, 251)

Today when people receive daily computerized and individual telephone solicitations and direct-mail requests from a wide variety of local, state, national, and even international charities, is it any wonder that many Americans simply hang up when they receive such unsolicited calls?

And third, Dodge notes that when propaganda is exposed as being half-truths or lies, the audience is likely to exhibit a "negativistic defensive reaction" (1920, 252). Thus, in effect, propagandists may, by making messages vulnerable to effective counterattacks, sow the seeds of their own destruction. Dodge, in reviewing World War I propaganda, notes: "There is evidence that the moral collapse of Germany under the fire of our paper bullets [propaganda] came with the conviction that they had been systematically deceived by their own propagandists"(1920, 252).

Similarly, in 1940, F. C. Bartlett observed yet a fourth potential boomerang of propaganda. Like Dodge's exhaustion of motive force, Bartlett notes an apparent exhaustive state related to levels of fear (1940, 77). Because propagandists recognize that propaganda often capitalizes on climates of fear and anxiety, Barlett observes that many propagandists attempt to produce or enhance such climates by emphasizing continuing threats to the audience's way of life. In short, propagandists work to inflame the in-group's fear of the designated out-group. But this may well backfire or boomerang, for the use of fear is a two-edged sword.

> When fear and anxiety are aroused there may be within them an uneasy suggestion that the opposing forces which are depicted to be at work may prove the stronger. Hence, while the stimulation of fear and anxiety is almost always a prominent motive in foreign propaganda, it is less safe to rely upon this motive to any extent for the purpose of internal propaganda. The initial effect of public fear may appear to be to produce greater social cohesion, but in the end it often gives rise to lowered *morale* and disintegration. (1940, 77; emphasis in original)

And in some unusual circumstances, propaganda isn't likely to work. For instance, as Choukas noted:

> Take the democratic system. Predicated as it is upon the continuous search for truth, and the development of the well-informed citizen, it fosters an atmosphere of freedom in which all channels of public communication may be used by any one, and to their capacity.
>
> One might say: but that's just what a propagandist dreams about: no official interference. And it is true. But this very freedom also works against him.
>
> Consider the well-informed citizen. To the extent that he is informed, he cultivates habits of thought which could only spell trouble for the propagandist. He is constantly on the alert, and capable of reasoning on any issue of general concern. He is not likely therefore to allow his thinking to fall into that dangerous trap, the either-or, black and white dichotomies, so common in propagandistic appeals. In short the limitations that pester the propagandist in his appeals to reason are very much in evidence in such a society. It may be said, that the more a society evolves along democratic lines, the greater is the difficulty of capturing and holding the minds of its people by propaganda, as such habits of thought would tend to diffuse and become generally accepted by larger and larger segments of its population. There is one standard for the acceptance of any idea that a democratic society tends to establish, and that is the rational validity of that idea. (1965, 225–26)

Similarly, Huxley wrote:

> Unlike the masses, intellectuals have a taste for rationality and an interest in facts. Their critical habit of mind makes them resistant to the kind of propaganda that works so well on the majority. Among the masses instinct is supreme, and from instinct comes faith. . . . Intellectuals are the kind of people who demand evidence and are shocked by logical inconsistencies and fallacies. They regard oversimplification as the original sin of the mind and have no use for their slogans, the unqualified assertions and sweeping generalizations which are the propagandist's stock in trade. (1971, 56–63)

A PRACTICAL CHECKLIST FOR SUCCESSFUL PROPAGANDA CAMPAIGNS

Through the work of Jowett and O'Donnell (1992) and Doob (1950; 1966), we have gleaned a number of characteristics that are associated with successful propaganda campaigns and are presenting them in a Successful Propaganda Campaign Checklist:

- Chooses a fertile context or climate
- Chooses an effective delivery mechanism, that is, the propagandist
- Creates resonance
- Builds source credibility
- Monopolizes mass communication sources
- Co-opts opinion leaders
- Utilizes interpersonal and group communication channels to reinforce mass communication channels
- Provides rewards for compliance and punishments (undesirable states) for noncompliance
- Utilizes strong visual symbols
- Utilizes widely shared symbols, stereotypes, and mythologies
- Utilizes emotional arousal through emotional appeals
- Adapts propaganda as the audience responds to increase effectiveness
- Effectively deals with counterpropaganda
- Evaluates the effects of the campaign to build an information base for future campaigns.

IN CONCLUSION

Propaganda is widely used among professional communicators such as advertisers, marketers, direct-mail specialists, PR professionals, and politicians. All of these professions engage in social marketing. The study of propaganda techniques and strategies yields not only more effective propaganda campaigns but counterpropaganda as well. An appreciation of propaganda analysis and construction is a necessity for effectively utilizing social marketing.

Appendix A

The Personality Strength (PS) Scale and Weighting

Item	Weight Yes	No
1. I usually count on being successful in everything I do.	13	7
2. I am rarely unsure about how I should behave.	14	7
3. I like to assume responsibility.	15	7
4. I like to take the lead when a group does things together.	17	8
5. I enjoy convincing others of my opinions.	15	7
6. I often notice that I serve as a model for others.	16	8
7. I am good at getting what I want.	14	7
8. I am often a step ahead of others.	18	9
9. I own many things others envy me for.	15	9
10. I often give others advice and suggestions.	12	6

Maximum score: 149
Minimum score: 75

Note: The procedure of weighting is detailed by Noelle-Neumann (1985) (Weimann 1994, 256).

Appendix B

Goebbels's Propaganda Machine

Following the aftermath of World War II, the once merely unpopular "propaganda" now became not only feared, but hated because of its association with the horror and human tragedy associated with Nazi Germany. Joseph Goebbels, Hitler's minister for popular enlightenment and propaganda (Reichsministerium für Volksaufklärung und Propaganda—RMVP or more widely known as the minister of propaganda, Reichspropagandaminister) (Welch 1987, 406) was primarily responsible for creating the Nazi political reality—the dream of a thousand-year rule for the Third Reich. Researchers attempting to explain how the Nazi movement orchestrated the consent of the German people have given the credit or, more accurately, blame to Goebbels. Researchers, in effect, viewed Goebbels as "brainwashing" the German people (Arendt 1951; Broszat 1966, 62; Friedrich and Brzezinski 1956; Ruge 1967, 354; Schoenbaum 1966; Welch 1987, 405; Zeman 1973, 32). A carefully crafted web of radio presentations, propaganda films, staged pseudoevents, national military parades, torchlight parades, and elaborate ritualized dramas were believed to have transformed the average German, in Goebbels's terms, "from a little worm into part of a large dragon" (Combs and Nimmo 1993, 72). And in so doing, Goebbels helped unleash one of the most horrendous regimes the world has ever seen.

Joseph Goebbels received his Ph.D. from Heidelberg in 1921. In 1923, he joined the National Socialist movement, quickly becoming a close confidant of Hitler, and was ultimately appointed "the agitator and propagandist" for the Third Reich in Nazi Germany (1933–1945) (Combs and Nimmo 1993, 68–69). Goebbels was heavily influenced by the writings of the noted American scholar Edward L. Bernays, *Crystallizing Public Opinion* (1923) and *Propaganda* (1928).

In his work, Bernays combined psychology, mass psychology (social psychology), the study of public opinion, and public relations. Bernays saw the potential for social science research findings to significantly enhance the influence of professional communicators. He believed that the role of social science was to "scientifically evaluate the hopes, aspiration, ignorance, knowledge, apathy and prejudices" (1923, 11–33) of the public in order to construct mass-communicated messages designed to achieve "the engineering of consent" (1923, 11–33). In addition to Bernays, Goebbels also turned to French scholar Gustav LeBon and his influential work *The Crowd: A Study of the Popular Mind* (1895; 1960). Bernays's and LeBon's influence may be seen in many of Goebbels's opinions about people and society.

Goebbels had rather a "fluid" interpretation of what constituted "truth." "Whatever is right for the advancement of the party is truth. If it should coincide with factual truth, so much the better; if it doesn't, adjustments must be made" (Goebbels, as cited in Combs and Nimmo 1993, 69). And in perhaps his most quoted statement concerning "truth," Goebbels succinctly declared, "truth is what I make it" (as cited in Combs and Nimmo 1993, 69). Goebbels found in Adolf Hitler another student of propaganda and a willing partner in manipulation and deceit. Thomson has written that three men in all of human history stand out as master propagandists. Hitler is one of them. Thomson writes that "Hitler shares with Julius Caesar and Napoleon Bonaparte, the distinction of not only making massive use of new methods of propaganda but also, of quite consciously and deliberately basing his entire career on planned propaganda" (1977, 111). Hitler's appreciation of propaganda is apparent in *Mein Kampf:*

> The truth must always be adjusted to fit the need. . . . The aim of propaganda is not to try to pass judgement on conflicting rights, giving each its due, but exclusively to emphasize the right which we are asserting. Propaganda must not investigate the truth objectively, and, in so far as it is favorable to the other side, present it according to the theoretical rules of justice; but it must present only that aspect of the truth which is favorable to its own side.

> The receptive powers of the masses are very limited, and their understanding is feeble. . . . All effective propaganda must be confined to a few bare essentials and these must be expressed as far as possible in stereotyped formulas.

> These slogans should be persistently repeated until the very last individual has come to grasp the idea that has been put forward . . . the greater the scope of the message that has to be presented, the more necessary it is for the propaganda to discover that plan of action which is psychologically the most efficient. (as cited in Combs and Nimmo 1993, 69)

Goebbels was quick to understand the potential power of mass communication, and he embraced the new medium of radio, ordering the mass production of the Volksempfänger (cheap one-channel radios), which translated means the "people's receiver" (see Combs and Nimmo 1993, 71; Jowett and O'Donnell 1992, 187). Eventually, Goebbels "introduced compulsory installation of radios with loudspeakers in restaurants, factories, and most public places" (Jowett and O'Donnell 1992, 187). And he staged periods of "collective listening" when all Germans stopped what they were doing and listened to the words of Der Führer or the Reichspropagandaminister. Such "National Moments" made every German feel a part of the "dragon" or the Third Reich (see Combs and Nimmo 1993, 71). Eventually, these National Moments became compulsory, and Goebbels introduced "radio wardens" who spot-checked homes and public places to make sure that people stopped what they were doing and listened to Nazi propaganda-based programming (Jowett and O'Donnell 1992, 187).

Goebbels obtained the engineered consent, at least tacitly, of the German people. Thus, Goebbels played an instrumental role in the extermination of 5.8 million Jews during the Holocaust. Few humans have been so universally reviled by the world. His very name brings repugnance and fear into the hearts of millions. In 1945, Goebbels committed suicide in the Führerbunker with Hitler and other Nazi figures.

However, it is important to recognize that Goebbels did not so much "brainwash" the German people as he was able to discover and capitalize on their preexisting attitudes. And therein rests the horror of what transpired. The German people resented their defeat in World War I and the Allied-imposed Versailles reparations, which amounted to $120 billion (Blum, Morgan, Rose, Schlesinger, Stampp, and Vann Woodward 1973, 570). The war had ravaged Germany's economy, and the country was in no position to pay reparations. Furthermore, the Treaty of Versailles established a "guilt clause" in that it laid the blame for World War I on the shoulders of the German people by specifying that it was "the aggression of Germany" that brought about the war (Blum, Morgan, Rose, Schlesinger, Stampp, and Vann Woodward 1973, 570). The German people never accepted that they were at fault, and therefore they resented both the huge reparation bill and the loss of territories that had been part of Germany since 1870 (particularly the natural resource–rich Alsace-Lorraine). For a few years, Germany had made reparation payments, but only with $2.6 billion in loans from U.S. banks. Finally in 1923, Germany defaulted on the reparations. The German government recklessly inflated its currency, creating a situation where people had to carry bushels of currency in order to buy a loaf of bread (Blum, Morgan, Rose, Schlesinger, Stampp, and Vann Woodward 1973, 600).

The resulting economic chaos was blamed on the Allies who had written the Treaty of Versailles and the German Jews who owned a number of prominent German banks. In short, the German people were angry—angry at the economic and political situation they found themselves in during the 1920s and early 1930s. Germany and its leaders looked for someone to blame for their societal ills, and, most predictably, it was the Allies and the Jews who eventually served as their scapegoats.

America was ill-prepared for the consequences of that anger. Stephen Ambrose noted:

> What Americans did not see was that Hitler was an authentic expression of a general German desire to set things right and establish German dominance over Europe. What had gone wrong in 1914–1918, most Germans reasoned, was not that they had fought, but that they had lost. (1971, 13–14)

In addition, few Americans understood the intensity of anti-Semitism in Germany at that time. Anti-Semitism had played a prevalent part in not only German but European history. The early segregation of Jews into walled ghettos, the Spanish Inquisition of the fifteenth century, and Czarist Russia's pogroms (an organized persecution and/or extermination) give testimony to that anti-Semitism (Hexter, Pipes, and Molho 1971). However, despite such anti-Semitism, the Jewish people in Germany ultimately prospered through hard work and frugality. And by the time of the Weimar Republic, many Jewish families were highly visible in the banking, clothing, and retail arenas (Carr 1985). The German Jewish population made up less than 1 percent of the total German population, roughly 500,000 Jewish residents (Carr 1985, 30). Seventeen percent of all bankers were Jewish, 16 percent of all lawyers, and 10 percent of all dentists and medical doctors (Carr 1985, 31). The non-Jewish Germans resented their success, and the mass media negatively portrayed Jews as being "self-seeking" and "parasitic" (Welch 1987, 415). German cartoons depicted Jews as either rats who scavenge their goods from refuse or as button mushrooms that feed off horse dung (see Carr 1985; Jowett and O'Donnell 1992).

In effect, Goebbels simply fueled the German people's resentment toward the Allied forces and the Jewish population, intensifying and amplifying that resentment until he achieved the public's support for both new military invasions and the "Final Solution" to the "Jewish Question" (Welch 1987; see sidebar 4). Goebbels, in short, discovered and capitalized on the German people's deep-seated resentments and cultural hatreds by crafting and disseminating resonating messages that channeled German efforts toward the achievement of Nazi objectives.

Understandably, news reporters, social critics, and academic researchers who were trying to explain how such horror as the Holocaust could occur in an industrialized, modern society (much like those represented by the Allied forces) focused on what they judged to be the work of two madmen, the Reichspropagandaminister Goebbels and the Führer Adolf Hitler. In effect, the world considered Goebbels, in particular, an extraordinary Nazi magician, a Rasputin of the modern communication age. For it was far more comforting to view the Holocaust as the result of an evil aberration, which gained control of German politics, than to consider the possibility of man's capacity for inhumanity to man (particularly such inhumanity from "men" who seemed very like themselves). This was particularly true in the United States, where the largest single immigrant group was German.

However, as scholars gained some temporal distance from the Holocaust, research emerged that indicated that the German people either supported the actions of the Third Reich or were indifferent to its actions (Carr 1985; Gordon 1984; Kershaw 1981, 1983a, 1983b, 1985, 1986, 1988; Kulka and Rodrigue 1984). Goebbels had merely tapped what was already there. Early research had suggested that the ordinary German people were paralyzed by the Nazis' so-called reign of terror (therefore freeing the ordinary German from any guilt), but it has become abundantly clear, as revealed through recent and more objective research, that this was not the case (Mayer 1955; Merkl 1975). An examination of the historical record reveals a stunning consistency in German public behavior. In 1935, The Nuremberg Laws were passed, eliminating German citizenship for Jews and criminalizing intermarriage (Gordon 1984, 171). No public outcry was heard. Soon after the passage of these laws, Jews were driven from their public posts, and their property was confiscated (as discussed in Kershaw 1988). And again, there was no public outcry. It was another three years before the internationally condemned Reichskristallnacht occurred (the night when thousands upon thousands of German Jews were seized from their homes and either killed or sent to concentration camps—known as the "Crystal Night" because of the millions of glass shards, from broken windows in Jewish homes and businesses, lying in the streets, reflecting the streetlights). And the German people still remained silent.

And, it is clear from Security Service (SS) public opinion reports (made public after the war), the working class favored the "euthanasia" of the mentally ill and the physically or mentally handicapped. The Nazi propaganda film *Ich klage an* (I accuse) promoted euthanasia as a benefit to society in eliminating the need for tax dollars to go to the perpetual care of such individuals. And the film suggested that such killings would "cleanse" the Aryan race of such dependent aberrations. More than 70,000 such people were killed (Welch 1987, 414).

Welch (1987) makes it abundantly clear that while researchers will never be able to show exactly how many people within Germany were aware of

Hitler's Final Solution, large numbers of Germans did in fact know, as evidenced by accounts in diaries, letters, and even in bureaucratic reports unrelated to the Final Solution discovered after the war (Kershaw 1988, 147–53). As early as 1942, underground newspapers in occupied territories provided highly accurate accounts of the Jewish plight:

> Of the 400,000 Jews of Warsaw no more than 40,000 remain. In Radom 228,500 Jews out of 300,000 were exterminated. In Vilno the entire Jewish population was massacred. . . . These are not the crimes of some isolated, low-ranking officers, but the premeditated and organized actions of the Hitlerite government. In applying this diabolic plan, the men fit for work are subject to intolerable sufferings in work-camps, where they die after a short time. The women, the children, the old, the sick, and the invalid are annihilated with a bestial savagery, unprecedented in history. All torments are put in effect: gas-chambers, shooting, mine-fields, electric current, etc. (Cohen 1988, 250)

Hitler, himself, on the founding anniversary of the Nazi Party on February 24, 1942, delivered a major address, alluding to the inevitable destruction of European Jewry, which he deemed a necessary and beneficial byproduct of the war. The next day, the German newspaper *Niedersaechsische Tageszeitung* used the headline *Der Jude wird ausgerottet* or "The Jew is being exterminated" to banner the news story covering the speech. Eventually church members and church officials called for a halt to the extermination of the infirm; however, no such organized protest was made to protect Europe's Jews. But not all Germans applauded what the Nazis were doing. Gestapo records indicate that the Third Reich recognized that the liberal intelligentsia, active churchgoers, and elderly Germans were more likely to be sympathetic toward the Jews. But because such individuals had concerns of their own and did not readily identify with members of a different ethnicity and religion as they had with the physically and mentally impaired, the plight of the Jews was not a priority. Therefore, little was said, and what was said focused on the fear of American and Jewish retaliation if the Nazi actions became known (Kershaw 1988, 153–54).

Kershaw concludes that the Germans became so accustomed to the dehumanizing of Jews by the dominant socioeconomic culture and by the repetitively consistent and pervasive Nazi propaganda, that the German people became, in effect, desensitized to Jewish suffering, eventually seeing the extermination of Jews as simply another act of war—that while unpleasant and ugly it was deemed necessary (1988, 152). And in the words of Leo Kuper:

> One is left with the troublesome thought that there may not have been much resistance at all to involvement in genocide, that it is no means foreign to man-in-

society, and that many features of contemporary "civilized" society encourage the easy resort to genocidal holocausts. (1981, 137)

Thus we can say with some certainty that Goebbels, while both brilliant and evil, was not a magician. Rather, Goebbels, as a social scientist and professional communicator, used resonance to bring out the very worst in the German psyche for his own political purposes.

References

Abercrombie, N., S. Hill, and B. S. Turner, eds. 1990. *Dominant ideologies.* London: Unwin Hyman.

Ackoff, R. L., and J. R. Emshoff. 1975. Advertising research at Anheuser-Busch, Inc. (1968–1974). *Sloan Management Review* 16: 1–15.

Adams, J. S. 1976. The structure and dynamics of behavior in organizational boundary roles. In *Handbook of industrial and organizational psychology,* ed. M. D. Dunnette, 1175–99. Chicago: Rand McNally.

———. 1980. Interorganization processes and organization boundary activities. In *Research in organizational behavior,* ed. L. Cummings and B. Staw, vol. 2, 321–55. Greenwich, Conn.: JAI.

Ajzen, I., and M. Fishbein. 1980. *Understanding attitudes and predicting social behavior.* Englewood Cliffs, N.J.: Prentice Hall.

Albig, W. 1956. *Modern public opinion.* New York: McGraw-Hill.

Allen, I. L., and J. D. Colfax. 1968. The diffusion of news of LBJ's March 31 decision. *Journalism Quarterly* 45: 321–24.

Allen, V. L., and D. A. Wilder. 1978. Perceived persuasiveness as a function of response style: Multi-issue consistency over time. *European Journal of Social Psychology* 8: 289–96.

Allison, G. 1971. *Essence of decision: Explaining the Cuban missile crisis.* Boston: Little, Brown.

Allport, G. W. 1968. The open system in personality theory. In *Modern systems research for the behavioral scientist,* ed. W. Buckley, 343–50. Chicago: Aldine.

———. 1985. The historical background in social psychology. In *The handbook of social psychology, vol. II.* 3rd ed., ed. G. Lindzey and E. Aronson, 1–42. New York: Random House.

Alpert, M. 1972. Personality and the determinants of product choice. *Journal of Marketing Research* 9: 89–92.

Altheide, D. L., and J. M. Johnson. 1980. *Bureaucratic propaganda.* Boston: Allyn and Bacon.

Alwin, D. F., and Krosnick, J. A. 1985. The measurement of values in surveys: A comparison of ratings and rankings. *Public Opinion Quarterly* 49: 535–52.

Alwitt, L. F. 1985. EEG activity reflects the content of commercials. In *Psychological process and advertising effects: Theory, research, and applications,* ed. L. F. Alwitt and A. A. Mitchell. Hillsdale, N.J.: Lawrence Erlbaum.

Ambrose, S. E. 1971. *Rise to globalism: American foreign policy, 1938–1970.* Baltimore, Md.: Penguin.

Anderson, J. A. 1988. Cognitive styles and multicultural populations. *Journal of Teacher Education* 39: 2–11.

Aquilino, W. S. 1993. Effects of spouse presence during the interview on survey response concerning marriage. *Public Opinion Quarterly* 57: 358–76.

Arendt, H. 1951. *The origins of totalitarianism.* New York: Harcourt Brace.

Aristotle. 1932. *The rhetoric of Aristotle.* Trans. L. Cooper. New York: Appleton-Century-Crofts.

Asch, S. E. 1951. Effects of group pressure upon the modification and distortion of judgments. In *Groups, leadership and men: Research in human relations,* ed. H. Guetzkow, 177–90. New York: Russell and Russell.

Ayers, B. 1986, January 13. Alabama's political detour coming to an end. *The Birmingham Post Herald,* p. 5.

Balandier, G. 1985. *Anthropo-logiques.* Paris: Librairie Générale Française.

Ball-Rokeach, S. J., and M. L. DeFleur. 1976. A dependency model of mass media effects. *Communication Research* 3: 3–21.

Ball-Rokeach, S. J., W. Grube, and M. Rokeach. 1981. *Roots: The Next Generation:* Who watched and with what effect? *Public Opinion Quarterly* 45: 58–68.

Bandura, A. 1969. *Principles of behavior modification.* New York: Holt, Rinehart and Winston.

———. 1977. *Social learning theory.* Englewood Cliffs, N. J.: Prentice Hall.

Banfield, E. C. 1961. *Political influence.* New York: The Free Press of Glencoe.

Bar-Tal, D., C. Graumann, A. W. Kruglanski, and W. Stroebe, eds. 1989. *Stereotyping, prejudice, and discrimination: Changing conceptions.* New York: Springer.

Bartlett, F. C. 1940. *Political propaganda.* Cambridge, U.K.: Cambridge University Press.

Basil, M. D., C. Schooler, D. G. Altman, M. Slater, C. L. Albright, and N. Maccoby. 1991. How cigarettes are advertised in magazines: Special messages for special markets. *Health Communication* 3: 75–91.

Baus, H. M., and W. B. Ross. 1968. *Politics battle plan.* New York: Macmillan.

Beatty, S. E., L. R. Kahle, P. Homer, and S. Misra. 1985. Alternative measurement approaches to consumer values: The list of values and the Rokeach value survey. *Psychology and Marketing* 2: 181–200.

Becker, B. W., and P. E. Connor. 1979. Personal values of the heavy user of mass media. *Journal of Advertising* 21: 37–43.

Berger, P., and T. Luckmann. 1966. *The social construction of reality.* Garden City, N.Y.: Doubleday.

Berlo, D. K. 1960. *The process of communication.* New York: Holt, Rinehart and Winston.

Bernays, E. L. 1923. *Crystallizing public opinion.* New York: Boni and Liveright.

———. 1928. *Propaganda.* New York: H. Liveright.

Bertalanffy, L. V. 1968. *General system theory: Foundations, development, applications.* Rev. ed. New York: George Braziller.

Bettelheim, B., and M. Janowitz. 1950. *Dynamics of prejudice.* New York: Harper.

Birdwhistle, R. 1952. *Introduction to kinesics.* Louisville, Ky.: University of Louisville Press.
————. 1970. *Kinesics and context.* Philadelphia: University of Pennsylvania Press.
Bloch, P. H. 1986. The product enthusiast: Implications for marketing strategy. *Journal of Consumer Marketing* 3: 51–61.
Blum, J., E. S. Morgan, W. L. Rose, A. M. Schlesinger Jr., K. M. Stampp, and C. Vann Woodward. 1973. *The national experience: Part two.* 3rd ed. New York: Harcourt Brace Jovanovich.
Blumer, J. G. 1951. Elementary collective behavior. In *New outline of the principles of sociology,* ed. A. M. Lee, 185–89. New York: Barnes & Noble.
Bogart, L. 1976. *Premises for propaganda: The U. S. Information Agency's operating assumptions in the cold war.* New York: Free Press.
Booth, A., and N. Babchuk. 1972. Informal medical opinion leadership among the middle aged and elderly. *Public Opinion Quarterly* 36: 87–94.
Botan, C. H., and F. Soto. 1998. A semiotic approach to the internal functioning of publics: Implications for strategic communication and public relations. *Public Relations Review* 24: 21–44.
Braungart, R. G., and M. M. Braungart. 1979. Reference groups, social judgment, and student politics. *Adolescence* 14: 135–39.
Brewer, M. B. 1979. In-group bias in the minimal intergroup situation: A cognitive-motivational analysis. *Psychological Bulletin* 86: 307–24.
Brody, E. W., and G. C. Stone. 1989. *Public relations research.* New York: Praeger.
Brody, R., and B. Page. 1975. The impact of events on presidential popularity: The Johnson and Nixon Administrations. In *Perspectives on the presidency,* ed. A. Wildavsky, 136–48. Boston: Little, Brown.
Broom, G. M., S. Casey, and J. Ritchey. 2000. Concepts and theory of organization-public relations. In *Public relations as relationship management: A relational approach to the study and practice of public relations,* ed. J. A. Ledingham and S. D. Bruning, 3–22. Mahwah, N.J.: Lawrence Erlbaum.
Broome, B. 1991. Building shared meaning: Implications of a relational approach to empathy for teaching intercultural communication. *Communication Education* 40: 235–49.
Broszat, M. 1966. *German national socialism.* Trans. K. Rosenbaum and I. P. Boehm. Santa Barbara, Calif.: Clio Press.
Brown, J. A. C. 1963. *Techniques of persuasion.* Baltimore, Md.: Penguin.
Brown, R. 1986. *Social Psychology.* 2nd ed. New York: Free Press.
Brownfield, A. C. 1984, May 4. *Washington Inquirer,* p. 6.
Brummett, B. 1976. Some implications of "process or intersubjectivity": Postmodern rhetoric. *Philosophy & Rhetoric* 2(1): 21–51.
Buchanan, P. 1993, September 12. As quoted in the *New York Times,* p. 37.
Buck, V. E. 1966. A model for viewing an organization as a system of constraints. In *Approaches or organizational design,* ed. J. D. Thompson, 103–72. Pittsburgh, Pa.: University of Pittsburgh Press.
Burgoon, J. K., and J. L. Hale. 1984. The fundamental topoi of relational communication. *Communication Monographs* 54: 19–41.
Burnett, N. F. S. 1989. Ideology and propaganda: Toward an integrative approach. In *Propaganda: A pluralistic perspective,* ed. T. Smith III, 115–26. New York: Praeger.

Campbell, J. D., A. Tesser, and P. J. Fairey. 1986. Conformity and attention to the stimulus: Some temporal and contextual dynamics. *Journal of Personality and Social Psychology* 51: 315–24.

Cantril, H., and G. W. Allport. 1933. Recent applications of *The Study of Values*. *Journal of Abnormal and Social Psychology* 38: 259–73.

Caplan, N., and S. D. Nelson. 1973. On being useful: The nature and consequences of psychological research on social problems. *American Psychologist* 28: 199–211.

Carr, W. 1985. November. A final solution? Nazi policy towards the Jews. *History Today* 35: 30–36.

Carroll, J. S., N. L. Kerr, J. J. Alfini, F. M. Weaver, R. J. Mac Coun, and V. Feldman. 1986. Free press and fair trial: The role of behavioral research. *Law and Human Behavior* 10: 187–201.

Chaffee, S. H., and J. L. Hochheimer. 1982. The beginnings of political communication research in the United States. In *The media revolution in America and Western Europe*, edited by E. M. Rogers and F. Balle, 263–83. Norwood: Ablex.

Chan, K. K., and S. Misra. 1990. Characteristics of the opinion leader: A new dimension. *Journal of Advertising* 19: 53–60.

Charters, W. W., Jr. and T. M. Newcomb. 1958. Some attitudinal effects of experimentally increased salience of a membership group. In *Readings in social psychology*. Rev. ed., ed. E. E. Maccoby, T. M. Newcomb, and E. L. Hartley, 276–81. New York: Holt, Rinehart and Winston.

Chase, S. 1956. *Guides to straight thinking*. New York: Harper and Row.

Cheskin, L., and L. B. Ward. 1948. Indirect approach to market reactions. *Harvard Business Review*, 572–80.

Choukas, M. 1965. *Propaganda comes of age*. Washington, D.C.: Public Affairs Press.

Cialdini, R. B., R. R. Reno, and C. A. Kallgren. 1990. A focus theory of normative conduct: Recycling the concept of norms to reduce littering in public places. *Journal of Personality and Social Psychology* 58: 1015–26.

Clark, R. D., III. 1971. Group-induced shift toward risk: A critical appraisal. *Psychological Bulletin* 76: 251–70.

Clawson, C. J., and D. E. Vinson. 1978, Human values: An historical and interdisciplinary analysis. In *Contributions to Consumer Research V*, ed. H. K. Hunt, 396–402. Chicago: Association for Consumer Research.

Cline, C. G., M. H. McBride, and R. E. Miller. 1989. The theory of psychological type congruence in public relations and persuasion. In *Public relations theory*, ed. C. H. Botan and V. Hazleton, Jr., 221–39. Hillsdale, N.J.: Lawrence Erlbaum.

Cobb, R. W., and C. D. Elder. 1983. *Participation in American politics: The dynamics of agenda-building*. Baltimore, Md.: John Hopkins University.

Cohen, A. 1988. The comprehension of the final solution in France and Hungary: A comparison. In *Comprehending the Holocaust: Historical and literary research*, ed. A. Cohen, Y. Gelber, and C. Wardi, 143–265. New York: Verlag Peter Lang.

Coleman, J., E. Katz, and H. Menzel. 1966. *Medical innovation: A diffusion study*. Indianapolis: Bobbs-Merrill.

Combs, J. E. 1973. *The dramaturgical image of political man: A modernist approach to political inquiry*. Dissertation, University of Missouri.

Combs, J. E., and D. Nimmo. 1993. *The new propaganda: The dictatorship of palaver in contemporary politics*. New York: Longman.

Cooley, C. H. 1909; 1916; 1929. *Social organization: A study of the larger mind.* New York: Scribner's Sons.

Cooper, M. D., and W. L. Nothstine. 1992. *Power persuasion: Moving an ancient art into the media age.* Greenwood, Ind.: Educational Video Group.

Copeland, G. A., and D. Slater. 1985. Television, fantasy, and vicarious catharsis. *Critical Studies in Mass Communication* 2: 352–62.

Corey, L. 1971. People who claim to be opinion leaders: Identifying their characteristics by self-report. *Journal of Marketing* 35: 48–53.

Crable, R., and S. Vibbert. 1986. *Public relations as communication management.* Edina, Minn.: Bellwether Press.

Craske, M. 1997. *Art in Europe 1700–1830: A history of the visual arts in an era of unprecedented urban economic growth.* Oxford: Oxford University Press.

Cravens, D. W. 1987. *Strategic Marketing.* 2nd ed. Homewood, Ill.: Irwin.

Creedon, P. J. 1993. Acknowledging the infrasystem: A critical feminist analysis of systems theory. *Public Relations Review* 19: 157–66.

Crossman, R. H. S. 1971. Supplementary essay. In *Psychological warfare against Nazi Germany: The Sykewar campaign, D-day to VE-day.* 2nd ed., ed. D. Lerner and R. H. S. Crossman. Cambridge, Mass.: MIT University Press.

Culbertson, H. M. 1989. Breadth of perspective: An important concept for public relations. In *Public relations research annual, Vol. I,* ed. J. E. Grunig and L. A. Grunig, 3–25. Hillsdale, N.J.: Lawrence Erlbaum.

Cutlip, S. M., A. H. Center, and G. M. Broom. 1985. *Effective public relations.* 6th ed. Englewood Cliffs, N.J.: Prentice Hall.

Dallin, A., and G. W. Breslauer. 1970. *Political terror in communist systems.* Stanford, Calif.: Stanford University Press.

Daniels, T. D., and B. K. Spiker. 1991. *Perspectives on organizational communication.* Dubuque, Iowa: Wm. C. Brown.

DeFleur, M. L., W. V. D'Antonio, and L. B. DeFleur. 1973. *Sociology: Human society.* Glenview, Ill.: Scott Foresman.

Demby, E. 1974. Psychographics and from whence it came. In *Life style and psychographics,* ed. W. D. Wells, 9–30. American Marketing Association.

Deutsch, M., and H. B. Gerard. 1955. A study of normative and informational, social influences upon individual judgment. *Journal of Abnormal and Social Psychology* 51: 629–36.

Deutschmann, P., and W. A. Danielson. 1960. Diffusion of knowledge of the major news story. *Journalism Quarterly* 37: 345–55.

Dewey, J. 1927. *The public and its problems.* Denver: Alan Swallow.

Dichter, E. 1964. *Handbook of consumer motivations: The psychology of the world of objects.* New York: McGraw-Hill.

Dion, K. L., R. S. Baron, and N. Miller. 1970. Why do groups make riskier decisions than individuals? In *Advances in experimental social psychology, Vol. 5,* ed. L. Berkowitz, 306–77. New York: Academic.

Dodd, C. H. 1973. *Homophily and heterophily in diffusion of innovations: A cross-cultural analysis in an African setting.* Paper presented at the Speech Communication Association Convention, New York, November.

Dodge, R. 1920. The psychology of propaganda. *Religious Education* 15: 241–52.

Doise, W., J. P. Gachoud, and G. Mugny. 1986. Influence directe et indirecte entre groupes dans des choix esthétiques. *Cahiers de Psychologie Cognitive* 6: 283–301.

Dominick, J. R., B. L. Sherman, G. A. Copeland. 1996. *Broadcasting/Cable and beyond.* 3rd ed. New York: McGraw-Hill.

Doob, L. W. 1935. *Propaganda: Its psychology and technique.* New York: Henry Holt.

———. 1948. *Public opinion and propaganda.* New York: Henry Holt.

———. 1950. Goebbels principles of propaganda. *Public Opinion Quarterly* 14: 419–42.

———. 1966. *Public opinion and propaganda.* Hamden, Conn.: Archon Books.

Dozier, D. M., and F. C. Repper. 1992. Research firms and public relations practices. In *Excellence in public relations and communication management,* ed. J. E. Grunig, 185–215. Hillsdale, N.J.: Lawrence Erlbaum.

Dumbauld, E., ed. 1955. *The political writings of Thomas Jefferson: Representative selections.* Indianapolis, Ind.: Bobbs-Merrill.

Durkheim, E. 1893; 1947. *The division of labor in society.* Glencoe, Ill.: Free Press.

Easton, D. 1953. *The political system.* New York: Knopf.

Edelstein, A. 1997. *Total propaganda: From mass culture to popular culture.* Mahwah, N.J.: Lawrence Erlbaum.

Ehrlich, H. 1973. *The social psychology of prejudice.* New York: Wiley.

Ellul, J. 1965; 1968. *Propaganda: The formation of men's attitudes.* Trans. K. Kellen and J. Lerner. New York: Knopf.

Evan, W. M. 1966. The organization-set: Toward a theory of interorganizational relations. In *Approaches to organizational design,* ed. J. D. Thompson, 173–92. Pittsburgh, Pa.: University of Pittsburgh Press.

Evans, F. B. 1959, October. Psychological and objective factors in the prediction of brand choice: Ford versus Chevrolet. *Journal of Business* X: 340–69.

Farace, R. V., and T. Mabee. 1980. Communication network analysis methods. In *Multivariate techniques in human communication research,* ed. P. R. Monge and J. N. Cappella, 365–91. New York: Academic.

Farace, R. V., P. R. Monge, and H. Russell. 1977. *Communicating and organizing.* Reading, Mass.: Addison Wesley.

Farley, C. J. 1999, September 13. Seriously Funny. *Time,* 154, 66–69.

Feather, N. T. 1984. Protestant ethics, conservatism and values. *Journal of Personality and Social Psychology* 46: 1132–41.

Fee, E., and N. Krieger. 1993. Understanding AIDS: Historical interpretations and the limits of biomedical individualism. *American Journal of Public Health* 83: 1477–86.

Feick, L. F., and L. L. Price. 1987. The market maven: A diffuser of marketplace information. *Journal of Marketing* 51: 83–97.

Ferguson, S. D., and S. Ferguson. 1988. The systems school. In *Organizational communication.* 2nd ed., ed. S. D. Ferguson and S. Ferguson, 38–60. New Brunswick, N.J.: Transaction.

Festinger, L. 1950. Informal social communication. *Psychological Review* 57: 217–81.

———. 1954. A theory of social comparison processes. *Human Relations* 7: 117–40.

Fine, M. G. 1993. New voices in organizational communication: A feminist commentary and critique. In *Transforming visions: Feminist critiques in communication studies,* ed. S. P. Bowen and N. Wyatt, 125–66. Cresskill, N.J.: Hampton Press.

Fisher, W. R. 1970. A motive view of communication. *Quarterly Journal of Speech* 56: 131–29.

Foster, G. M. 1965. Peasant society and the image of limited good. *American Anthropologist* 67: 293–315.

Fraser, C. 1971. Group risk taking and group polarization. *European Journal of Social Psychology* 1: 493–510.

Fraser, C., and M. Billing. 1971. Risky shifts, caution shifts, and group polarization. *European Journal of Social Psychology* 1: 7–29.

Freeman, R. E. 1984. *Strategic management: A stakeholders approach.* Boston: Pitman.

Friedrich, C. J., and Z. Brzezinski. 1956. *Totalitarian dictatorship and autocracy.* Cambridge, Mass.: Harvard University Press.

Fromm, E. 1941. *Escape from freedom.* New York: Rinehart and Winston.

Gans, H. 1979. *Deciding what's news.* New York. Vintage.

Garceau, O. 1951. Research in the political process. *American Political Science Review* 45: 69–85.

Gardner, J. W. 1961. *Excellence.* New York: Harper and Row.

Garreau, J. 1981. *Nine nations of North America.* Boston: Houghton Mifflin.

Gitlin, T. 1978. Media sociology: The dominant paradigm. *Theory and Society* 6: 205–53.

Glazer, N., and D. P. Moynihan. 1963. Beyond the melting pot; the Negroes, Puerto Ricans, Jews, Italians, and Irish of New York City. Cambridge, Mass.: Harvard University Press.

Goffman, E. 1974. *Frame analysis: An essay on the organization of experience.* Cambridge, Mass.: Harvard University Press.

Goldhaber, G. M., M. P. Yates, T. D. Porter, and R. Lesniak. 1978. Organizational communication: 1978. *Human Communication Research* 5: 76–96.

Goldsmith, R. E., M. T. Stith, and J. D. White. 1987. Race and sex differences in self-identified innovativeness and opinion leadership. *Journal of Retailing* 63: 411–25.

Gordon, S. 1984. *Hitler, Germans, and the "Jewish Question."* Princeton, N.J.: Princeton University Press.

Gouge, C., and C. A. Fraser. 1972. A further demonstration of group polarization. *European Journal of Social Psychology* 2: 95–97.

Gould, S. J. 1997. The use of psychographics by advertising agencies: An issue of value and knowledge. In *Values, lifestyles, and psychographics,* ed. L. R. Kahle and L. Chiagouris, 217–29. Mahwah, N.J.: Lawrence Erlbaum.

Gove, P. B. 1986. *Webster's third new international dictionary of the English language unabridged.* Springfield, Mass.: Merriam-Webster.

Graham, W. K., and J. Balloun, J. 1973. An empirical test of Maslow's need theory. *Journal of Humanistic Psychology* 13: 97–108.

Greenberg, B. S. 1964a. Diffusion of the news about the Kennedy assassination. *Public Opinion Quarterly* 28: 225–32.

———. 1964b. Person to person communication in the diffusion of news events. *Journalism Quarterly* 41: 489–94.

Grice, H. P. 1975. Logic and conversation. In *The logic of grammar,* ed. D. Davidson and G. Harman, 65–75. Belmont, Calif.: Dickenson

———. 1978. Further notes on logic and conversation. In *Syntax and semantics, vol. 9, Pragmatics,* ed. P. Cole and J. L. Morgan, 113–28. New York: Academic.

Grube, J. W., I. L. Weir, S. Getzlaf, and M. Rokeach. 1984. Own values systems, value images and cigarette smoking. *Personality and Social Psychology Bulletin* 10: 306–13.

Grunert, S. C., K. G. Grunert, and K. Kristensen. 1991. The cross-cultural validity of the List of Values (LOV): A comparison of nine samples from five countries. In *Development and applications in structural equation modeling*, ed. J. J. G. Schmeets, M. E. P. Odekerken, and F. J. R. van de Pol, 89–99. Amsterdam: Sociometric Research Foundation.

Grunig, J. E. 1976. Organizations and public relations: Testing a communication theory. *Journalism Monographs* 46: 1–59.

————. 1984. Organizations, environments, and models of public relations. *Public Relations Research & Education* 1: 6–29.

Grunig, J. E., and F. C. Repper. 1992. Strategic management, publics, and issues. In *Excellence in public relations and communication management*, ed. J. E. Grunig, 117–57. Hillsdale, N.J.: Lawrence Erlbaum.

Guiltinan, J. P., and K. B. Monroe. 1980. Identifying and analyzing consumer shopping strategies. In *Advances in consumer research, vol. 7*, ed. J. Olson, 745–48. Ann Arbor, Mich.: Association for Consumer Research.

Guthrie, G. M. 1972. The shuttle box of subsistence attitudes. In *Attitudes, conflict, and social change*, ed. B. T. King and E. McGinnies, 192–210. New York: Academic.

Gutman, J. 1982. A means-end chain model based on consumer categorization processes. *Journal of Marketing* 46: 60–72.

Hall, A. D., and R. E. Fagen. 1968. Definition of system. In *Modern systems research for the behavioral scientist*, ed. W. Buckley, 81–92. Chicago: Aldine.

Hall, E. 1963. A system for the notation of proxemic behavior. *American Anthropologist* 65: 1003–26.

————. 1966. *The hidden dimension*. New York: Random House.

Hall, E. T. 1959. *The silent language*. New York: Doubleday.

Hamilton, D. 1981. *Cognitive processes in stereotyping and intergroup behavior*. Hillsdale, N.J.: Lawrence Erlbaum.

Hardin, C. D., and E. T. Higgins. 1996. Shared reality: How social verification makes the subjective objective. In *Handbook of motivation and cognition, vol. 3*, ed. R. M. Sorrentino and E. T. Higgins, 28–84. New York: Guilford.

Harrell, G. D. 1986. *Consumer Behavior*. San Diego, Calif.: Harcourt Brace Jovanovich.

Haworth, L. 1960. The experimental society: Dewey and Jordon. *Ethics* 71: 27–40.

Heath, M. R., and S. J. Bekker. 1986. *Identification of opinion leaders in public affairs, educational matters, and family planning in the township of Atteridgeville*. Pretoria: Human Sciences Research Council.

Heider, F. 1946. Attitudes and cognitive organization. *Journal of Psychology* 21: 107–12.

Henry, W. A. 1976, May. Cultural values do correlate with consumer behavior. *Journal of Marketing Research* 13: 121–27.

Hensehl, A. M. 1971. The relationship between values and behavior: A developmental hypothesis. *Child Development* 42: 1997–2007.

Heston, C. 1997. Private speech as president of the National Rifle Association, invitation fundraiser, Tuscaloosa, Alabama, The Hinton Mansion.

Hexter, J. H., R. Pipes, and A. Molho. 1971. *Europe since 1500*. New York: Harper & Row.

Higie, R. A., L. E. Feick, and L. L. Price. 1987. Types and amount of word-of-mouth communications about retailers. *Journal of Retailing* 63: 260–78.

Hill, R. J., and C. M. Bonjean. 1964. News diffusion: A test of the regulatory hypothesis. *Journalism Quarterly* 41: 336–42.

Hirschman, E. C., and M. B. Holbrook. 1982, Summer. Hedonic consumption: Emerging concepts, methods and propositions. *Journal of Marketing* 46: 92–101.

Hitler, A. 1943; reprinted in 1971. The struggle of the early period—the significance of the spoken word. From *Mein Kampf* by Adolf Hitler, translated by Ralph Manheim. Copyright 1943, by Houghton Mifflin Company. In *Readings in speech.* 2nd ed., ed. H. A. Bosmajian, 74–89. New York: Harper & Row Publishers, 1971.

Ho, Y. C. 1969. *Homophily in the diffusion of innovations in Brazilian villages.* Master's thesis, East Lansing, Mich.: Michigan State University.

Hobbes, T. 1909. *Hobbes' Leviathan.* Oxford: Clarendon.

Hollander, E. P. 1975. Independence, conformity, and civil liberties: Some implications from social psychological research. *Journal of Social Issues* 31: 55–67.

———. 1976. Independence, conformity, and civil liberties. In *Current perspectives in social psychology,* ed. E. P. Hollander, and R. G. Hunt, 412–19. London: Oxford University Press.

Homer, P., and L. R. Kahle. 1988. A structural equation test of values-attitude-behavior hierarchy. *Journal of Personality and Social Psychology* 54: 638–46.

Horton, D., and R. Wohl. 1956. Mass communication and para-social interaction: Observations on intimacy at a distance. *Psychiatry* 19: 215–29.

Horton, R. L. 1979, May. Some relationships between personality and consumer decision-making. *Journal of Marketing Research* X: 244–45.

Howard, J. A. 1977. *Consumer behavior: Application and theory.* New York: McGraw-Hill.

Hustad, T., and E. Pessemier. 1974. The development and application of psychographic, life style, and associated activity and attitude measures. In *Life style and psychographics,* ed. W. Wells, 33–67. Chicago: American Marketing Association.

Huxley, A. L. 1971. Propaganda in a dictatorship. In *Readings in speech.* 2nd ed., ed. H. A. Bosmajian, 56–63. New York: Harper and Row.

Hyman, H. H., C. R. Wright, and R. K. Hopkins. 1962. *Application of methods of evaluation: Four studies of the Encampment for Citizenship.* Berkeley, Calif.: University of California Press.

Inkeles, A. 1954. The totalitarian mystique. In *Totalitarianism,* ed. C. J. Friedrich. Cambridge, Mass.: Harvard University Press.

Jackman, M. R., and M. S. Senter. 1983. Different, therefore unequal: Beliefs about trait differences between groups of unequal status. *Research in Social Stratification and Mobility* 2: 309–35.

Jackson, G. 1973. A preliminary bicultural study of value orientations and leisure attitudes. *Journal of Leisure Research* 5: 10–22.

Jackson, J. M. 1965. Structural characteristics of norms. In *Current studies in social psychology,* ed. I. D. Steiner and M. Fishbein, 301–9. New York: Holt, Rinehart and Winston.

Janis, I. L. 1954. Personality correlates of susceptibility to persuasion. *Journal of Personality* 22: 504–18.

———. 1972. *Victims of groupthink.* Boston: Houghton Mifflin.

———. 1973. Groupthink. *Yale Alumni Magazine* 36: 16–19.

———. 1976. Groupthink. In *Current perspectives in social psychology,* ed. E. P. Hollander and R. G. Hunt, 406–8. London: Oxford University Press.

Johnson, J. D. 1993. *Organizational communication structure.* Norwood, N.J.: Ablex.

Johnson (aka Johnson-Cartee), K., G. Copeland, and M. Huttenstine. 1988. *Perceived differences in men and women as expert news sources in analytical and historical presentations.* Unpublished paper. University of Alabama.

Johnson-Cartee, K. S., and G. A. Copeland. 1991. *Negative political advertising: A coming of age.* Hillsdale, N.J.: Lawrence Erlbaum.

———. 1997a. *Inside political campaigns: Theory and practice.* Westport, Conn.: Praeger.

———. 1997b. *Manipulation of the American voter: Political campaign commercials.* Westport, Conn.: Praeger.

Johnson-Cartee, K. S., G. A. Copeland., A. Marquez, J. Buford, and J. Stephens. 1998. Examining the demise of the National Republican Coalition. *International Harvard Journal of Press/Politics* 3(2): 34–54.

Johnson-Cartee, K., C. Elebash, and G. A. Copeland. 1992. *The political advertising of George Corley Wallace of Alabama: A case study of negativity.* Paper presented at the annual convention of the Association of Education in Journalism and Mass Communication. Boston, Mass., in August 1992.

Johnston, A., and A. B. White. 1994. Communication styles and female candidates: A study of the political advertising during the 1986 senate elections. *Journalism Quarterly* 71: 321–29.

Jowett, G. S., and V. O'Donnell. 1992. *Propaganda and persuasion.* 2nd ed. Newbury Park, Calif.: Sage.

———. 1993. *Propaganda and persuasion.* 3rd ed. Thousand Oaks, Calif.: Sage.

Kahle, L. R. 1986. The nine nations of North America and the value basis of geographic segmentation. *Journal of Marketing* 50: 37–47.

Kahle, L. R., S. E. Beatty, and P. Homer. 1986. Alternative measurement approaches to consumer values: The List of Values (LOV) and Values and Life Styles (VALS). *Journal of Consumer Research* 13: 405–9.

Kahle, L. R., P. M. Homer, R. M. O'Brian, and D. M. Boush. 1997. Maslow's hierarchy and social adaptation as alternative accounts of value structures. In *Values, lifestyles, and psychographics,* ed. L. R. Kahle and L. Chiagouris, 111–35. Mahwah, N.J.: Lawrence Erlbaum.

Kahle, L. R., B. Poulos, and A. Sukhdial. 1988. Changes in social values in the United States during the past decade. *Journal of Advertising Research* 28: 35–41.

Kamakura, W. A., and J. A. Mazzon. 1991. Value segmentation: A model for the measurement of values and value systems. *Journal of Consumer Research* 18: 208–18.

Kaplan, N. 1968. Reference groups and interest group theories of voting. In *Readings in reference group theory and research,* ed. H. H. Hyman and E. Singer. New York: Free Press.

Kassarjian, H. H. 1971, November. Personality and consumer behavior: A review. *Journal of Marketing Research* 8: 409–18.

———. 1981. Low involvement: A second look. In *Advances in consumer research, vol. 8,* ed. K. B. Monroe, 299–303. Ann Arbor, Mich.: Association for Consumer Research.

Kassin, S. M., L. N. Williams, and C. L. Saunders. 1990. Dirty tricks of cross-examination: The influence of conjectural evidence on the jury. *Law and Human Behavior* 14: 373–84.

Katz, D. 1964. The motivational basis of organizational behavior. *Behavioral Science* 9: 131–46.

Katz, D., and R. Kahn. 1966. *The social psychology of organizations.* New York: Wiley.

Katz, E. 1957. The two-step flow of communication: An up-to-date report on an hypothesis. *Public Opinion Quarterly* 21: 69–78.

Katz, E., J. G. Blumer, and M. Gurevitch, 1974. Utilization of mass communication by the individual. In *The uses of mass communication: Current perspectives on gratifications research,* ed. J. G. Blumler and E. Katz, 19–32. Beverly Hills, Calif..: Sage.

Katz, E., and P. Lazarsfeld. 1955. *Personal influence.* New York: Free Press.

———. 1960. *Personal influence.* Glencoe, Ill.: Free Press.

Kecskemeti, P. 1973. Propaganda. In *Handbook of Communication,* ed. I. de Sola Pool, F. F. Frey, W. Schramm, N. Maccoby, and E. B. Parker, 844–70. Chicago: Rand McNally.

Keller, K. L. 1987. Memory factors in advertising: The effect of advertising retrieval cues on brand evaluations. *Journal of Consumer Research* 14: 316–33.

Kelley, H. H. 1952. Attitudes and judgments as influenced by reference groups. In *Readings in social psychology.* Rev. ed., ed G. E. Swanson, T. M. Newcomb, and E. L. Hartley, 410–14. New York: Holt, Rinehart and Winston.

———. 1955. Salience of membership and resistance to change of group-anchored attitudes. *Human Relations* 8: 275–89.

Kennamer, J. D. 1989. Deceptive advertising and the power of suggestion. In *Propaganda: A pluralist perspective,* ed. T. Smith III, 141–49. New York: Praeger.

Kennedy, J. F. 1956. *Profiles in courage.* New York: Harper.

Kennedy, P. F., R. J. Best, and L. R. Kahle. 1989. An alternative method for measuring value-based segmentation and advertising positioning. In *Current issues and research in advertising,* ed. J. L. Leigh and C. R. Martin, Jr. Ann Arbor: University of Michigan Press.

Kershaw, I. 1981. The persecution of the Jews and German popular opinion in the Third Reich. In *Yearbook of the Leo Baeck Institute, vol. 26.* London: Leo Baeck Institute.

———. 1983a. How effective was Nazi propaganda? In *Nazi propaganda: The power and the limitations,* ed. D. Welch, 180–205. London: Leo Baeck Institute.

———. 1983b. *Popular opinion and political dissent in the Third Reich.* Oxford: Oxford University Press.

———. 1985. *The Nazi dictatorship, problems, and perspectives of interpretation.* London: Leo Baeck Institute.

———. 1986. German popular opinion and the "Jewish Question," 1939–43; some further reflections. In *Die Juden im Nationalsozializtichen Deutschland 1933–43/The Jews in Nazi Germany 1933–43,* ed. A. Panchenfed. London: Leo Baeck Institute.

———. 1988. German popular opinion during the "Final Solution": Information, comprehension, reactions. In *Comprehending the Holocaust: Historical and literary research,* ed. A. Cohen, Y. Gelber, and C. Wardi, 145–58. New York: Verlag Peter Lang.

Kimball, R. K., and E. P. Hollander. 1974. Independence in the presence of an experienced but deviate group member. *Journal of Social Psychology* 93: 281–92.

Kingdon, J. W. 1970. Opinion leadership in the electorate. *Public Opinion Quarterly* 34: 256–61.

Klapper, J. T. 1960. *The effects of mass communication.* Glencoe, Ill.: Free Press.

Kluckhorn, C. 1951. Values and value orientations in the theory of action: An exploration in definition and classification. In *Toward a general theory of action,* ed. T. Parsons and E. Shils, 388–433. Cambridge, Mass.: Harvard University Press.

Knapp, M. L. 1972. Nonverbal communication in human interaction. New York: Holt Rinehart and Winston.

Knietal, T. 1982, December. Secrets of propaganda broadcasting. *Popular communication: The monitoring magazine,* 8–21.

Knower, F. H. 1935. Experimental studies of change in attitude: I. A study of the effect of oral argument on changes of attitude. *Journal of Social Psychology* 6: 315–47.

Koenig, F. 1985. *Rumor in the marketplace: The social psychology of commercial hearsay.* Dover, Mass.: Auburn House.

Koestler, A. 1967. *The ghost in the machine.* New York: Macmillan.

Kogan, N., and M. A. Wallach. 1964. *Risk-taking: A study in cognition and personality.* New York: Holt.

Koponen, A. 1960, September. Personality characteristics of purchasers. *Journal of Advertising Research* 1: 6–12.

Kornhauser, W. 1953. *The politics of mass society.* Glencoe, Ill.: Free Press.

Kramer, N. J. T. A., and J. de Smit. 1977. *Systems thinking: Concepts and notions.* Leiden: Martinus Nijhoff.

Kraus, S., and D. Davis. 1976. *The effects of mass communication on political behavior.* University Park: Pennsylvania State University Press.

Krauthammer, C. 1992, March. Buchanan explained. *Washington Post Weekly Edition,* 9–15, p. 28.

Kruglanski, A. W., and O. Mayseless. 1987. Motivational effects in the social comparison of opinions. *Journal of Personality and Social Psychology* 53: 834–42.

Kulik, J. A., and S. E. Taylor. 1980. Premature consensus on consensus? Effects of sample-based versus self-based consensus information. *Journal of Personality and Social Psychology* 39: 871–79.

Kulka, O. D., and A. Rodrigue. 1984. The German population and the Jews in the Third Reich. Recent publications and trends in research on German society and the "Jewish Question." *Yad Vashem Studies* 16: 421–35.

Kuper, L. 1981. *Genocide: Its political use in the twentieth century.* New Haven, Conn.: Yale University Press.

Lasswell, H. D. 1927; 1938; 1972. *Propaganda technique in the World War.* New York: Garland Publishing.

———. 1934. *Propaganda. In the Encyclopedia of the social sciences. Vol. 12,* 521–28. New York: Macmillan.

———. 1935. The person: Subject and object of propaganda. *The Annals of the American Academy of Political and Social Science* 197: 187–93.

———. 1948. The structure and function of communication in society. In *The communication of ideas,* ed. L. Bryson, 37. New York: Harper & Row.

———. 1958. *Politics: Who gets what, when, how.* New York: Meridian.

Lasswell, H. D., and Blumsenstock, D. 1939. *World revolutionary propaganda: A Chicago study.* New York: Knopf.

Latané, B., and J. M. Darley. 1969. Bystander "apathy." *American Behavioral Scientist* 57: 244–68.

Lau, R. R. 1980. *Negativity in political perceptions.* Unpublished manuscript, University of California, Department of Psychology, Los Angeles.

———. 1982. Negativity in political perception. *Political Behavior* 4: 353–78.

————. 1985. Two explanations for negativity effects in political behavior. *American Journal of Political Science* 29: 119–38.

Lazar, W. 1963. Life style concepts and marketing. *Conference Proceedings Series.* Chicago: American Marketing Association, 130–39.

Lazarsfeld, P. F. 1970. Sociology. In *Main trends of research in the social and human sciences.* Paris: UNESCO.

Lazarsfeld, P. F., B. Berelson, H. Gaudet. 1948. *The people's choice.* New York: Duell, Sloan, & Peard.

LeBon, G. 1895; 1960. *The crowd: A stuff of the popular mind.* New York: Viking.

Lee, A. M., and E. B. Lee, eds. 1939. *The fine art of propaganda.* New York: Harcourt Brace.

Lenart, S. 1994. *Shaping political attitudes: The impact of interpersonal communication and mass media.* Thousand Oaks, Calif.: Sage.

Leonard-Barton, D. 1985. Experts as negative opinion leaders in the diffusion of a technological innovation. *Journal of Consumer Research* 11: 914–26.

Levine, J. M. 1989. Reaction to opinion deviance in small groups. In *Psychology of group influence,* ed. P. B. Paulus. Hillsdale, N.J.: Erlbaum.

Levine, J. M., L. M. Bogart, and B. Zdaniuk. 1996. Impact of anticipated group membership on cognition. In *Handbook of motivation and cognition, vol. 3: The interpersonal context,* ed. R. M. Sorrentino and E. T. Higgins, 531–69. New York: Guilford.

Levine, J. M., and R. L. Moreland. 1991. Culture and socialization in work groups. In *Perspectives on socially shared cognition,* ed. L. B. Resnick, J. M. Levine, and S. D. Teasley. Washington, D.C.: American Psychological Association.

Levine, J. M., and C. J. Ranelli. 1978. Majority reaction to shifting and stable attitudinal deviates. *European Journal of Social Psychology* 8: 5–70.

Levy, S. J. 1966. Social class and consumer behavior. In *On knowing the consumer,* ed. J. W. Newman, 146–60. New York: Wiley.

Lewin, K. 1948. *Resolving social conflicts: Selected papers on group dynamics.* New York: Harper & Row.

Lewis, S. A., C. J. Langan, and E. P. Hollander. 1972. Expectation of future interaction and the choice of less desirable alternatives in conformity. *Sociometry* 35: 440–47.

Likert, R. 1967. *The human organization: Its management and value.* Hightstown, N.J.: McGraw-Hill.

Lippmann, W. 1965. *Public Opinion.* New York: Free Press.

Littlejohn, S. W. 1992. *Theories of human communication.* 4th ed. Belmont, Calif.: Wadsworth.

Lochner, L. P., trans. and ed. 1948. *The Goebbels diaries.* New York: Doubleday.

Loden, M. 1985. *Feminine leadership or how to succeed in business without being one of the boys.* New York: Times Books.

Loden, M., and J. B. Rosener. 1991. *WORKFORCE AMERICA! Managing employee diversity as a vital resource.* Homewood Hills, Ill.: Business One Irwin.

Lowi, T. J. 1995. *The end of the Republican era.* Norman: University of Oklahoma Press.

Luchins, A. S., and E. H. Luchins. 1955. On conformity with true and false communications. *Journal of Social Psychology* 42: 283–303.

MacDonald, J. F. 1989. Propaganda and order in modern society. In *Propaganda: A pluralistic perspective,* ed. T. Smith III, 23–35. New York: Praeger.

Mackie, D. M. 1986. Social identification effects in group polarization. *Journal of Personality and Social Psychology* 50: 720–28.

Maier, N. R. F., and L. R. Hoffman. 1965. Acceptance and quality of solutions as related to leader's attitudes toward disagreement in group problem-solving. *Journal of Applied Behavioral Science* 1: 373–86.

Mailer, N. 1973. *Marilyn.* New York: Galahad.

Mancuso, J. R. 1969. "Why not create opinion leaders for new product information?" *Journal of Marketing* 33: 20–25.

Mansfield, M. 1990. Political communication in decision-making groups. In *New directions in political communication: A resource book,* ed. D. L. Swanson and D. Nimmo, 255–30. Newbury Park, Calif.: Sage.

March, J., and H. Simon. 1958. *Organizations.* New York: Wiley.

Martilla, J. A. 1971. Word-of-mouth communication in the industrial adoption process. *Journal of Marketing Research* 8: 73–78.

Martin, L. J. 1971, November. Effectiveness of international propaganda. *Annals of the American Academy of Political and Social Science* 398: 61–70.

Maslow, A. 1970. *Motivation and personality.* 2nd ed. New York: Harper & Row.

Matthews, D. R. 1960. *U. S. Senators and their world.* New York: Vintage.

Mayer, M. 1955. *They thought they were free: The Germans 1933–1945.* Chicago: Chicago University Press.

McCarty, J. A., and L. J. Shrum. 1993a. The role of personal values and demographics in predicting television viewing behavior: Implications for theory and application. *Journal of Advertising* 22: 77–101.

McCauley, C. R. 1972. Extremity shifts, risky shifts and attitude shifts after group discussions. *European Journal of Social Psychology* 2: 417–36.

McQuail, D. 1994. *Mass communication theory: An introduction.* 3rd ed. London: Sage.

McQuarrie, E. F., and D. Langmeyer. 1985, Winter. Using values to measure attitudes toward discontinuous innovations. *Psychology and Marketing* 2: 239–52.

Mentzel, H., and E. Katz. 1955. Social relations and innovation in the medical profession. *Public Opinion Quarterly* 19: 337–52.

Merkl, P. 1975. *Political violence under the Swastika: 581 early Nazis.* Princeton, N.J.: Princeton University Press.

Merton, R. K. 1949. Patterns of influence. In *Communication research,* ed. P. F. Lazarsfeld and F. N. Stanton, 180–219. New York: Harper and Brothers.

———. 1957. Social theory and social structure. Glencoe, Ill.: Free Press.

Miethe, T. D. 1985. The validity and reliability of value measurements. *Journal of Psychology* 119: 441–53.

Mill, J. S. 1956. *On Liberty.* Ed. by C. V. Shields, first printed in 1859. Indianapolis, Ind.: Bobbs-Merrill.

Miller, J. G. 1978. *Living systems.* New York: McGraw-Hill.

Miller, G. R. 1980. On being persuaded: Some basic distinctions. In *Persuasion: New directions in theory & research,* ed. M. E. Rologg and G. R. Miller, 11–28. Newbury Park, Calif.: Sage.

———. 1987. Persuasion. In *Handbook of communication science,* ed. C. R. Berger and S. H. Chaffee, 446–83. Beverly Hills, Calif.: Sage.

Mitchell, A. 1983. *The nine American lifestyles: Who we are and where we are going.* New York: Macmillan.

Mitchell, M. G., ed. 1970. *Propaganda, polls, and public opinion.* Englewood Cliffs, N.J.: Prentice Hall.

Moch, M. K. 1980. Job involvement, internal motivation, and employees' integration into networks of work relationships. *Organizational Behavior and Human Performance* 25: 15–31.

Moffitt, M. A. 1994, Summer. Collapsing and integrating concepts of 'public' and 'image' into a new theory. *Public Relations Review* 20: 159–70.

Monge, P. 1977. The systems perspective as a theoretical basis for the study of human communication. *Communication Quarterly* 25: 19–29.

————. 1982. System theory and research in the study of organizational communications: The correspondence problem. *Human Communication Research* 8: 245–61.

Moore, B. 1954. *Terror and progress—USSR.* Cambridge, Mass.: Harvard University Press.

Moore, M. 1975. Rating vs. ranking in the Rokeach Value Survey: An Israeli Comparison. *European Journal of Social Psychology* 5: 405–8.

Morrison, A. M. 1992. *The new leaders: Guidelines on leadership diversity in America.* San Francisco, Calif.: Jossey-Bass.

Mortensen, C. D. 1972. *Communication: The study of human interaction.* New York: McGraw-Hill.

Moscovici, S. 1976. *Social influence and social change.* London: Academic.

————. 1985. Social influence and conformity. In *The handbook of social psychology, vol. II.* 3rd ed., ed. G. Lindzey, and E. Aronson, 347–412. New York: Random House.

Moscovici, S., and C. Faucheux. 1972. Social influence, conformity bias, and the study of active minorities. In *Advances in experimental social psychology, vol. 6,* ed. L. Berkowitz, 149–202. New York: Academic.

Moscovici, S., and E. Lage. 1976. Studies in social influence III: Majority versus minority influence in a group. *European Journal of Social Psychology* 6: 149–74.

Moscovici, S., and M. Naffrechoux. 1969. Influence of a consistent minority on the responses of a majority in a color perception task. *Sociometry* 32: 365–79.

Moscovici, S., and C. Nemeth. 1974. Minority influences. In *Basic group processes,* ed. P. Paulus. New York: Springer-Verlag.

Moscovici, S., and P. Neve. 1972. Studies on group polarization of judgments III: Majorities, minorities and social judgments. *European Journal of Social Psychology* 2: 221–44.

Moscovici, S., and M. Zavollini. 1969. The group as a polarizer of attitudes. *Journal Personality and Social Psychology* 12: 125–35.

Mugny, G. 1982. *The power of minorities.* London: Academic.

Mugny, G., C. Kaiser, and S. Papastamou. 1983. Influence minoritaire, identification et relations entre groupes: Étude expérimentale autour d'une votation. *Cahiers de Psychologie Sociale* 19: 1–30.

Mugny, G., and S. Papastamou. 1980. When rigidity does not fail: Individualization and psychologization as resistances to the diffusion of minority innovations. *European Journal of Social Psychology* 10: 43–61.

Mugny, G., and J. A. Pérez. 1985. Influence sociale, conflit et identification: Étude expérimentale autour d'une persuasion "manquée" lore d'une votation. *Cahiers de Psychologie Sociale* 6: 1–13.

————. 1991; 1987. *The social psychology of minority influence.* Trans. by V. W. Lamongie (Le Déni et la raison). Cambridge: Cambridge University Press.

Munson, J. M., and S. H. McIntyre. 1979, February. Developing practical procedures for the measurement of personal values on cross-cultural marketing. *Journal of Marketing Research* 16: 48–52.

Munson, J. M., and E. F. McQuarrie. 1988. Shortening the Rokeach Value Survey for use in consumer research. *Advances in Consumer Research* 15: 381–86.

Munson, M. J., and W. A. Spivey. 1981. Product and brand-user stereotypes among social classes: Implications for advertising strategy. *Journal of Advertising Research* 21: 37–46.

Murry, J. P., Jr., J. L. Lastovicka, and J. R. Austin. 1997. The value of understanding the influence of lifestyle trait motivations on consumption beliefs. In *Values, lifestyles, and psychographics*, ed. L. R. Kahle and L. Chiagouris, 45–68. Mahwah, N.J.: Lawrence Erlbaum.

Myers, J. H., and T. S. Robertson. 1972. Dimensions of opinion leadership. *Journal of Marketing Research* 4: 41–46.

Nemeth, C. J., and B. M. Staw. 1989. The tradeoffs of social control and innovation in groups and organization. In *Advances in experimental social psychology, vol. 22*, ed. L. Berkowitz, 175–210. New York: Academic.

Newcomb, T. M. 1950. *Social psychology.* New York: Dryden.

———. 1953. An approach to the study of communication acts. *Psychological Review* 60: 393–404.

Nie, N. H., S. Verba, and J. R. Petrocik. 1976. *The changing American voter.* Cambridge, Mass.: Harvard University Press.

———. 1979. *The changing American voter.* Cambridge, Mass.: Harvard University Press.

Nimmo, D. 1978. *Political communication and public opinion in America.* Santa Monica, Calif.: Goodyear.

Nimmo, D., and J. Combs. 1983. *Mediated political realities.* New York: Longman.

Noelle-Neumann, E. 1973. Return to the concept of powerful mass media. *Studies of Broadcasting* 9: 67–112.

———. 1981. Mass media and social change in developed societies. In *Mass media and social change*, ed. E. Katz and T. Szecsko. Beverly Hills, Calif.: Sage.

Novack, T. P., and B. MacEvoy. 1990. On comparing alternative segmentation schemes: The List of Values (LOV) and Values and Life Styles (VALS). *Journal of Consumer Research* 17: 105–9.

Nugent, J. W. (undated). *Murder in the first degree.* New York: The Wall Street Underground.

O'Donnell, V., and G. S. Jowett. 1989. Propaganda as a form of communication. In *Propaganda: A pluralist perspective*, ed. T. Smith III, 49–64. New York: Praeger.

O'Donnell, V., and J. Kable. 1982. *Persuasion: An interactive dependency approach.* New York: Random House.

Ornstein, N. J. 1983. The open Congress meets the President. In *Both ends of the avenue*, ed. A. King, 185–211. Washington, D.C.: American Enterprise Institute for Public Policy Research.

Ornstein, N. J., R. L. Peabody, and D. W. Rohde. 1985. The Senate through the 1980s: Cycles of change. In *Congress reconsidered.* 3rd ed., ed. L. C. Dodd and B. I. Oppenheimer, 13–33. Washington, D.C.: Congressional Quarterly Press.

Oxford Analytica. 1986. *America in perspective: Major trends in the United States through the 1990s.* Boston, Mass.: Houghton Mifflin.

Packard, V. 1957. *The hidden persuaders.* New York: David McKay.

Palmgreen, P., II, and J. D. Rayburn. 1985a. A comparison of gratification models of media satisfaction. *Communication Monographs* 52: 334–46.

———. 1985b. An expectancy-value approach to media gratifications. In *Media gratification research: Current perspectives,* ed. K. E. Rosengren, L. A. Wenner, and P. Palmgreen, 61–72. Beverly Hills, Calif.: Sage.

Palmgreen, P., L. A. Wenner, and K. E. Rosengren. 1985. Uses and gratifications research: The past ten years. In *Media gratifications research: Current perspectives,* ed. K. E. Rosengren, L. A. Wenner, and P. Palmgreen, 11–37. Beverly Hills, Calif.: Sage.

Parsons, T. 1969. Suggestions for a sociological approach to the theory of organizations. In *A sociological reader on complex organizations,* ed. A. Etzioni, 32–46. New York: Holt, Rinehart and Winston.

Pattl, C. H., and C. F. Frazer. 1988. *Advertising: A decision-making approach.* Chicago: Dryden.

Pavlik, J. V. 1987. *Public relations: What research tells us.* Newbury Park, Calif.: Sage.

Pearson, R. 1990. Ethical values or strategic values: The two faces of systems theory in public relations. *Public Relations Research Annual* 2: 219–34.

Peffley, M., and J. Hurwitz, J. 1993. *The political impact of racial stereotypes.* Paper presented at the annual meeting of the American Political Science Association. Washington, D.C., September 2–5.

Peirce, C. S. 1960. *Collected papers of Charles Sanders Peirce.* Ed. C. Hartshorne and P. Weiss. Cambridge, Mass.: Harvard University Press.

Perez, J. A., G. Mugny, and P. Roux. 1989. Evitement de la confrontation idéologique: Quelques déterminants psychosociaux des stratégies persuasives. *Revue Internationale de Psychologie Sociale* 2: 153–63.

Perris, A. 1985. *Music as propaganda: Art to persuade, art to control.* Westport, Conn.: Greenwood.

Pettigrew, T. 1979. The ultimate attribution error: Extending Allport's cognitive analysis of prejudice. *Personality and Social Psychology Bulletin* 5: 461–76.

———. 1981. Extending the stereotype concept. In *Cognitive processes in stereotyping and intergroup behavior,* ed. D. L. Hamilton, 301–31. Hillsdale, N.J.: Lawrence Erlbaum.

Phillipe, R. 1980. *Political graphics: Art as a weapon.* New York: Abbeville.

Pitts, R. E. Jr., and A. G. Woodside. 1983. Personal values influences on consumer product and brand preferences. *Journal of Social Psychology* 119: 37–53.

Plummer, J. 1971–1972. Life style patterns: A new constraint for mass communications research. *Journal of Broadcasting* 16: 78–89.

Plummer, J. T. 1985, January. How personality makes a difference. *Journal of Advertising Research* 24: 27–31.

Pratkanis, A., and E. Aronson. 1991. *Age of propaganda: The everyday use and abuse of persuasion.* New York: Freeman.

Prensky, D., and C. Wright-Isak. 1997. Advertising, values, and the consumption community. In *Values, Lifestyles, and psychographics,* ed. L. R. Kahle and L. Chiagouris. Mahwah, N.J.: Lawrence Erlbaum.

Presthus, R. 1978. *The organizational society.* Rev. ed. New York: St. Martin's.

Price, L. L., and L. F. Feick. 1995. Everyday market helping behavior. *Journal of Public Policy & Marketing* 14: 255–66.

Price, L. L., and A. Guskey-Federouch. 1988. Couponing behaviors of the market maven: Profile of a super couponer. *Advances in Consumer Research* 1(5): 354–59.

Price, V., and H. Oshagan. 1995. Social-psychological perspectives on public opinion. In

Public opinion and the communication of consent, ed. T. Glaser and C. T. Salmon, 177–206. New York: Guilford.

Pruitt, D. G. 1971. Choice shifts in group discussion: An introductory review. *Journal of Personality and Social Psychology* 20: 339–60.

Psy-Ops Bonanza. 1991, June 17. *Newsweek,* 23–24.

Qualter, T. H. 1962. *Propaganda and psychological warfare.* New York: Random House.

———. 1985. *Opinion control in the democracies.* New York: St. Martin's.

Radway, L. I. 1969. *Foreign policy and national defense.* Atlanta: Scott Foresman.

Rank, H. 1984. *The pep talk.* Park Forest, Ill.: The Counter-Propaganda Press.

Rankin, W. L., and J. W. Grube, J. W. 1980. A comparison of ranking and rating procedures for value system measurement. *European Journal of Social Psychology* 10: 233–46.

Ransom, H. H. 1964. *Can American Democracy Survive Cold War?* Garden City, N.Y.: Doubleday.

Rao, A. G., and E. M. Rogers. 1980. Caste and formal education in interpersonal diffusion of an innovation in two Indian villages. *Indian Journal of Extension Education* 16: 1–19.

Rayburn, J. D., and P. Palmgreen. 1984. Merging uses and gratifications and expectancy value theory. *Communication Research* 2: 537–62.

Redding, W. C. 1979. Organizational communication theory and ideology: An overview. In *Communication yearbook 3,* ed. D. Nimmo, 309–41. New Brunswick, N.J.: Transaction.

Reis, A., and J. Trout. 1986. *Positioning: The battle for your mind.* New York: Warner.

Revett, J. 1968, December 30. Market research '68 term: Psychographics. *Advertising Age,* 16.

Reynolds, E. V., and J. D. Johnson. 1982. Liaison emergence: Relating theoretical perspectives. *Academy of Management Review* 7: 551–59.

Reynolds, T. J., and A. B. Craddock. 1988, April/May. The application of the MECCAS model to the development and assessment of advertising strategy: A case study. *Journal of Advertising Research* 28: 43–54.

Reynolds, T. J., and J. Gutman. 1988, February/March. Laddering theory, method, analysis, and interpretation. *Journal of Advertising Research* 28: 11–31.

Rice, R. E., and C. Atkin. 1994. Principles of successful public communication campaigns. In *Media effects: Advances in theory and research,* ed. J. Bryant and D. Zillmann, 365–88. Hillsdale, N.J.: Lawrence Erlbaum.

Richards, W., Jr. 1985. Data, models, and assumptions in network analysis. In *Organizational communication: Traditional themes and new directions,* ed. R. McPhee and P. Tompkins, 109–28. Newbury Park, Calif.: Sage.

Richey, M. H., R. J. Koenigs, H. W. Richey, and R. Fortin. 1975. Negative salience on impressions of character: Effects of unequal proportions of positive and negative information. *The Journal of Social Psychology* 97: 233–41.

Richmond, V. P. 1977. The relationship between opinion leadership and information acquisition. *Human Communication Research* 4: 38–43.

———. 1980. Monomorphic and polymorphic opinion leadership within a relatively closed communication system. *Human Communication Research* 6: 111–15.

Rieken, G., and U. Yavas. 1986. Seeking donors via opinion leadership. *Journal of Professional Services and Marketing* 2: 109–16.

Riesman, D., N. Glazer, and R. Denney. 1950. *The lonely crowd: A study of the changing American character.* New Haven, Conn.: Yale University Press.

Riley, J. W., Jr., and M. W. Riley. 1959. Mass communication and the social system. In *Sociology today,* ed. R. K. Merton, L. Broom, and L. S. Cottrell, 537–78. New York: Basic.

Roberts, D. F., and N. Maccoby. 1985. Effects of mass communication. In *Handbook of social psychology, vol. II.* 3rd ed., ed. G. Lindsey and E. Aronson, 539–98. New York: Random House.

Roberts, K. H., and C. A. O'Reilly III. 1979. Some correlations of communication roles in organizations. *Academy of Management Journal* 4: 283–93.

Robertson, T. S., J. Zielinski, and S. Ward. 1984. *Consumer behavior.* Glenview, Ill.: Scott Foresman.

Robinson, J. P. 1974. The press as kingmaker. *Journalism Quarterly* 51: 587–94.

———. 1976. Interpersonal influence in election campaigns: Two step flow hypothesis. *Public Opinion Quarterly* 40: 304–19.

Rogers, E. M. 1969. *Modernization among peasants.* New York: Holt.

———. 1973a. *Diffusion of innovations.* 3rd ed. New York: Free Press.

———. 1973b. Mass media and interpersonal communication. In *Handbook of Communication,* ed. I. de Sola Pool, F. F. Frey, W. Schramm, N. Maccoby, and E. B. Parker, 290–310. Chicago: Rand McNally.

———. 1983. *The diffusion of innovations.* 3rd ed. New York: Free Press.

———. 1995. *Diffusion of innovations.* 4th ed. New York: Free Press.

Rogers, E. M., and R. Agarwala-Rogers. 1976. *Communication in organizations.* New York: Free Press.

Rogers, E. M., and D. L. Kincaid. 1981. *Communication networks: Toward a new paradigm of research.* New York: Free Press.

Rogers, E. M., and F. Shoemaker. 1971. *The communication of innovations: A cross cultural approach.* New York: Free Press.

Rogers, E. M., and L. Svenning. 1969. *Modernization among peasants: The impact of communication.* New York: Holt, Rinehart and Winston.

Rokeach, M. 1960. *The open and closed mind.* New York: Basic.

———. 1973. *The nature of human values.* New York: Free Press.

Rokeach, M., and S. Ball-Rokeach. 1984. *Influencing behavior and belief through television.* New York: Free Press.

Roper, E. 1975. *Trends in public opinion toward television and other mass media 1959–1974.* New York: Television Information Office.

Rosenberg, M. 1957. *Occupations and values.* Glencoe, Ill.: Free Press.

Rubin, A. M., and S. Windahl. 1986. The uses and dependency model of mass communication. *Critical Studies in Mass Communication* 3: 184–99.

Rubin, R. B., and M. P. McHugh. 1987. Development of parasocial interaction relationships. *Journal of Broadcasting & Electronic Media* 31: 279–92.

Ruge, W. 1967. *Deutschland von 1917 bis 1933: Von der grossen Sozialistischen Oktoberrevolution bis zum ende der Weimarer Republik.* Berlin: Deutscher Verlagder.

Sapir, E. 1935. Communication. In *Encyclopedia of the social sciences.* New York: Macmillan.

Saunders, J. J., L. L. Davis, and D. M. Monsees. 1974. Opinion leadership in family planning. *Journal of Health and Social Behavior* 15: 217–27.

Saussure, R. 1916. *Course in general linguistics.* Trans. W. Baskins. New York: Philosophical Library.

Schattschneider, E. E. 1960. *The semi-sovereign people: An elitist's view of democracy in America.* New York: Holt, Rinehart and Winston.

Schiffman, L. G., and V. Gaccione. 1974. Opinion leaders in institutional markets. *Journal of Marketing* 38: 49–53.

Schlesinger, A. M., Jr. 1965. *A thousand days.* Boston: Houghton Mifflin.

Schoenbaum, D. 1966. *Hitler's social revolution: Class and status in Nazi Germany, 1933–1939.* Garden City, N.Y.: Doubleday.

Schutz, A. 1962. *Collected Papers vol. 1, The problem of social reality.* Ed. Maurice Natanson. The Hague: Martinus Nijhoff.

———. 1967. *The phenomenology of the social world.* Evanston, Ill.: Northwestern University Press.

———. 1970. *On phenomenology and social relations.* Chicago: University of Chicago Press.

Schwartz, M. 1993. *New times in the old South or why Scarlett's in therapy and Tara's going condo.* New York: Harmony.

Schwartz, T. 1972. *The responsive chord.* Garden City, N.Y.: Anchor.

———. 1976. The inside of the outside. In *The new style in election campaigns,* ed. R. Agranoff, 344–58. Boston: Holbrook.

Scott, J. C., III, and D. O'Hair. 1989. Expanding psychographic concepts in public relations: The composite audience profile. In *Public relations theory,* ed. C. Botan and V. Hazelton Jr., 203–19. Hillsdale, N.J.: Lawrence Erlbaum.

Sears, D. O. 1969. Political behavior. In *The handbook of social psychology 5.* 2nd ed., ed. G. Lindzey and E. Aronson, 315–458. Reading, Mass.: Addison Wesley.

Shannon, C. E., and W. Weaver. 1949. *The mathematical theory of communication.* Urbana: University of Illinois Press.

Sherif, M. 1936. *The psychology of social norms.* New York: Harper.

Shibutani, T. 1955. Reference groups as perspectives. *American Journal of Sociology* 60: 562–69.

Shils, E. A., and M. Janowitz. 1948. Cohesion and disintegration in the Wehrmacht in World War II. *Public Opinion Quarterly* 12: 289–315.

Short, K. R. M., ed. 1983. *Film and radio propaganda in World War II.* Knoxville: University of Tennessee Press.

Shultz, R. H., and R. Godson. 1984. *Dezinformatsia: Active measures in Soviet strategy.* Washington, D.C.: Pergamon-Brassey's.

Siegel, A. E., and S. Siegel. 1957. Reference groups, membership groups, and attitude change. *Journal of Abnormal and Social Psychology* 55: 360–64.

Sigelman, L., and S. A. Tuch. 1997. Metastereotypes: Black's perceptions of whites' stereotypes of Blacks. *Public Opinion Quarterly* 61: 87–101.

Simmel, G. 1922. *Conflict and the web of group affiliations.* Trans. R. Bendix in 1955. Glencoe, Ill.: Free Press.

Slama, M. E., and A. Tashchian. 1985. Selected socioeconomic and demographic characteristics associated with purchasing involvement. *Journal of Marketing* 49: 72–82.

Smith, D. R., and L. K. Williamson. 1977. *Interpersonal communication.* Dubuque, Iowa: Wm. C. Brown.

Smith, T., III, ed. 1989a. Propaganda: And the techniques of deception. In *Propaganda: A pluralistic perspective,* ed. T. Smith III, 65–97. Westport, Conn.: Praeger.

———. 1989b. *Propaganda: A pluralistic perspective.* Westport, Conn.: Praeger.

Smith, W. A. 1997. Social marketing: Beyond the nostalgia. In *Social marketing: Theoretical and practical perspectives,* ed. M.E. Goldberg, M. Fishbein, and S. E. Middlestadt, 21–28. Mahwah, N.J.: Lawrence Erlbaum.

Snyder, M., W. Mischel, and B. E. Lott. 1960 or 1972. Value, information, and conformity behavior. *Journal of Personality* 28: 333–41.

Sproule, J. M. 1991. Propaganda and American ideological critique. In *Communication Yearbook 14,* ed. J. A. Anderson, 211–38. Newbury Park, Calif.: Sage.

Stanton, W. J. 1978. *Fundamentals of Marketing.* 5th ed. New York: McGraw-Hill.

Stern, B. B., and S. J. Gould. 1988. The consumer as financial opinion leader. *Journal of Retail Banking* 10: 4–52.

Stern, E., and S. Keller. 1953. Spontaneous group references in France. *Public Opinion Quarterly* 17: 208–17.

Storm over Tropical Fantasy. 1991, April 22. *Newsweek,* 34.

Stroebe, W., and C. Insko. 1989. Stereotype, prejudice, and discrimination: Changing conceptions in theory and research. In *Stereotyping and prejudice: Changing conceptions,* ed. D. Bar-Tal, C. Graumann, A. Kruglanski, and W. Stroebe, 3–34. New York: Springer.

Suchman, E. A., and H. Menzel. 1955. The interplay of demographic and psychological variables in the analysis of voting surveys. In *The language of social research: A reader in the methodology of social research,* ed. P. Lazarsfeld and M. Rosenberg, 148–55. New York: Free Press.

Sue, S., R. E. Smith, and C. Caldwell. 1973. Effects of inadmissible evidence on the decisions of simulated jurors: A moral dilemma. *Journal of Applied Social Psychology* 3: 345–53.

Szanto, G. H. 1978. *Theater and propaganda.* Austin: University of Texas Press.

Tajfel, H. 1969. Social and cultural factors in perception. In *The handbook of social psychology, vol. 3,* ed. G. Lindzey and E. Aronson, 30–45. Reading, Mass.: Addison Wesley.

———. 1972. Experiments in a vacuum. In *The context of social psychology,* ed. J. Israel and H. H. Tajfel, 45–55. London: Academic.

———. 1982. The socialpsychology of intergroup relations. *Annual Review of Psychology* 33: 1–39.

Thayer, L. 1968. *Communication and communication systems: In organization, management, and interpersonal relations.* Homewood, Ill.: Richard D. Irwin.

Thomas, R. R., Jr. 1991. *Beyond race and gender: Unleashing the power of your total work force by managing diversity.* New York: American Management Association.

Thomson, O. 1977. *Mass persuasion in history.* Edinburgh: Paul Harris.

Thorelli, H. B., H. Becker, and J. Engledow. 1975. *The information seekers.* Cambridge, Mass.: Ballinger.

Thorelli, H. B., and S. V. Thorelli. 1977. *Consumer information systems and consumer policy.* Cambridge, Mass.: Ballinger.

Tichenor, P. J., G. A. Donohue, and C. N. Olien. 1977, Winter. Community research and evaluating community relations. *Public Relations Review* 3: 96–109.

Tjosvold, D. 1991. *The conflict-positive organization: Stimulate diversity and create unity.* Reading, Mass.: Addison Wesley.

Troldahl, V. C., and R. Van Dam. 1965. A new scale for identifying public-affairs opinion leaders. *Journalism Quarterly* 42: 626–34.

Turner, J. C. 1975. Social comparison and social identity: Some prospects for intergroup behavior. *European Journal of Social Psychology* 5: 5–34.

———. 1982. Towards a cognitive redefinition of the social group. In *Social identity and intergroup relations,* ed. H. Tajfel, 15–40. Cambridge: Cambridge University Press.

———. 1983. Some comments on 'The measurement of social orientations in the minimal group paradigm.' *European Journal of Social Psychology* 13: 351–67.

———. 1985. Social categorization and the self-concept: A social cognitive theory of group behavior. In *Advances in group processes, vol. 2,* ed. E. J. Lawler, 77–122. Greenwich, Conn.: JAI.

———. 1987. *Rediscovering the social group: A self-categorization theory.* Oxford: Basil Blackwell.

Turner, J. C., and P. J. Oakes. 1989. Self-categorization theory and social influence. In *Psychology of group influence.* 2nd ed., ed. P. B. Paulus, 233–78. Hillsdale, N.J.: Lawrence Erlbaum.

Turner, J. H., and L. Beeghley. 1981. *The emergence of sociological theory.* Homewood, Ill.: The Dorsey Press.

Turner, R. H. 1956. Role-taking, role standpoint, and reference group behavior. *American Journal of Sociology* 61: 316–28.

Van Dijk, T. A. 1995. Elite discourse and the reproduction of racism. In *Hate speech,* ed. R. K. Whillock and D. Slayden, 1–27. Thousand Oaks, Calif.: Sage.

Van Maanen, J. 1977. Experiencing organization: Notes on the meaning of careers and socialization. In *Organizational careers: Some new perspectives,* ed. J. Van Maanen. New York: Wiley.

Van Maanen, J., and E. H. Schein. 1979. Toward a theory of organizational socialization. In *Research in organizational behavior: An annual series of analytical essays and critical reviews,* ed. B. M. Staw. Greenwich, Conn.: JAI Press.

Veblen, T. 1948. *The portable Veblen.* Ed. Max Lerner. New York: Viking.

Vinokur, A. 1971. A review and theoretical analysis of the effect of group processes upon individual and group decisions involving risk. *Psychological Bulletin,* 231–50.

Vinson, D. E., and J. M. Munson. 1976. Personal values: An approach to market segmentation. In *Marketing: 1877–1976 and beyond,* ed. K. L. Bernhardt, 313–17. Chicago: American Marketing Association.

Vinson, D. E., J. E. Scott, and L. M. Lamont. 1977, April. The role of personal values in marketing and consumer behavior. *Journal of Marketing* 41: 44–50.

Vonnegut, K. 1963. *Cat's cradle.* New York: Dell.

Walsh, R. H., M. Z. Ferrell, and W. T. Tolone. 1976. Selection of reference group, permissiveness attitudes, and behavior: A study of two consecutive panels. *Journal of Marriage and Family* 38: 495–507.

Ward, L. W. 1985. *The motion picture goes to war: The U.S. government film effort during World War I.* Ann Arbor, Mich.: UMI Research Press.

Waterston, A. 1997. Anthropological research and the politics of HIV prevention: Towards a critique of policy and priorities in the age of AIDS. *Social Science Medicine* 44: 1381–91.

Watzlawick, P. 1967. *Pragmatics of human communication: A study of interaction patterns, pathologies, and paradoxes.* New York: Norton.

Watzlawick, P., J. H. Beavin, and D. Jackson. 1967. *Pragmatics of human communication.* New York: Norton.

Wegner, D. M., R. Wenzlaff, R. M. Kerker, and A. E. Beattie. 1981. Incrimination through innuendo: Can media questions become public answers? *Journal of Personality and Social Psychology* 40: 822–32.

Weimann, G. 1982. On the importance of marginality: One more step into the two-step flow of communication. *American Sociological Review* 47: 764–73.

———. 1991. The influentials: Back to the concept of opinion leaders? *Public Opinion Quarterly* 55: 267–79.

———. 1994. *The influentials: People who influence people.* Albany: SUNY Press.

Weiss, M. J. 1988. *The clustering of America.* New York: Harper & Row.

Weissberg, R. 1976. *Public opinion and popular government.* Englewood Cliffs, N.J.: Prentice Hall.

Welch, D. 1987. Propaganda and indoctrination in the Third Reich: Success or failure? *European History Quarterly* 17: 403–22.

Wells, W. D. 1975. Psychographics: A critical review. *Journal of Marketing Research* 12: 196–213.

Wells, W. D., and D. J. Tigert. 1971, August. Activities, interests, and opinions. *Journal of Advertising Research* 11: 27–35.

Wenner, L. A. 1985. The nature of news gratifications. In *Media gratifications research: Current perspectives,* ed. K. A. Rosengren, L. A. Wenner, and P. Palmgreen, 171–93. Beverly Hills, Calif.: Sage.

Westley, B. 1971. Communication and social change. *American Behavioral Scientist* 14: 719–42.

Whillock, R. K. 1995. The use of hate as a stratagem for achieving political and social goals. In *Hate speech,* ed. R. K. Whillock and D. Slayden, 28–54. Thousand Oaks, Calif.: Sage.

Whorf, B. L. 1956. *Language, thought, and reality; selected writings.* Ed. John B. Carroll. Cambridge, Mass.: Technology Press of the Massachusetts Institute of Technology.

Whyte, W. H., Jr. 1956. *The organization man.* New York: Simon & Schuster.

Wilder, D. A. 1981. Perceiving persons as a group: Categorization and intergroup relations. In *Cognitive processes in stereotyping and intergroup behavior,* ed. D. L. Hamilton, 213–57. Hillsdale, N.J.: Lawrence Erlbaum.

———. 1984. Predictions of belief homogeneity and similarity following social categorization. *British Journal of Social Psychology* 23: 323–33.

Wilensky, H. L. 1967. *Organizational intelligence.* New York: Basic.

Williams, R. M., Jr. 1959. Friendship and social values in a suburban community. *Pacific Sociological Review* 1: 3–10.

Winograd, T. 1977. A framework for understanding discourse. In *Cognitive processes in comprehension,* ed. M. A. Just and P. E. Carpenter, 63–88. Hillsdale, N.J.: Lawrence Erlbaum.

Woolf, L. 1953. *Principia politica.* London: Hogarth.

Wright, C. R., and M. Cantor. 1967. The opinion seeker and avoider: Steps beyond the opinion leader concept. *Pacific Sociological Review* 10: 33–43.

Young, S., and B. Feigin. 1975, July. Using the benefit chain for improved strategy formulation. *Journal of Marketing* 39: 72–74.

Zeman, Z. A. B. 1973. *Nazi propaganda.* Rev. ed. Oxford, England: Oxford.

Ziff, R. 1974. The role of psychographics in the development of advertising strategy and copy. In *Life style and psychographics,* ed. W. D. Wells, 129–55. American Marketing Association.

Zotti, E. 1985. Thinking psychographically. *Public Relations Journal* 41: 26–30.

Index

absolute information, 70
attitudes versus values, 91
audience, 75–76

Bay of Pigs, 39
brainwashing, 4

censorship, 183
Claritas, 102
cognitive traits, 12; communication inter-
    action, 51; linear models, 51; "one can-
    not not communicate," 52;
    transactional, 51–54; transaction
    defined, 51–52
conformity, 38–42
congruence model, 62–63; convergence,
    63; physical level, 62; psychological
    level, 62–63; social level, 63
conspicuous consumption, 81
co-orientation theory, 56–60; A-B-X
    model, 57–60; asymmetry, 57; attrac-
    tion among members, 60; complemen-
    tarity, 59; homogeneity of orientation,
    60; homogeneity of perceived consen-
    sus, 60; symmetry, 57
counterpropaganda, 184–85
cultural configurations, 13–14; and politi-
    cal mythology, 14
cultural traits, 12–15
culture, 10

demographics, 82–84
dependency model, 127–30, 136
direct effects paradigm, 109–11
discriminatory in-group behavior, 21
distributed information, 70
divergence of meanings, 63

Elmira County voting study, 111
ethnocentrism defined, 21

fact-by-conspiracy reasoning, 157
formal groups, 26
functionalist communication approach,
    130

geo-demographics, 101–4
GeoVALS, 104
group conformity, 55
group decision-making problems, 39–40
group norms, 26–27; and deviant behavior,
    43; independence, 43–46; indepen-
    dence and innovation, 44–46; innova-
    tion stages, 45–46
groups, 26–31; defined, 26; diffusion of
    responsibility, 42; informational influ-
    ence, 27; new member indoctrination,
    56; normative influence, 27; personal
    detachment, 42; polarization effect, 42;
    and risky-shift phenomenon, 42
groupthink, 39–42; decision rationaliza-

tion, 40; direct pressure, 40; illusion of invulnerability, 40; inherent morality, 40; methods to avoid, 41; *mind guards,* 40; self-censorship, 40; stereotypes, 40

hedonic consumption, 88
hierarchical value map (HVM), 106–7
Hierarchy of Needs, 89–90
hypodermic needle theory, 110

ideology, 13
individual-blame, 60
influentials, 124–27; identifying, 126; and market opinion leadership, 125
information circuits, 63
informational groups, 26
in-groups, 20–21; behaviors, 47–50; defined, 20; reasoning, 21
innovation, 45
Institute for Propaganda Analysis (IPA), 163–64
interpersonal communication effects, 110, 113
intragroup cohesion, 22
iVALS, 100–101

Janus effect, 68

laddering, 104–7; preference-consumption differentials, 104; inferring values from product preference, 105–6; triadic sorting, 104
LeisureStyles, 101
lifestyles, 84–89, 94–96; defined, 94–95; surveys, 84–89, 96
limited media effects, 113–19
List of Values (LOV), 93–94

magic bullet theory, 110
magnification of perceived differences, 22
market opinion leaders, 119–24; activation, 121; market mavens, 122–24
market segmentation, 79–80
Maslow, Hierarchy of Needs, 89–90
mass, 25–26
mass society theory, 110
material traits, 12

media effects levels, 129. *See also* two-step flow theory
Mediamark Research, Inc., 101
media use by voters studies, 111
message system, levels of: denotative, 53; interpretive, 53; relational, 53
metastereotype, 22
mob anarchy, 25
mothers' club, 18–20
motivational research, 85–88
motives: "because of," 176; "in order to," 176
multistep flow, 118–19
mutual identification, 23

network analysis, 70–74; boundary spanners, 74; groups, 73; isolates, 74; liaisons, 73; links, 72; nodes, 71; symmetry, 72
network convergence model, 60–64; web of group affiliations, 62
nonconformity, 43–50
nonverbal communication, 52–53; content, 52; gesture, 53; proxemics, 53
normative traits, 12
norms, 27; conforming to a group, 28–29, 35; descriptive, 27; injunctive, 27; internalization of, 28; patterns of, 29; patterns of in sororities, 32–33; public compliance, 28

opinion leadership, 111–19; activism, 114–15; community, 115; cosmopolites, 112; culture, 116; horizontal sources, 117; information exposure, 116; information processing, 116; and innovations, 114–15; interest cluster, 115; localites, 111–12; monomorphs, 112; polymorphs, 112; public individuation, 116; social dimensions, 113; spheres of influence, 112
out-group behavior, 46–50; defined, 20, 46–47; negotiation style, 46

Peace Corps, 17
peasantry, 16–20

personality tests, 85

person blame, 60–61

persuasion, 2–3; emotional, 2–3; facts, 2–3; feedback, 6; shared characteristics with propaganda, 6

Planned Parenthood Federation of Korea (PPFK), 17–20

political communication, 152

political mythology, 14

Potential Rating Index for Zip Markets (PRIZM), 102–4; clusters defined, 102–4

powerful media effects, 134–35

propaganda, 2–6, 137–92; accidental suasion, 150–51; agitation, 145–46; analytical tools, 175–76; art, 141–42; boomerangs, 189–91; bureaucratic, 148–49; cartoons, 142–43; components of, 152–61; cultural overcoating, 180–82; defined, 4–5; deflective source, 153; and desired outcomes, 145–51; disinformation, 156–58; disintegrative, 147; domains, 138–41; effects, 161; external, 160–61; facilitative, 147–50; factoid, 156–58; false identification, 153; fear appeals, 190–91; front groups, 153; information/disinformation, 155–60; information flow control, 183–84; integration, 146–47; internal, 160; long-term, 183; modern campaigns, 177–91; music, 143–44; myth, 181–82; orthopraxy, 144–45; primitive patterns, 182; processual model, 177; as reasoned act, 6; rumor, 158–60; shared characteristics with persuasion, 6; short-term, 183; and sociological mechanisms, 7; sources, 153–55; strategic goals, 185–86; symbolic fiction, 155; tactics, 186–89; timing, 183

propaganda techniques, smoke and mirrors, 164–68; asymmetrical definition, 164; card stacking, 166; desirable by association, 165–66; fallacy of impossible certainty, 167; fallacy of limited alternatives, 167; false analogies, 167; glittering generality, 165; guilt by association, 166; implacatures, 167–68; juxtaposition, 165; name calling, 164; negative testimonial, 166; negative transfer, 166; overgeneralizing, 166; polarizing, 167; positive testimonial, 165; positive transfer, 165; secret sources, 168; slinging, 164; statistical proof, 166; tautological appeals, 167

propaganda techniques, familiar and comfortable, 168–69; bandwagon appeal, 168; granfalloon, 168–69; plain folks, 168; self-evident truths, 169; superiority appeals, 169; wise men can't be wrong, 169

propaganda techniques, emotion ignitions, 169–71; absurdity appeals, 170; cathartic identification, 170–71; fear appeals, prospective, 169–70; fear appeals, retrospective, 170; hate speech, 170, 171–75; personal attacks, 170

pseudoevents, 155

psychographics, 88–92, 94–101; first used, 94; and marketing, 95; marketing strategies, 100; variables, 95

psychosocial identification, 47

publics, 76–79; creation, 76–77, 78; defined, 76, 77

reference groups, 33–38, 81; comparative functions, 36; defined, 35; functions, 36; imagined groups, 37; negative, 36; normative functions, 36; positive, 36; primary, 36; theory, 33–35

resonance strategy, 4

Rokeach Value Scale, 92–93; instrumental values, 93; terminal values, 92–93

Rovere election study, 111

rural ethic, 15

Sapir–Whorf hypothesis, 135–36

segmentation, 79–80; macro approaches, 104; micro approaches, 104–7

self-categorization theory, 22

semiotics, 77–78; and publics, 77

shared reality, 55–56

Simmons Market Research Bureau (SMRB), 83

small-town pastoralism, 15
social categorization, 20, 23–25; defined, 20; perceptual tendencies, 21; versus organized groups, 20
social cohesiveness, 22
social comparison theory, 54–60
social conformity, 22
social construction of reality, 135–36
social control, 31
social-emotional contagion, 25
social frames, 10
social influence, 127–34; and mass media, 127–34
social marketers, 1; distrust of, 1–2; versus social control, 2
social organizations, 20–38
social rankings, 31
social relationships, 10
social roles, 31
social sanctions, 31; negative, 31, 33; positive, 31, 33
social self-identification, 23
social solidarity, 22
society, 62
SRI Consulting Business Intelligence, 96, 100

status conferral function, 156
Strength of Personality Scale (Personlichkeitsstärke), 125
subculture, 15–20
system theory, 64–69, 130; and communication, 69; attributes of all, 64–67; open systems, 66–67
system theory boundary, 67

terror, 173–75
two-step flow theory, 111; compared to multistep flow, 119; criticism of, 117–18

ultimate attribution error, 21
uses and dependency theory, 134
uses and gratifications, 130, 132–33

VALS, 96–99, 102, 104, 126; basis, 96; segments, 96–99
value–attitude–behavior hierarchy, 91
values, 90; traits, 12; research, 90–91
Values Instrumentality Inventory (VII), 94
verbal communication content, 52

"white guys in ties" (WGITS), 24

About the Authors

Karen S. Johnson-Cartee is professor in the Department of Advertising and Public Relations and in the Department of Communication Studies at The University of Alabama. She has also taught at the University of Alabama at Birmingham and the Universitat Klagenfurt in Klagenfurt, Austria. Dr. Johnson-Cartee has coauthored *Negative Political Advertising: Coming of Age* (with Copeland, 1991), *Manipulation of the American Voter: Modern Political Commercials* (with Copeland, 1997), and *Inside Political Campaigns: Theory and Practice* (with Copeland, 1997). Her research has appeared in such scholarly journals as *Presidential Studies Quarterly, Journalism and Mass Communication Quarterly, Newspaper Research Journal,* and *The Harvard International Journal of Press/Politics.* For nearly twenty years, Dr. Johnson-Cartee has worked as a political consultant for numerous federal, state, and local electoral campaigns. She teaches undergraduate and graduate courses in political communication theory, political advertising and public relations, political campaign communication, political news analysis, and lobbying.

Gary A. Copeland is professor in the Department of Telecommunication and Film and in the Department of Communication Studies at The University of Alabama. He has also taught at the Universitat Klagenfurt in Klagenfurt, Austria. Dr. Copeland is primarily known for his research in political advertising, although he has written in several scholarly areas. In addition to his three books with Dr. Johnson-Cartee, he has coauthored *Broadcasting/Cable and Beyond,* 3rd ed. (with Joseph R. Dominick and Barry L. Sherman, 1996). He is coeditor of *Critical Questions: Invention, Creativity, and the Criticism of Discourse and Media* (with William L. Nothstine and Carole Blair, 1994). His work has appeared in such publications as *The Harvard International Journal of Press/Politics, Critical Studies in Mass Communication, Journalism Quarterly,* and *Journal of Broadcasting and Electronic Media.*